One Man's Search

To grace
my life's companion
more precious each year
now more than ever
Love
Obert

One Man's Search

ADDRESSES BY
OBERT C. TANNER

□

University of Utah Press
Salt Lake City
1989

Frontispiece: Original portrait by Randall Lake.

Library of Congress Cataloging-in-Publication Data

Tanner, Obert C. (Obert Clark), 1904–
   One man's search.

   Includes index.
   I. Title.
AC8.T18 1989   081   88–28045
ISBN 0–87480–306–3

Dedicated to those who wonder

Contents

FOREWORD   *Sterling M. McMurrin*

PREFACE   *Obert C. Tanner*

I.   WORLD PEACE

Introduction: *Eric Ashby*

If Peace Comes to America.   5

Is There a Need for World Government?   16

Economic Competition and World Peace   23

A New Internationalism   36

Where Peace Begins.   51

The Greatest Honor.   58

The Individual and the United Nations   64

II.   TRUTH AND EDUCATION

Introduction: *Chase Peterson*

The Teacher and America Today   75

Plato's Trinity as Problem and Promise   86

The Profession of Teaching   94

Truth and Myth as Competitors for the Mind 101

vii

Power Structures and Reason *110*
A University and the Adventure of Great Ideas. *122*
Freedom in Business and Freedom in the
    Classroom. *129*

III. RELIGION

Introduction: *Carolyn Tanner Irish*
A New Religion for a New Age *145*
Is Religion an Aid to International Understanding? . . *153*
Religion Today in America. *167*
Seven Minutes About Brotherhood *177*

IV. FREEDOM AND DEMOCRACY

Introduction: *Warren E. Burger*
The Supreme Values of Democracy *187*
Home Democracy: Difference, Tolerance
    and Cooperation *198*
Western Civilization and Utah *211*
If Free Men Stay Free. *219*
Freedom's Best Fight *225*
The Constitution and Freedom *231*

V. VALUES

Introduction: *L. Jackson Newell*
Life Is a Many-Sided Thing *243*
Think Your Way Through Life *257*
Moral Aspects of the Invasion of Privacy *275*
Are Moral Values Absolute? *291*
Commitment to Beauty. *299*
Business and the Good Society *315*

Foreword

The Several Lives of Obert C. Tanner

Sterling M. McMurrin

☐

Recently I was asked, "What does Obert Tanner do?" I said, "He does good." "Yes, but what does he do to do good?" My response was immediate: "He calls for freedom!" *Freedom* is the Tanner hallmark. The demand for freedom permeates his thought and is diffused throughout his conversation. And certainly it is at the heart of his public statements.

Now freedom is various and complex, and the very word "freedom," perhaps fortunately, has about it a quality of ambiguity. There is not one freedom; there are many. There are "freedoms from" and there are "freedoms for"; freedom *from* such things as political and ecclesiastical tyranny, economic poverty, racial and sexual discrimination, ignorance, boredom, and loneliness; freedom *for* independent thought and action, creative work, the right to be an individual.

There is a sense in which freedom is an ingredient, and certainly a necessary condition, for the other human values. This is clearly the case for Obert Tanner, whose life has been a dedi-

Dr. McMurrin is E. E. Ericksen Distinguished Professor Emeritus
of the University of Utah
and former United States Commissioner of Education.

cation to the realization of those values. For him no freedom would mean no authentic truth, no beauty, no goodness. Freedom is the *sine qua non* of whatever in life has genuine worth.

The interesting thing about Obert Tanner is that this intoxication with the value of freedom not only pervades his thoughts, his teachings, and his public and private admonitions, it is equally evident in his private affairs, his business, his public service, and his philanthropic work. To an impressive degree, his behavior conforms to his principles. This is no mean accomplishment in a world in which cooperation is yielding to more ruthless competition and the social order is increasingly invaded by irresponsibility, moral malfeasance, and crime. Obert Tanner is a free spirit who wants the spirit of freedom to engage everyone. Not the freedom of abandon and irresponsibility, but freedom with responsibility, good sense, composure, decency, restraint, and reason.

A full portrait of Obert Tanner would be a complex of his several lives, a fascinating story of hard work, faith, academic study, romance, grief, courage, service, and philanthropy.

There is the Obert of the early years who learned the meaning of hard work as a child on the farm, herding sheep when only ten or eleven, laboring on a railroad crew and in a mining camp, a youth whose spiritual life and intellectual aspirations were cultivated and nourished by association with a mother who was to inspire him throughout his life.

Then there is Tanner the L.D.S. missionary, teacher of religion, Stanford chaplain, and author of religious studies, whose religious faith, in the encounter with scientific knowledge and philosophic wisdom, moved from an early orthodoxy to a naturalistic and humanistic piety, but whose devotion to his church, its traditions and its people, constantly strengthened rather than weakened.

Tanner the intellectual and academic, the professor of philosophy, was perhaps an inevitable issue of a childhood and youth where question, inquiry, and discussion were the rule rather than the exception. It is not surprising that this Tanner would achieve in the academic world: as student in three universities—Utah, Harvard, and Stanford—with degrees in law and philosophy; hold faculty posts in two institutions, Stanford and the University of Utah; and receive honorary degrees among other academic recognitions. What is surprising is that his academic pursuits, as student and teacher, were never interrupted while at the same time he was creating from scratch, beginning at a work bench in his mother's basement, a remarkably successful industry and business, the largest of its kind in the country. But that's another Tanner. This academic Tanner seems to have been obsessed with the ancient injunction that the unexamined life is not worth living, and for more than half a century he inspired students with a passion for knowledge and a commitment to reason and truth.

Just how the industrial and business Tanner managed to be such an eminent success while all the time disguising himself as a university philosophy professor is something of a mystery even to his closest friends. Not since the father of Greek philosophy, Thales, in the sixth century, B.C., managed to corner the wine industry in the eastern Mediterranean, had a philosopher pulled off such a coup. At the university he was Obert Tanner, the champion of academic freedom; downtown he was O. C. Tanner, manufacturing jeweler. And many of his colleagues and students were not aware that Obert and O. C. were one and the same person. But succeed in business he did, a fortunate success for the community, state, and nation, for not only is the Tanner enterprise an important civic economic asset, it also has provided the means for countless philanthropies and the opportunity for extensive public service.

No doubt a combination of things accounts for Tanner's success in business—his capacity to make decisions, and to change his mind, to listen, to judge human character, his concern for others, his sense of humor, a remarkable instinct for timing, and just plain brains and good judgment. And perhaps good motives has had a great deal to do with his success. In countless discussions with Obert on many things which sometimes related to his business, I have never heard him talk about profits. His speech reveals his pride in his company and his concern for its stability as an element of the community's economy; but references to his business mainly relate to two things: his interest in creating something of beauty (and his manufacturing firm and retail stores are works of art), and especially his concern for his employees – their working conditions, their security, their happiness, and the quality of their lives. Obert is not against profits; he is a defender of the capitalist system (though I am aware that he once successfully defended a card-carrying communist who faced excommunication from his church). But his interest seems to be in human beings more than in money and what money can buy. Unlike so many in today's society, he does not use money to make more money.

Now what about the romance? Despite their down-to-earth realism, I think "romantic" is the word to describe Obert and his wife, Grace, a queenly, unpretentious, and wise woman. By "romantic," I refer to their sense of adventure, their vision, their native energy, their life affirming idealism, their remarkable zest for life. They lost three children, boys in their early years, yet in the face of this cruel suffering their courage has been nothing less then heroic. Obert had said, "We do not intend to be symbols of tragedy for our friends." They have been symbols of the love of life.

In public service Obert has been a star in the firmament of both state and nation – as chairman of the Utah State Bicentennial Commission, as a leader in UNESCO and the United Nations Association, as a member of the President's Commission on the Bicentennial of the United States Constitution, as an American delegate to several international conferences devoted to the cause of peace and world understanding, to mention only the more obvious. In these and in other positions where he has given his time, energy, and means to further the public good he has won wide esteem and admiration.

And by their countless philanthropies, committed especially, as Obert has said, to the two B's—beauty and brains—the Tanners have made a difference in the quality of life of innumerable persons. Their support of music, symphony and opera, ballet, the theatre; their funding of over half a hundred fountains, library and other rooms to beautify public places; their endowment of numerous lectureships for colleges, universities, and learned societies, crowned by the now illustrious international Tanner Lectures on Human Values; their financing of publications in the humanities—these are only the more obvious gifts of the Tanners. Those who know them best can testify of much else, sometimes gifts for organizations, sometimes assistance for promising students; and then, of course, there are the usual charities and the countless things that are done in secret, that are known to no one else. It is not without reason that among his many honors Obert should receive in 1988 the Governor's Award in the Humanities from the Governor of Utah and the National Medal of Arts from the President of the United States.

Well, these are the lives of Obert Tanner as I see them and as I see him—a most uncommon, generous, compassionate person. What he has said in his public addresses deserves the attention of all of us.

Preface

One Man's Search

Obert C. Tanner

☐

This volume is a collection of a few addresses I gave while on the faculty of philosophy at the University of Utah. It is no more than one man's search among ideas and ideals that I thought were of major importance.

On the occasion of these addresses, I selected a subject that I thought would be of special interest to the particular audience. I discussed with them matters I considered important, ideas and ideals that guided me as a citizen and teacher. I did not expect the audience to agree with me. My hope was to define and clarify a problem, and search with them for possible solutions.

I am eighty-four years old. It is now time to clear out my study and give away my books.

Giving away books can be quite pleasant, although as I recently glanced at some of them, I felt a little sadness that I would not be seeing them again. Some of these books were landmarks in my life as a student and teacher.

Disposing of my papers and correspondence is a little more difficult. As I looked over papers that included these addresses, I could see why I had filed them away. They were concerned with ideas I cared about very deeply.

The addresses I have selected for this volume deal with problems that face us today, as they did when I gave them: ideas about world peace, economic justice, better education, the quality of religion, the meaning of democracy, and the endless search for human happiness.

For example, the first address in this volume, "If Peace Comes to America," though given twenty-eight years ago, analyzes the problem of world peace in much the same way that it is now analyzed by President Ronald Reagan and Chairman Mikhail Gorbachev.

And the address, "Think Your Way Through Life," in the last section of the book, a case is made that young people are more likely to be successful and achieve happiness, if they try to think their way through life, rather than follow impulse and emotion. Some methods for careful thought are suggested.

In summary, this volume is a search among ideas, ideas that one might believe, or doubt, or disbelieve. It is a search among ideals that may be helpful to the individual person in a search for happiness and in the creation of a better world.

In this searching for what to believe and how to live, each person must find his or her own way. This volume describes just one man's search. To repeat, these addresses are not solutions. At best they are no more than a modest attempt to identify and clarify a problem.

I was fortunate to engage the services of Margery Ward, a professional editor, who helped me select these addresses from among my papers. I want to thank her and my secretary, Dionne Williams, for their help and encouragement.

I

WORLD PEACE

Introduction

Eric Ashby

□

When Obert Tanner was a child, armies still rode into battle on horseback, and civilians, unless their loved ones were at war, remained comfortably at home. Today, a finger on a button is sufficient to set off a battle, and the forces released could wipe out the populations of cities. Obert has survived to witness this terrifying change; and, being the man he is, he decided not to be terrified but to seek some way of coming to terms with it.

For him, "coming to terms" does not mean passive resignation; it means an active search for ways in which Americans could live at peace "in a world with a billion communist neighbours." There is a passage somewhere in Plato where he argues that the ideal state will either have no neighbours or at least no contact with them. That sort of state could pursue its interests and ideals without risk of clashes with competing interests and ideals. But a message from Moscow can now reach Utah at the speed of light and a missile could arrive in minutes. In

Lord Ashby is former Chancellor of the Queen's University, Belfast, former Master of Clare College, Cambridge, and former Vice-Chancellor of the University of Cambridge.

these speeches, given over a period of thirty years, Obert Tanner confronts this situation with sober realism.

"Peaceful coexistence" is not sufficient for him, for it implies shutting the door and pulling down the blinds against communist states. It would be much more honest and objective to exert "peaceful opposition to communism" through a greatly increased interchange of people, information, and commercial products between capitalist and communist countries. Indeed, in commercial competition he sees a process, as old as the trade that brought spices and silk from the East to the shores of Italy, which demands trust and confidence between peoples of different race and religion and politics. It is a plea to the young people of America based on all that they have in common with the young people of the Soviet Union, without for a moment compromising about the beliefs that separate them and will continue to do so. It is "a kind of North Star" as Obert puts it, "that guides but is never reached."

If Peace Comes to America

Salt Lake Rotary Club
November 1, 1960

☐

If peace is to come to America, we must solve the problem of communism.

The problem of communism is how we live in freedom and also at peace on the same planet with a billion people now living within the communist bloc of nations.

All of us want peace and we also want to maintain our freedom. Can we achieve both? Can we live in peace and freedom in this world which is one-third communist?

We in America are determined to keep our freedom against the threat of communism; yet we are not sure we can do so without war, or at least without great risk of war. But if we have to choose peace under communist slavery or accept a war for our freedom, we would accept war. Such a dilemma—peace under communism or war to avoid communist slavery—is a terrible one. Perhaps we do not have to choose between one or the other. Perhaps we *can* have both peace and freedom. Is it possible to live in freedom and also in peace when the world is divided between communists and free men? This is our problem. It is the problem of communism.

Is there any solution to it, at least any very clear-cut solution? Apparently not; that is, none we can see very clearly now.

So let us face it, this problem of communism – of how America can live at peace in freedom in a world with a billion communist neighbors – seems presently insoluble. Those who say they can solve it are making far greater claims than they can deliver. The challenge for America is to survive these next decades and centuries without a third world war against communism and to keep her free way of life among so many communist nations; but no one is now able to tell us how to accomplish this almost miraculous achievement.

This sobering conclusion does not mean that peace with freedom is an impossibility. However, it does seem that the problem of keeping both the peace and our freedom is of staggering proportions. The best we can do is work on the problem, be patient in our failures, and cautious in our optimism.

How is America trying to solve this problem today? Primarily, our present course is a military solution. That is, our immediate answer to the communist threat is to make ourselves militarily strong. Most Americans agree with this necessity. Military power can at least prevent the aggressive march of communism, and this is of great and first importance.

But the military solution raises the question of whether military power is adequate. It is pressingly necessary, but is it sufficient? One fact about this military determination is that it gives many, if not most Americans, a sense of safety and security. Is this a false sense of security that we now enjoy?

Both presidential candidates – Vice-president Richard Nixon and Senator John Kennedy – stress the importance of this military solution. Neither candidate has ventured very far beyond it. Both claim they would make America militarily stronger. They both maintain that if we are stronger militarily, we will be in a better position to negotiate with the communists.

Such is our present solution to the communist problem. The question is whether we can now be satisfied with this solution. To be sure, we will always need a strong military to protect us against communist aggression; but will we need more than the military if we are to live in peace with the communist nations?

My answer is affirmative. We must experiment with new solutions. While we do so, the military stands watch over us. As we go forth with peaceful efforts, the military looks over our shoulder to prevent any double-cross by the communists. In other words, the military not only stops communist military aggression, it also gives us the necessary safety and security we need while we try to solve the problem of communism on a peaceful basis.

Many Americans today are doubtful that any solution other than a military one will be successful against communism. They believe that only superior military power will provide real security and peace against the communists.

Let us look more closely at this military solution. There are three different viewpoints held by those who rely upon it.

First, there are those who believe that a military showdown with the communist nations is not only inevitable, but imminent. The communists, they maintain, will launch a military attack whenever they feel the time is opportune, and this time of attack is not far away.

This impending attack requires an urgent response in building our military strength so that the communist nations will be destroyed when the attack comes, while our destruction from the communist enemy will be as minimal as possible. This point of view frankly faces the possibility that a nuclear war might destroy us, but justifies such an eventuality with the reasoning that it is better to die in defense of our freedom than to live in communist slavery. This viewpoint, charged with great emotion, has a great many supporters in America today.

The answer to this solution of the communist problem is not simple. However, it is not known for certain that the communists will attack at the first opportune moment. Millions of Americans claim they know this to be true, but they really do not know. Probably the communists themselves do not know what they will do. No one can be absolutely certain about the future, a vast unknown time into which no man's foot has ever trod. No one should claim to know more than he does, in fact, know.

To assume the inevitability of imminent attack from the communist nations creates conditions that are full of danger to peace, not the least of which is that it produces a sense of futility, and working for peace becomes a meaningless effort. Also, if war is expected as a certainty, that very expectation will help bring it about. Thoughts precede actions and help determine what actions will be. We often say that a man finds what he is looking for; so, too, many a nation finds what it expects as unavoidable. In addition, if war is inevitable, then any peace effort can be regarded as dangerous to war preparation. This attitude is common among millions of Americans today. Indeed, a short time ago, the very use of the word "peace" created suspicion in many audiences. Even today those who work for peace are considered unrealistic, soft on communism, or possibly unconscious allies of the communist cause.

Let us now look at the second position taken by those who stress the military solution to the problem of communism. This is no less pessimistic than the first position. It holds that while war is not inevitable, it is very probable. This position is, however, more optimistic about the outcome of a war, stating that if war comes, there will not be total destruction, that millions of Americans will survive to carry on in freedom.

This viewpoint shares some of the weaknesses of the first. It claims to know too much. War may not in fact be very probable. It may in fact be true that *peace* instead of war is very probable.

In any case, to believe that war is likely to come gives people a sense of futility, helps create an acceptance of the tragedies of war, and, finally, creates the belief that because it is reasonable to expect war, it is unreasonable to do anything else other than prepare for it. This reasoning again creates great mistrust against those who work on behalf of peace.

As to the argument that millions of Americans will survive to carry on in freedom, is this so sure? And even if it is, how good is a solution that kills outright fifty or one hundred million Americans and perhaps another two or three hundred million other people?

The third military solution to the problem of communism is less pessimistic than the previous two. It holds that war is neither inevitable, probable, nor even likely. It advocates that the sure road to peace is for America and her allies to have a stronger military capability than the communist bloc of nations. The argument maintains that if we are stronger, the communists will not dare start a war; hence, the way to peace is through great military power. The advocates of this solution contend that the only thing a communist understands is force. Confronted by a superior power, a communist will mind his business. Moreover, we need not fear war too much because we have good defenses even if the communists start something.

This argument, that we are so strong the communists would not dare risk a war, has more believers in America today than the other two military solutions. Millions among us feel secure and safe because of our superior military strength.

The optimism of this viewpoint, that there will be peace through power, would be persuasive if it were not for nuclear weapons. Nuclear weapons give nations armed with inferior missiles power to wipe out nations armed with superior missiles. There is really no such thing as a "stronger" nation anymore. Any nation armed with nuclear weapons has a military power that is absolute. It makes little difference that a missile goes a little slower or that it takes two of them instead of one to destroy a city.

As for adequate defense weapons, there really are none. Missiles go into the stratosphere and come down by the pull of gravity. A few could be intercepted, but many would hit their targets.

My conclusion is that these three military solutions to the communist problem are not adequate. They protect us for the present, that is all. Without some non-military solutions, our days are probably numbered.

America is trusting too much in military solutions, and inevitably we move day by day and month by month closer to war. We should see military solutions for what they are—temporary and uncertain, valuable only while other solutions to the communist problem are being worked out.

What are some of the non-military solutions to the communist problem? What other courses lie open to us? What must America do to remove the dark threat of a nuclear war that could possibly exterminate all life on this planet?

There are a hundred, a thousand steps we could take that would place our feet firmly on the highway of peace and involve no loss to our free way of life.

Here are only three such steps. They are not all-inclusive, fully adequate, or certified solutions. However, they are beginnings, and they should give us margins of success over failure. Moreover, they are desperately necessary if we are to reverse our present trend toward war.

First, America needs new faith in peaceful possibilities as against our present reliance on military strength.

Second, America must find ways and means to exercise greater wisdom in our foreign policies.

Third, America must launch a new foreign service program.

I am suggesting that to solve the communist problem we need a new faith in peace, a new wisdom in foreign policy, and a new service to the less fortunate nations that might otherwise adopt communism.

Let us be frank with ourselves. If we have no genuine faith in peace, if we do not support programs intended to achieve peace and, worse, if we are deeply suspicious of those who do, and if we applaud and primarily support our military efforts, then here is the future we are probably making–not certainly making, there are no certainties–but here is the high probability of our future: the Salt Lake valley will be empty of homes, of children, of friends, and of people. There will be no buildings, no trees, no games, no gardens, no one to see the sunsets, and no one to awaken with the dawn.

When someone speaks easily about war, as though it were something that could be won if we are strong, I want to tell them what we are making in this valley. We are making a Minuteman missile whose warhead is small enough to fit inside the trunk of an automobile but whose explosive power is greater than a train of boxcars loaded with TNT stretching from Chicago to Honolulu. Each one of these Minuteman missiles can make a hole in the earth larger than a city. We are stockpiling them; so are the Russians. And we have four other weapons programs, each of absolute military capability. Are you clear on what that term "absolute" means?

A military eventuality is unthinkable–yet we do not realize it. We still place most of our faith in a military solution to the communist problem. It is really no solution unless death is a solution. But we lack real faith in any alternative. The chances are good that we may go on cursing communism into our own oblivion. We will be in the right, if war comes, but we will also be dead.

First of all we need a new faith, a new confidence in negotiation, a strong belief that in peaceful competition with the communists we are more than a match for them. For example, we need a new faith in the United Nations. Again, let us be frank with ourselves. Americans have not had much faith in the United Nations; they have hardly supported it at all. Many, in great ignorance, have viciously attacked it. Yet the United Nations is the political conscience of the world. Here world opinion and even world action are possible to help prevent or halt the spread of war.

Another example is our need for faith that the problem of communist China can be solved peacefully. We have no such faith now, and the price for its lack may be disastrous. Ten years from now, more or less, our children may be faced by a great hostile nation, three times our size, heavily armed with thermonuclear weapons. But you and I might possibly help create a friendly China for them to deal with. There is now none, or very little faith in this possibility. This is why we need a new faith. We really have no choice but to live with the communists or die with them. Our present faith points in one of those directions, not the other. We must reverse ourselves.

If someone wants to object that it is no wonder we lack any real faith by pointing out our past failures in dealing with communists – their past aggressions, their present boasts, and their future intent of world domination – I would agree. They have been impossible in the past. They are presently arrogant and boastful. They do intend world domination. But there is still solid ground for a strong faith in successful negotiations. Here are three bases for great hope and faith.

First, as military weapons become more lethal, the communists can clearly see that if war comes, they too will be dead.

This will make them think twice, as it also gives us some second thoughts. Today the communists may negotiate in good faith or at least with more earnestness than they have in the past.

Second, in our past dealings with the communists we have not always been blameless in the failures. Take, for example, our U-2 flights mapping military targets on their May Day, just prior to the summit conference.* If we are more careful and thoughtful in the future, our chances for success may be greater. Who can say?

Third, if we do not have a war, I believe that the free world in open competition with the communist world will outstrip the communist nations on every level and in every race you can name. Our economic system, for example, is at least two or three times more efficient than the communist system—notwithstanding all reports to the contrary. Our educational, scientific, medical, political—in fact, every institution of the free world—surpasses in efficiency and achievement its counterpart in the communist world. I know, I have seen and observed all of them.

Why then are we afraid of their boasts? Why then do we put our money and trust in military security every time we hear them say they will bury us or dominate the world? We ought rather to learn the facts, be calm, and be prepared for peaceful competition. We simply do not believe in ourselves enough and so we trust in our guns. This is a mistake. We need more faith.

The second change necessary if peace is to come to America is new wisdom in our foreign policies. We have a desperate need for this. Our State Department, good enough for a small country, is woefully inadequate for a nation with the responsibility for world leadership. America is constantly surprised by events in

---

*An American U-2 spy plane was shot down by Soviet missiles on the eve of the scheduled summit conference in Paris in May 1960. Russian communist party chairman Nikita Khrushchev walked out on this conference when U.S. President Dwight Eisenhower did not apologize for the spy plane.

other parts of the world. We need to be less surprised by knowing more than we presently do about the world.

Needed far more than facts about the world are men of great wisdom who understand the forces at work in the world. We cannot afford many more foreign policy mistakes if peace is to come to America. Wiser men in our State Department might have counseled us better concerning World War II alliances and in our dealings with communist nations. The free world has lost half of Europe to the communists, not to mention China, possibly South America, and now Cuba. Rather than one man or only a few in the State Department advising the president, we desperately need the collective judgment of many knowledgeable and wise men to guide our relationships within the world family of nations. Presently, we are woefully lacking in this respect. We particularly lack wisdom in our dealings with the communist nations. Certainly, if peace is to come to America, this particular wisdom is absolutely necessary.

Finally, if peace is to come to America, we must train a new army of civilian scientists, doctors, engineers, and educators who will, in lieu of two years' military service, serve the 1200 million people of the underdeveloped nations and thus help turn them from the tragic alternative of communism.

Americans give money but, except in rare cases, they do not give of themselves. Our young people with their idealism, their true democratic spirit, their willingness to put up with hardships are the patriotic soldiers of tomorrow who will increase America's chances of avoiding a future world of communism and a future death from a nuclear war. The day is past when our armies made us safe by going abroad to fight. Now a new army must be on the move, armed with the skills of science and the democratic spirit to turn the future loyalties of men toward freedom instead of allowing them to turn to slavery. This service by young people will be absolutely necessary if peace is to come to America.

As a last comment and by way of hope, let us remember that great as the problem of communism is for us, we do in fact have more in common with the communist peoples than our vast differences would imply. We have our common humanity – the love of life, of creative work, of sharing, of falling in love, of seeing our children, of reading books, of playing games, and of feeling that the world was better because we lived in it. We have all this in common with what we think are evil communists. Are they so evil? And if they are, can we not handle them like a wayward adolescent – with patience and kindness rather than by clubbing them for their mistakes?

I have traveled widely in the communist nations and have negotiated with communists at six conferences at Geneva and Warsaw. I know their theories and practices. I believe that if we keep our powder dry, our hearts warm, and our heads clear and cool we are more than sufficiently resourceful to solve the communist problem so that peace and freedom will come to us here in America and eventually to all the other members of the family of nations.

Is There a Need for World Government?

Annual Utah Education Association Institute
October 10, 1963

□

There is one truly great need for a world government. This pressing need is for a world government to maintain world peace. There is no greater need. The world is getting on in other matters about as well as can be expected, with this one exception. This exception, or flaw, or present failure of our world, needs to be corrected to avoid an international holocaust.

The world does not face a clear and present need for a world government in order to achieve a better economic life, a better religious life, or a better social life. World trade and world cultures are doing quite well and promise much greater progress without a world government.

But the world's political life needs a world government. Politically, the world is in desperate need, for if there is political failure it will probably be absolute. That is, world political failure means war, and war probably means the end of man's life on this planet—not certainly but probably, not necessarily the death of every single soul, but nearly everyone.

If there is a world business depression, many people will probably starve; but a great many will survive. If there is a world failure of cultural life, darkness will come; but not permanently.

Yet if there is world political failure, both darkness and death might be universal and permanent.

A world government conceivably can help or hinder world trade, and either way the final result may not be very important. A world government may enrich or impoverish human cultural life, but either way it is not final. A world government limited to keeping world peace may succeed or fail, yet here the failure, unlike economic and cultural failures, could result in total annihilation.

In summary, there may be some need for a world government in many areas of man's life, yet these needs are not certain to be satisfied by any world government. But there is one overriding need, the need for life itself. A world government is absolutely necessary to satisfy such a need.

If this is so, what kind of world government has the best chance to maintain world peace?

The answer is that a world government with the best chance for keeping world peace is a realizable world government. An unrealizable, unworkable, impracticable world government has no chance at all to maintain peace.

What is a presently possible and presently workable world government?

It certainly is not a world government vested with great powers that would undermine strong nationalisms now prevalent everywhere on earth. A totalitarian world government is an utter impossibility. So also is a world government patterned after our strong federal United States government. Even a loose federation of national states is presently an utterly impossible dream. The present rise of new nations and the surge of national patriotism everywhere make impracticable the surrender of national sovereignties required of even a loose form of world federalism.

The conclusion is that a realizable, practicable world government capable of the political success necessary for world peace is a world government as now constituted in our present United Nations organization. Granted, that although we do not refer to the United Nations as a world government, it is one de facto. And if a more powerful world government is presently impossible, it is also true that a less powerful world government than our present UN would have a small chance of maintaining peace.

Ideally, we do not want a stronger world government than our present UN organization. Ideally, we want a world of free and independent nations, each stressing their own cultures, histories, institutions, and unique characteristics. Negatively stated, a world government able to keep the peace only at the price of lost freedoms to the nations might be preferable to war and death, but it is hardly an ideal to work for.

What is it that presently exists in the United Nations that gives it preference over any other form of world government?

The answer is that, in substance, the UN is no more than a continuous conference of nations with the sole purpose of keeping world peace. The charter of the United Nations does not establish a government such as we have in the United States or as governments exist elsewhere in the world. The charter of the UN provides only for the machinery whereby dangers of war can be faced by all nations and where a forum for negotiation is possible.

The United Nations conference place, an arena or peaceful battleground, is located beside the East River in New York City. Here the giant Goliath-nations and the small David-nations gather to hurl words rather than missiles. Here the hatreds from history are brought to light, the bullies are exposed, and the last and the least of nations fight the oldest and the largest nations using with equal force the weaponry of words. Here world opinion is formed, nations vote, and friends and foes count costs and consider future results, all without military application.

Here gather the oppressor and the oppressed, the ambitious and the zealous, the greedy and the intolerant, the helpful and the hopeless, the hungry and the suffering, the lost and the forgotten. In turn they take the center of the world's stage to plead, to dissent, to threaten, to intimidate, and to pressure; but also to cool off and vote, to discuss and agree, and to share and even cooperate. What other world government is possible or practicable in our present world, filled as it is with emotional nationalisms, desires, and ideologies?

The United Nations takes the world about as far as it can presently go in world government. As such it holds out three great possibilities to the human race:

1. The real possibility of keeping our world at peace.
2. The real freedom and independence of every nation.
3. The healing of deep wounds that cause wars – ignorance, poverty, and suffering.

What is this United Nations organization as a government, or if we cannot call it a government, what is it as an organization? How does it keep the peace?

The UN is staffed by approximately 25,000 persons – 5,000 assigned to political problems and 20,000 to non-political work in such specialized agencies as UNESCO and the World Health Organization. The United Nations presents to the world a new type of public official – a Secretary-General and staff who are international civil servants bound by oath to administer impartially to all nations, according to the charter.

The UN has the power to help nations settle disputes by diplomacy, mediation, conciliation, and adjudication. It can, under the charter, adopt "police" measures that are political, economic, and military. It can empower a regular fighting force, as it did in the Congo in 1960 and in Korea from 1950 to 1953, or the armed buffer force or patrol on the border of Egypt and Israel in 1952. It has powers of truce supervision such as in 1948 between India and Pakistan or in the Near East. It can control subversive border crossings as in Greece in 1952. It has the authority to administer a territory while a transfer of sovereignty is made as it did in west New Guinea in 1946. The United Nations has what is called a UN "presence," as when it sends observers to secure information about subversion or violence or when the Secretary-General visits troubled spots.

To save succeeding generations from the scourge of war, the UN can involve itself in a war using armaments and soldiers. This is a paradox – war by a peace organization. But in our kind of world, no world government could keep the peace without using force occasionally, as no local government can keep the peace without a policeman.

The United Nations is a form of voluntary world government with a charter that insures not only the greatest possible political freedom and independence of each nation but, in addition to this primary burden of political and military activity, is also deeply involved in specialized agencies of freedom – freedom from hunger, from ignorance, from disease, from many of the miseries that plague the people on this planet. Away from the harsh and dangerous political clashes within the arena of the United Nations building beside the East River, there is the UN in all parts of the world. This is a UN world government of mercy, of giving, of sharing, of creating, of changing mankind's miserable existence to a life of gladness and hope. Diseases have been stamped out, rivers harnessed, crops increased, schoolbooks provided, navigation safety improved, among numerous other things.

Finally, there is in the United Nations world government a staff of strange new public servants. Indeed, this organization is staffed almost exclusively by a singular kind of human being. Like many others, UN employees do not stop working at the end of eight hours. For many years, more than in any office building I have seen in New York City, workers in the UN headquarters building toil long into the night. Yet this is not unique. Nor is it singular that men are here who live religion as John Dewey defined it: the joining of the ideal with the real, the "is" with what "ought" to be. What is almost unique is that these men and women, applying great energies to safeguard and transform the world, are people with minds and hearts of universal sympathetic understanding. Loving their own countries, they also love all other countries. The barriers within our lives, our limited ideas and small sympathies, are overcome by these people. UN workers rise above these barriers. They see the world, all the nations and peoples with their hopes and despairs, with all mankind's goodness and evil. And, seeing this, these UN workers are devoted to everyone – the last and the least, the strong and the weak, the poor and the rich, the educated and the ignorant, the ambitious and the humble, the belligerent and the peaceful, and the fanatic and the thoughtful. They are almost a new breed of human being on this planet. They are almost a unique type of public servant.

These workers approach a new type of sainthood. Here is the ancient religious ideal of universalism made real. Here is the thought of great philosophers brought into actual being. Gradually the world, with nations large and small, is beginning to see that a human being is capable of purging his earlier narrow loyalties in favor of a universal loyalty, each nation counting for one – no more and no less. Such a person is the Secretary-General of the United Nations, whose qualifications are scrutinized and whose appointment is agreed upon unanimously. Such people are on his staff. Nowhere on earth, including churches and governments, are there people who surpass or equal these officials who labor on behalf of mankind's dream for a peaceful world.

Such people are coming to be trusted by all nations. They are the peacemakers who replace soldiers and armaments. Without such people no perfectly conceived world government could long preserve peace; but with them a weak world organization is made strong enough to keep the peace.

The conclusion is that the world needs a world government to keep world peace. Such a world government should not be totalitarian, or federal, or strong in central authority. Rather, it should be a government of nation-states voluntarily signing a charter to band together, voluntarily paying their dues, and voluntarily meeting in assembly to settle issues that might otherwise lead to war. Such a world organization is the presently existing United Nations.

But it is more than that. It is an organization whose greatest total effort is to heal the deep wounds on our planet—hunger, ignorance, exploitation, and suffering. In attempting to do this, with some eighteen years of more success than failure, a new order of sainthood has emerged in this century—the international civil servant whose labor, open mind, and great heart have won the necessary preliminary battles of respect over antagonism, of trust over suspicion, and of esteem over contempt, even from avowed antagonists.

Here then is our United Nations organization—a gathering of nations whose representatives hammer out peaceful solutions and whose civil servants not only labor for peace, but also for food and literacy for the health of both the body and mind. All these people bring hope in place of despair and light to the darkness.

Economic Competition and World Peace

Great Issues Forum, University of Utah
February 20, 1963

☐

The question before us now is whether economic competition helps or hurts our chances for world peace. Is international economic competition a pathway leading us in the direction of peace or war? Is economic competition compatible with world peace?

My answer to this difficult question will be attempted with the following three propositions:

1. International economic competition probably has a greater potential for world peace and also a greater potential for world war than does the success or failure of any other international relationship, such as those in the fields of diplomacy, education, religion, or cultural exchanges.

2. Bad or distorted international economic competition has an enormous potential for war.

3. Good or sound international economic competition has an enormous potential for world peace.

My first proposition, that world trade may be a greater factor for peace or war than is education, diplomacy, cultural exchanges, or religion, is not to downgrade other international efforts for peace, but rather to say that world trade as a profound influence for peace or war should receive more of our attention. We possibly are not fully aware of a most fundamental influence that could lead us to either peace or war, namely, the enormous goodwill resulting from successful international business relationships and the enormous bad will resulting from unsuccessful international business relationships.

To be sure, other factors, such as the quality of education in the schools of the various nations, might lead to peace or war. And in world diplomacy, the United Nations could fail, and that failure could mean war; or the UN may succeed and thus keep the peace. Religion alone may inflame our emotions toward war or warm our hearts sufficiently for peace. Cultural exchanges, including the Peace Corps, together with travel and the exchange of artists, athletes and their events, scientists, and educators, if successful, can do much to keep us on the pathway to peace.

But no human activity in the long run is as successful in battering down the walls of national tensions that lead to war as is sound and mutually profitable international trade and commercial relationships. Contrariwise, in the long run, nothing will more certainly generate mistrust and ill will that could lead to war than economic failures, lack of economic opportunities, or unfair advantages taken in man's economic life. Put simply, business success easily makes friends, and business failure easily makes enemies. Trust of friends and fear of enemies is the stuff of which war is made.

Granted man does not live by bread alone, but he does live by bread. In our search for peace, we must find those factors that promise the greatest success; and probably no single factor is so full of promise in preventing war as is world trade through sound international economic competition. In making this point, we are reminded of the emphasis Karl Marx gave to economics. But Marx overstated the case. Contrary to his conclusions, regardless of the prevailing economic system, man is quite capable of being objective as he weighs truth-claims and appraises cultural values. Nor did Marx appreciate man's undying upward reach for a religious interpretation of life – including the possibility of a religious interpretation courageously criticizing current economic injustices.

Yet most of us would agree that Marx was correct in assuming that economics is a bedrock element in man's life. How profoundly economics affects all facets of man's life – religious, educational, political – is difficult to say. But I am sure that world peace has great hope if there is a flourishing world trade, and hopes of world peace will end in despair if economic competition is distorted by numerous failures.

Europe can be cited as an example of this point. Europe has had essentially one religion, one educational system, and one area for tourists and frequent exchange of diplomats; but it has also had two world wars. The Schuman plan of combining coal and iron production for larger common use emerged finally into the Common Market,* and the Common Market promises a peace in Europe that no common religion, common education, or common political assemblies have ever been capable of achieving. However, the story of the Common Market success in achieving peace is not complete. France may turn it to a war potential.

Why is economic competition a two-edged sword that successfully dissolves tensions in favor of peace yet also builds tensions that lead to war? What is economic competition?

Economic competition is a business relationship that necessarily helps some of the parties involved and necessarily hurts others. In all competition, whether in sports, education, or busi-

---

*Robert Schuman (1886-1963) helped formulate the plan which bears his name, in which the rich coal basin of central Europe was to be operated as a cooperative rather than a competitive venture among the central European nations. Organized in 1951, it helped inspire the larger cooperative venture of the European Economic Community (EEC) or Common Market, begun in 1957.

ness, there are winners and losers. In sports the losers need only show good sportsmanship. In education the losers try again or select other fields quite as attractive. But in economic competition the losers do not partly lose or partly win, they totally win or totally lose. A competitor in business who wins second place wins nothing. A competitor who wins first place takes all.

Those who lose in competitive business can go hungry, become angry, lose their business, or go into another business. They can also change their present business operations. Failing this, they sometimes resort to bad business practices such as false representations, conspiracies with competitors, briberies, or secret attempts to destroy competitors.

The point is that when a competitor takes second place in economic competition, he always suffers the hurt of not achieving. To repeat, in sports second place is a great honor. In education, a second choice can be quite agreeable; but in world trade, second place can mean starvation.

Only two parties are greatly favored in economic competition. One is the consumer or buyer who can choose the lowest price, best service, and/or the finest quality. The other favored party is the successful competitor. All others lose totally and completely. World trade competitors oppose each other, and this is one of the real war potentials of international economic competition. That is, nations and international firms losing as competitors may go hungry, but they may also choose to try for economic success by distorting competition with violence or with war.

At this point we might ask, is economic competition necessary? Must men and nations oppose each other as competitors? What about economic cooperation? What about economic planning? If economic competition is so fraught with war potential, why not give it up? Is it really necessary? What about applying the life of reason to world trade; that is, study the means-and-end relationships whereby nations plan their goals and their strategy of attaining these goals and eliminate all the waste and risks of war involved in competition? Couldn't the wear and tear of international competition that builds up tension and could lead to war be replaced by thoughtful forms of international economic cooperation?

This question divides men as no other. There are those on the side of cooperation and those on the side of competition. To use James's descriptive phrase, the competition-minded are the tough-minded, and the cooperation-minded are the tender-minded—and the world of men and nations divides itself on this issue between the tough- and tender-minded. Our congressmen are divided, our legislators are divided, and so are most of us.

Essentially the question is whether there is a more humane way to practice economic life and replace harsh economic competition. This question forms the great economic divide, a great watershed of beliefs and practices concerning man's economic life.

The answer I believe is that while cooperative theories and practices can replace competitive theories and practices, the replacement can never be more than temporary. All cooperative programs, great and necessary as they are under many circumstances, will ultimately face the various tests of competition. Competition will show up sooner or later as the supreme judge of all the cooperative efforts of man. Competition is the basic law of life. Cooperation is basic for the best life, but competition is life's harsh and ultimate reality. Forms of cooperation are among the highest of man's achievements, but none are immune from the tests of competition.

The lion and the lamb may lie down together, but for a short time only. Competition always comes back to haunt the cooperators, to test their programs, and everlastingly insist that changes be made.

Why is this so? Why does competition always have the last word about our thousand-and-one forms of excellent cooperation? Competition has the last judgment because our world is one of constant change. Nothing abides, and with inevitable change come the possibilities for improvement. With improvements come rewards to those who create them. With these greater rewards come greater and greater efforts from those who now become competitors. Successful competitors overwhelm successful co-operators. Cooperators are rather peaceful. Competitors are not so peaceful. The realistic appraisal of life for man and for nations on this planet appears to be that competitors win out over cooperation.

Arnold Toynbee's challenge-response interpretation of history is but a restatement of competition winning over coopera-tion. A new competitor replaces an older and once successful competitor who has since turned to the life of cooperation. In such an evolution the political order of cooperation finally becomes another of history's dead empires. This is the life of nations. It is also the life of free business enterprise. Every business today needs to change for the better, and those who excel in this need for improvement survive, while those failing to improve finally go under.

Facing the harsh realities of such an economic life and try-ing to avoid them, men have devised every dodge, theory, and practice imaginable. A few escapes from economic competition presently known to all of us are religious united orders, commu-nism, socialism, consumer unions, collectives, mergers, monop-olies, and cooperatives. These systems are, in a way, escape hatches from the unhappy and sometimes unsuccessful life of economic competition.

These systems do mitigate the harshness of competition. They do avoid much waste and the general destructiveness of competition, especially the wear and tear on the human nervous system. They do give more peace of mind. But always these col-lective walls against competition crumble before the onslaught of inevitable change. Competitors destroy them. To use a metaphor, these cooperatives and collectives are like a lake frozen in wintertime, peaceful and quiet. But the springtime of competition returns and cracks the ice. It breaks up monopolies, economic empires, and protective schemes designed to keep out innovation, novelty, and competition. The once-still lake is churned by winds and waves. Flow and change now revolutionize what was once fixed and peaceful. Now damaging floods are possible. But life-giving irrigation becomes possible too. Between the stasis and the flux, men and institutions succeed and fail, live and die—hopefully without war, but sometimes by violence and sudden death.

If competition is inevitable, and nowhere more than in man's economic life, does it hold more hope for peace than for war? Our answer is affirmative. Competition has much that favors world peace even though it also carries the risk of war.

Consider two very broad distinctions, two very general types of competition. As in so many important aspects of man's social life, there is the good and the bad, the fair and the foul, the constructive and the destructive. Ethical or moral theories of relativity may harass us as we use the words "good" and "bad," but for all that these two words are significant and meaningful for our present discussion.

We are trying to answer the question of whether economic competition is compatible with world peace. Thus far we have affirmed that for better or worse the life of economic competition is always with us more insistently than any other form of international relationship. Now let us attempt to explain this broad distinction between good and bad economic competition. Our conclusion is that while good economic competition cannot guarantee peace, it can be a large factor favoring peace, whereas bad economic competition can easily balance the scales on the side of war. With this distinction in mind, we turn now to our second proposition that bad or distorted international economic competition has an enormous war potential.

What is bad or distorted international economic competition? Good or sound economic competition will be explained in our third proposition, but a brief statement about it is necessary to explain the meaning of bad economic competition that might lead to war.

Good competition is a business relationship favoring both the buyer and the seller. The buyer is favored by the lower price, the better service, and the finer product. The seller is favored by retaining and acquiring additional wealth made possible by the margin between the cost of producing and the selling price.

Distorted or bad economic competition is a failure of one or more of the three necessary parties involved in all economic competition. The three parties are the consumer and two or more competitors.

The variety of possible failures between these three parties, or the failure of any one of them, is as numerous as are the sands of the sea. Only a few need be mentioned. They are failures that antagonize, frustrate, and distort the promise of a good economic life. They produce results that sometimes lead nations to war.

First, there is the failure of the buyer or consumer. He may refuse to apply the standards of sound competition, namely, to buy at the best price, quality, and service. Nations do this in a hundred ways and for as many reasons—tariffs to protect domestic industry, trade agreements to keep friendly relationships, or trade agreements to perpetuate hostile relationships. Sometimes the buyer is bribed by one competitor or influenced to ignore sound competitive considerations. That nations frequently do not trade with each other on a sound competitive basis is a present threat to peace. They do not produce and trade on the most favorable competitive basis.

Then there is the failure of one, or more than one, of the competitors. Here deviations from sound competition are by far the most numerous and variable. One can easily understand the temptations of men and nations to win by other than fair practices. The stakes are high. These stakes are no less than wealth or poverty, food or hunger, happiness or misery, recreation or worry, learning or ignorance, power or servitude, friends or isolation, life or death.

Some of the words competitors use to describe their life of competition, the life they live in separate business transactions, and the life they sometimes live from morning to night from year to year also describe the life of international competition. They are noted here to indicate some of the reasons for the failures of competition and to indicate the war-potential of these failures. Men and nations naturally do not like an economic life described by such words as "cold-blooded," "ruthless," "mean," "fierce," "vicious," "bitter," "tough," "harsh," "severe," "keen," "hot," "sharp," "dishonest," "unfair," "double-crossing," "slugging," or "no-holds barred." There is little wonder that competition described this way fails so frequently. The risks of economic loss in fair competition are so many and so unpleasant that they produce many escapes and distortions. To avoid these risks conspiracies between competitors, such as price-fixing, sometimes occur. Rather than face economic failure, there are also thousands of misrepresentations a competitor may make to win regardless of the real merits of the product. Sometimes one competitor will secretly plan to destroy another competitor.

Then there is the great failure of competition we know as monopoly—the unwillingness to even enter the field of sound competition where the rules are fair and the real merits are decisive and frequently disastrous to the loser. We live today with growing monopolies, business mergers, international cartels, communist blocs, and other giant associations. Perhaps someday there will be only two divisions on earth, the eastern and western hemispheres. In any case, giants of economic monopoly are destructive to competition. Whatever competition monopolists allow will not be healthy and sound. It will be a distortion or a denial of competition. So the results may finally end in a war of giants and the tragic abolition of life, or a peace forced by one giant and the nearly equal tragedy of tyranny for all.

The real hope of competition for world peace lies not in any of its distortions. Real hope is only found in sound and healthy competition.

We turn now to our third proposition: that good or sound international economic competition has an enormous potential for world peace.

Harsh and cruel as competition may be – and surely it is to a large extent an unhappy reality of life – it can be a great factor for world peace. Three reasons that this may be so we classify as (1) material, (2) intellectual, and (3) methodological.

1. Material. Sound competition will out-produce any other economic system. It makes the consumer the benefactor and final judge of competitors who will also profit when able to give the best in service, quality, and price.

World peace is advanced nearer to reality if people do not face the choice of hunger or violence. The greater the production, the less chance of war from privation and hunger. Competition is the key to the largest output of the world's desired material satisfactions. Russian communism has proven to be no match for western competition. So they have continuously altered their system. They now provide bonuses and better living conditions to the more successful competitors. They are still far behind us and will remain so unless they more realistically face the value of competition as a means to a higher standard of living.

But this favorable balance of more goods and services for more people is not a decisive factor on the side of peace. Great cooperative or dictatorial means of production can satisfy a people's demand for a better standard of living short of the danger of recourse to war.

2. Intellectual. We turn now to a more important aspect of life that thrives in a competitive economy.

A sound competitive economy does not create an intellectual life, but it lives compatibly with lively intellectual interests. It might even be said that a free competitive economy is a precondition for the free life of the mind. What is this relationship? It is the priceless relationship of freedom. If business life is free, intellectual freedom is encouraged. If business life is coercive, as in Russia, intellectual life will also be coerced. The power to control economic life automatically means the use of power to control intellectual life. Why? Because economic dictation is a power so great as to find intellectual dissent unbearable and unnecessary.

What is the relationship of world peace to a free intellectual life? My reply is that world peace is not really threatened by economic inefficiencies and even by economic exploitations. War is more an intellectual issue, a matter of the mind, of ideas and attitudes. Above all, the issue of peace or war is a problem so difficult that it can be solved only by free minds. The free mind can doubt, dissent, experiment, and create. It can face a new challenge with new ideas and more promising solutions. We cannot look to Russia for a solution to world peace. We must look to ourselves, where there is freedom of the intellect.

A free competitive economy offers its greatest contribution to world peace by encouraging freedom of the mind. Contemporary history records that the front line of freedom is economic. When economic freedom collapses, intellectual freedoms disappear. Real economic freedom must always be competitive as real intellectual freedom is also competitive.

World peace is a gigantic problem, the ultimate solution of which requires the help of large populations, numerous professions, and great diplomats free to wonder, question, probe, and create new possibilities. A great contribution for such a world of intellectual freedom is made by a free competitive economy. Free businessmen, free professional men, and free farmers mean free classrooms, free pulpits, and free elections. Such freedom holds out great hope for world peace.

3. Methodological. The third reason that a sound economic system has a potential for world peace is methodological. Sound competition is self-corrective. There are only two ways of correcting all the abuses I have named. One is by force – political force – and the other is by increased competition. In Russia political force is used. In America, except in extreme cases, we count on new competitors to weed out corruption. In this way freedom is better maintained. Each man is free to try his hand, and the failures of some competitors become the free opportunities for others.

Here we face a particularly difficult problem that relates economics to world peace. In our own country the government can step in if economic competition is excessively corrupt and if this corruption is uncorrected by other competitors. But who is to act to control the extremes of economic corruption in world trade? What is to stop an aggressive nation from pillaging the economy of a weaker nation as has so frequently happened in the past? What is to stop international cartels and monopolies from practices that incite international tension leading to war?

The basic answer is more competition. This answer of self-corrective competition is more inclusive than one might suspect. Small nations and underdeveloped nations are neither deaf nor blind to competing offers. Colonialism is nearly dead except in the new Russian colonialism of the communist bloc countries. And with nationalism on the rise, old economic exploitations are declining. A new world is now in the making where healthy economic competition is emerging. This new healthy economic competition is a stride forward to peace because excessive exploitations are largely self-corrected by ready opportunities from numerous competitors.

The family of nations, however, is not without some protection in cases of excessive exploitation. The influence of the United Nations is nearly everywhere. It is a spotlight on troubled places. Tyranny and exploitation are highlighted by the UN for all the world to see. World opinion is the new world force. The UN marshals this power of world opinion, which makes older forms of economic exploitation difficult.

My conclusion is optimistic. World economic competition can triumph over its inevitable failures. It is enormously successful in breaching international tensions. Its freedom encourages man's intellectual freedoms now so necessary in solving the greatest problem humanity has ever faced – the problem of life or death.

A New Internationalism

Utah State University Faculty Dinner
September 19, 1959

□

This year of 1959 is turning over to American colleges a new assignment of such magnitude as to outdate all our previous thinking. The cold war ends in 1959. The burden of the free world to meet the challenge of communism has now shifted from the military and political fronts to the whole field of education.

The days of the importance of the military are ending. The days of the importance of political debate are ending. The days of the cold war are numbered.

Something new in mankind's international life is now emerging. The thirteen years from 1946 to 1959 were the years of the cold war. A new internationalism is now in the making. The burden of creating this new world is not a military one. It is not a political assignment. The future will be a peaceful world of severest competition between a way of life that promises freedom to private conscience as against a way of life that promises security through social controls.

Which one of these systems will win out is now to be answered in our schools. On this one point there is no question: If the way of individual freedom and personal dignity should finally win, the victory will come by way of the classroom.

Let us first turn back to appraise the cold war which is now ending. In the main, the cold war period was one of success for the free world. For all the reverses freedom has suffered, in balance the cold war has favored the free nations.

One achievement of the cold war is a free world strong in military power to oppose communist aggression. And this military capability must be kept as a deterrent to future communist aggression. Communism at its base is less a social reform and more a struggle for power. Therefore, the West has made a great gain for freedom by maintaining sufficient military strength to stop the military march of communism.

A second achievement of the cold war has been the vast educational program that informed millions of people all over the world about the real nature of communism – that behind its promises of equality and security was the fatal price tag of lost freedoms. Comparable to the gains of past centuries made for man's personal dignity, communism finally came to be understood. It is a throwback to a tribal ethic of total social control resulting in personal enslavement. This understanding on the part of millions has finally emerged and is probably the cold war's greatest victory.

Another achievement of the cold war has been our understanding of the way communism spreads: with unlimited promises to the hungry, with the deception of those who are friendly, and with an iron hand of brute force when such power can be used.

To be sure, there were also defeats in the cold war. Millions who were not communists are now communists or are under communist control. Some are enslaved and some are true believers in the communist way of life. The cold war fight for men's minds has witnessed many converts to communism.

Next, we ask these questions: Why did the cold war come to an end? Why couldn't the war against communism be fought on cold war principles to final victory?

There are many who would take this course. Several countries and millions of people would fight the cold war unremittingly and without reservation until death or final victory. But the cold war came to an end because the majority of countries and their people are now willing to try some new policy.

Why has the majority of the world's population turned their backs upon a continuation of the cold war? The answer is this: After the cold war began, military weapons progressed in destructive power until now any recourse to war means death to all. Facing this possibility, the majority of people are now turning away from cold war tactics. The logic is clear that cold war is the last step before entering a hot war. Therefore, a cold war is risky business. With nuclear weapons available to foe and friend, a cold war forces the human race to walk a tightrope, balancing day by day and year by year between life and death.

Historians will probably mark the year 1959 as the date when mankind decided to end the cold war. However, repudiation of the cold war is by no means a unanimous, if indeed a final, decision. There are millions of individuals and hundreds of institutions whose cold war convictions are as strong as ever, if not stronger.

The cold war has not ended for some religions. These religions can be identified by their responses to the 1959 visit of Mr. Khrushchev to the United States. In some public utterances of religious leaders, one finds the ageless clash between institutional loyalty and the ideals of love and tolerance. When their institutional life appears to be threatened, leaders generally favor their institution. Their ideal of love is not given up, but their institution comes first.

The cold war has not ended for some veterans' organizations. Patriotic men who fought for their country are unwilling to change for some larger and perhaps nobler patriotism.

The cold war has not ended for military men who now protect us from communist aggression. These men are united in thought necessary for an emergency.

The cold war has not ended for some labor unions. The hard fight against communist infiltration of the unions has created within their ranks an inevitable antagonism toward communism as a whole. It is now difficult to modify this antagonism.

The cold war has not ended for many businessmen. Those successful in the free enterprise system have always correctly considered communism devoted to their destruction. Many therefore prefer that the cold war be continued.

The cold war has not ended for many who labor for their country in the field of foreign affairs. In diplomatic relations the communists work by deceit and frustration which test human patience to the utmost and make it nearly impossible that even a small margin of goodwill is attained.

The cold war has not ended for millions of ordinary men and women who listen, read, see, and are influenced by the media. For a dozen years, most people had only a diet of anti-communism through the mass communication media. Following the Second World War during which free and communist nations cooperated, the communists became mortally opposed to their former allies of the free world. The challenge of free nations then became the difficult task of educating their common citizens to the real meaning of communism. In this necessary educational process, the pendulum of anti-communism swung so far that Americans of the McCarthy era fell to destroying each other in a manner more insidious than the outright methods of destruction by communism. The overall result to the free world of these years of educating citizens to the communist danger is that millions of people think any policy toward the communists other than the cold war is suspicious if not outright treasonous.

This divergence of American opinion about the cold war— whether to support it or change it—was illustrated by the division of opinion among the American delegates who attended the World Federation of the United Nations Associations in Geneva.* On the one hand there were those who wanted to retain the cold war policies in every resolution. If America's cold war policy was not supported by every resolution they wanted to marshal our allies and oppose that resolution. The attitude of these delegates advocating a continuation of the cold war was to achieve unconditional victory and refuse to compromise.

On the other hand, there were American delegates seeking some way out of the cold war, trying to establish some common ground of understanding to lessen international tension. One such delegate, Professor Arthur Holcombe of Harvard, approached the chairman of the Russian delegation and suggested that the United States and the USSR jointly sponsor a resolution to indicate some common agreement in order to promote international understanding. The Russian delegate agreed to such an effort, and each drew up a resolution. When the two resolutions were exchanged, the American delegation rejected the entire Russian resolution. On the other hand, the entire American resolution was accepted by the Russian delegation. Assuming as we must that Russian delegations always act according to the instructions of their government, it was significant that the Russians apparently were also seeking a cessation of the cold war. Certainly, America had her way and Russia agreed to support the resolution presented to them by the American delegation.

The following is the resolution jointly sponsored by the two great powers at Geneva two weeks ago:

> Taking into account the necessity of easing international tension;

---

*The World Federation of United Nations Associations Fourteenth Plenary Assembly, held in Geneva from 31 August to 5 September, 1959.

OBSERVING the success of recent efforts to reduce such tension, under USA-USSR Agreement for Cultural Exchanges, notably the Soviet Union's exhibition at New York and the United States exhibition at Moscow;

WELCOMING the announcement of the forthcoming exchange of visits between the Chairman of the Council of Ministers of the USSR and the President of the USA;

AND WELCOMING ALSO the unilateral cessation of nuclear weapons tests until the end of this year, and looking forward to the permanent cessation of such tests;

EXPRESSES its pleasures at these gratifying developments, and its hope that the reduction of tension will be continued by these and other measures now in prospect, including vigorous measures for expanding the exchange of visitors, of goods, and of ideas.

(submitted by the Delegations
of the USSR and the USA)

Needless to say, this non-controversial resolution passed unanimously, although some American delegates refused to work for its passage. It was quite apparent that they thought it was a mistake.

However, the cold war policy differences among the American delegates soon found a battlefield. This came about with a resolution sponsored by England and Poland calling for the establishment of zones freed from nuclear weapons. Such a resolution ran counter to American cold war policy. The American delegates who advocated continuing the cold war won the decision to fight the resolution at the plenary session in the presence of all the nations of the federation. The fight occurred, but the voting was unanimously against America. This vote against the American position was not, in my opinion, a vote on the specific resolution concerning zones freed of nuclear weapons; it was a vote against America by the other countries because they had reached the end of yielding so much to American cold war policies. When all votes go one way there is usually some clear reason. My own explanation for such an overwhelming vote against America is that on all previous issues the other nations, including the Russians, had yielded rather generously to the American position in the interest of lessening international tension. The American delegation approached the vote on this last issue like one who has received nine of the ten slices of bread on a table and is now arguing for the tenth. Getting the tenth slice if you can, an old practice of the cold war, was first instituted by the Russians. When, in typical cold war fashion, American delegates tried this, every nation voted against her.

The point is that today the countries of the world will not stand by cold war friends in violation of the principle of reasonable compromise. While the bonds of cold war alliances may be strong when war is feared, they are not as strong when reasonable compromise will promote world peace. Other bonds are now necessary.

This example illustrates also that the cold war will still be fought by many Americans for a long time to come. The cold war is not yet so cold it is dead. Nevertheless, in spite of a large minority who support it, the cold war is ending. The tide of public opinion favors a new policy. Millions of people and hundreds of institutions are turning away from the cold war in search of some new and better policy. And even the millions who appear to favor a continuation of the cold war, and the institutions defending this continuation, are feeling some frustration about their position.

To sum up the situation: A cold war is the last step before a hot war. Since the cold war began in 1946, people have had time to produce sophisticated weapons that could mean the annihilation of the human race. Reflecting upon such a possible result of the cold war, people are expending great effort to find some new international policy to promote understanding and world peace.

What will replace the cold war? It is difficult to say, but it is certain that the new internationalism will continue the opposition between the communist and the free world. Like it or not, free men everywhere will continue to be committed to opposing communism for all the foreseeable years ahead. Nevertheless, this opposition must be something other than military if we are to survive.

What term or phrase will be substituted for the term "cold war"? History has yet to answer that question. Some of the phrases now used to describe this new policy of international relations incorporate some old but challenging ideas such as:

> a policy of cautious tolerance;
> a fair market of free competition in goods and ideas;
> one world without iron or bamboo curtains;
> a world without nuclear weapons, but a world with various social systems;
> a world of freedom with justice;
> a world of live and let live;
> a world whose common humanity outweighs all the differences of nations or races or social systems; and
> a federation of nations united for peace yet independent and free and equal for all other purposes.

Such are the words and phrases that give some indication of the nature of this new internationalism.

Some events leading to a cessation of the cold war may give us some idea of the world to be. These events were:

> the unilateral cessation of nuclear tests;

the signing of cultural exchange agreements between the communist nations and the free world;

the increasing moral and physical presence of the United Nations organization;

the fourteen thousand American tourists who visited Russia this summer of 1959;

the exchange of United States and Russian exhibitions in Moscow and New York;

the Russian tour of Vice-president Richard Nixon;

the present exchange visits between the Chairman of the Council of Ministers of the USSR and the President of the United States;

the new trade agreements between the communist and free nations.

Underlying all these specific events which lessened international tension is a new will to achieve peace that is surging forth everywhere in the world. People have had second thoughts about settling international disputes with force and violence. The new weapons that would be used with such a policy are now too ultimate, too absolute, too final. The cold war is a preparation to use such weapons. The cold war is a preparation of people's minds to use such weapons. And if the mind is resolved and the weapons are available, the doom of this world is sealed.

Where will men turn to find a better alternative than a cold war with all its risks of annihilation?

The answer lies in the classrooms of free schools and free universities. Other institutions may help to achieve a peaceful world, but the great burden and the great promise of a peaceful world will be found in a free classroom.

Why is this so? Because a free classroom is the one place on earth that most fairly and objectively seeks to find and live by truth.

The end of the cold war does not mean the end of the struggle between the communist and free worlds. Opposition to communism will go on as long as men love freedom. Can we peacefully oppose communism successfully by any other means than by the truth?

From the beginning of this modern era, we have been crying over and over, "The facts, the facts, give us the facts." Where does one best find the facts? What institution devotes itself only to the facts? Indeed, does not every institution think and act in terms of its own well-being first and last–with one exception, a free classroom? Here there is no loyalty to supercede the loyalty to truth. Again, is there a better chance for three billion people to live in peace other than through an education that finds and teaches only the facts? And if America is thrust into a place of leadership among these three billion people, can it ever succeed by any other means than by possessing the facts?

Moreover, wars are made in the heat of strong emotions. But nothing is more true of human psychology than that awareness of the facts cools off emotions. Plain, simple facts, accurately understood, drive out irrational emotions and facilitate calm deliberation.

Those of us engaged in the higher education of a free nation are deeply involved in this transition toward a new internationalism. If we are still fighting the cold war, we are out-of-date. If we are not of some aid in this pioneering for the survival of humanity, we fail in that which society has a right to expect of us.

There has been one mistaken assumption made these past two or three years by nearly all of us. It is the fallacy that by concentrating on the physical sciences we can make America safe and secure. To stress the physical sciences is of great value, but to assume that science will have survival value to our nation is an illusion. Why is this so?

It is so because military weapons have already, and for some time, reached the saturation point of absolute destruction. Little more need be added to our present ability to give us the power to vaporize all life on this planet. Therefore, if America would survive, let no one suppose that a new large investment in the physical sciences will be of much help. Rather, if America would survive, let our concentration now be in the social sciences and in the humanities.

At this point there is a strange attitude about education in our American culture. It is that the businessman lives by the creed of free enterprise, fair competition, and ultimately upon the judgment of the buyer as to the best product, the best service, and the fairest price. By this system, which is the best ever yet devised to benefit the consumer, the businessman lives and generally thrives. He fights against social controls that kill incentive and thereby ultimately hurt the consumer. He fights for his freedom. But, strangely enough, he also fails to join his best ally – a good teacher in a classroom. It is false to say that there is no clash between the business community and the educational community. There has been a continual clash between them throughout American history. Businessmen give generously to charities but grudgingly to education – especially for schools of excellence. Lately, some businessmen have yielded to the argument of investing in education for the teaching of science in our schools.

Alas! If American free enterprise survives and if America as a nation survives by taking the wise course of some new internationalism, the center of power and knowledge for such a survival is not in science or in armaments where nearly all our money is spent. Rather, our destiny depends upon that education now receiving little attention – the social sciences and the humanities. The minds of men are influenced on the great issues of life by teachers in the social sciences and humanities. Here in these classrooms are fought the issues and ideas of freedom and communism.

Why does not the American business community understand this and support the free classroom as its strongest ally? The case now is not just for a free economic system at home. It is for the very survival of America. We will win if we know languages, histories, and cultures other than our own. We will lose without such knowledge.

Will the business community rise up to strengthen our schools so that America will remain free and safe among the nations of the world? It is doubtful. The clash is as old as America, and even now in a desperate hour of need, America will go on to suffer a hazardous future because of poorly supported public schools and universities.

There is, however, one sure method, even with average schools, to win a new and better internationalism. It is to diligently apply what we understand as the scientific method. Science begins and ends with the facts, but between this beginning and end there is a theory or law or hypothesis which science uses to account for the facts. Now this hypothesis or scientific theory is always held as provisional, tentative, and subject to modification or even total rejection. This humility about its laws, generalizations, and hypotheses is the very genius of science.

This scientific method is now submitted as the best procedural way to achieve a replacement of our cold war theory.

The same humility involved in the scientific method can also transform our understanding of the human world. If one were to indicate the greatest block to world peace today, it would be that segment of the human race, the communists, committed to a method that denies tentativeness to their theory. They believe the theory of the class struggle with a finality that refuses the possibility of compromise. With such dogmatism, a communist is the present problem-child of the human race. And anyone who holds a theory or belief as final and absolute is thereby a potential peace problem to his neighbors and to the world.

Education at its best for world peace would be the application of the scientific method to world problems. We must find the facts as best we can, organize those facts under a workable hypothesis, verify our hypothesis with new facts, and change the hypothesis whenever new facts require us to do so. In the past our facts justified a cold war policy, but new facts are now present. We and our opposition now possess lethal weapons. We therefore need a new hypothesis to guide our international relations. If we placed the cold war theory of opposition to communism side-by-side with a theory of peaceful opposition to communism, the results would be something like this:

The cold war theory puts great confidence in vast military preparation.

The peaceful opposition theory agrees in the need for great military strength but denies that such strength justifies much confidence for the future.

The cold war theory considers communism as wholly unworthy of trust and even incapable of the ordinary decencies of mankind.

The peaceful opposition theory is also unwilling to trust communism but holds that the dangers of being injured by too much trust can be matched by the danger of trusting too little. A person or a nation believed to be wholly depraved and without common decency may, in desperation, become very dangerous.

The cold war theory would trade little if at all with communist nations.

The peaceful opposition theory would reduce tensions by encouraging trade, except in strategic materials.

The cold war theory would reluctantly agree to minimum cultural exchanges.

The peaceful opposition theory would welcome cultural exchanges on a vast scale as a sure way to break the communist lie and also as a sure way to goodwill and the eventual banishment of war.

The cold war theory would condition human emotions with large measures of ill will and animosity toward communism as a dangerous enemy.

The peaceful opposition theory would purge ill will and animosity as unworthy of decent men and even hazardous when dealing with a serious problem like communism.

In summary, the cold war theory uses every weapon against communism short of force and violence, whereas the peaceful opposition theory is centered upon the goal of ultimate peace, and proposes to use every means available for its achievement, short of relinquishing freedom.

I would conclude by suggesting a phrase for this new era that is now replacing the cold war. It is "peaceful opposition to communism." Other terms to describe our new world may be less accurate and even dangerous. The term "peaceful coexistence" implies two existences living on either side of the iron or bamboo curtains. This double-world existence builds up tensions through fear and ignorance and is dangerous.

The term "one world" implies that there is no real division, but the division is real. The issue of individual freedom or collective coercion is clear. There never can be "one world" with people divided on this fundamental issue.

The ultimate fact of our world is that communism and the free world oppose each other. They will do so for years to come. If they oppose each other peacefully, the world may benefit. If they oppose each other forcefully, the world is finished. Therefore, let us give up the propagation of the cold war, which is lethally dangerous. In its place let us enter a new era of peaceful opposition.

I repeat what I said at the beginning of this speech: this year of 1959 is turning over to American colleges a new assignment of such magnitude as to outdate all our previous thinking. The cold war ends in 1959. The burden of the free world to meet the challenge of communism has now shifted from the military, the political, and even the scientific arenas to the free classrooms of the social sciences and the humanities.

Will America respond? The answer is not yet available.

Where Peace Begins

Utah State University Peace Center
February 23, 1969

□

In this peace center, one question will always be asked: "Where does peace begin?" Today I offer my own reply with the hope you will correct or replace it with a better answer.

Peace begins with the citizen of clear mind and warm heart who squarely faces the issues of peace and war, solves these issues by walking the middle of the road, and avoids solutions offered by the extreme right or extreme left. Stated another way, peace begins with a middle-of-the-roader whose reasoning is based upon facts, and whose attitude toward all men on earth is one of reverence, respect, and sympathy.

Put negatively, peace can hardly begin with extremists on the right or left, and scarcely at all with an individual whose mind is clouded and whose heart is cool toward any person, religion, race, nation, or group of nations. Stated in other negative terms, a person belonging to a group with radical commitments, right or left, and whose clear mind is not matched by a warm heart, or whose warm heart is not matched with a clear mind, presents a combination destined to fail.

Is such a reply adequate for world peace? Hardly. Peace or war may have nothing to do with a wise, warm, moderate individual. Peace or war will probably be decided in Washington or Moscow, or in the Near East or the Far East. Peace or war may result from the acts of some leader who is ill in mind or body; war may come from some failure of communication, possibly a careless technician or even a short circuit.

Nevertheless, however peace or war is achieved, we can choose one of two attitudes. We can believe that peace or war is beyond anything we can do, and, therefore, give up. Or, we can believe that each individual can do something and simply refuse to give up. However, it is clear that whatever course we take, it will be only a slight beginning toward peace.

We should be realists about our own small place in the world. Our hopes may be too high in believing that we can find good answers to the enormous problems of world peace; but I do believe that each individual should make every effort toward world peace.

As a young man I assumed that answers to my questions were just around the corner. In our youthful years and even later, there abides, perhaps in all of us, an optimism that some final answer will be found in a great book, or in some lecture, or in some college course, or most certainly in a whole college education. Life is full of opportunities to find answers, and maybe most of our countless questions are answered rather well.

However, some questions are not answerable. Some problems cannot be solved. The most that can be done with these questions is to whittle away at them. In some areas, every answer or solution is only temporary. With some difficult problems, we can do no better than muddle along.

I believe it is this way with the problem of world peace. There is no solution, no answer. In our optimism, we feel we are making progress—and perhaps we are. Yet, we cannot be sure. Old wars will not be repeated, but what of a hydrogen war?

Let us face it. The collapse of nineteenth-century optimism tells us, among other realities, that peace is a far-off goal. World peace is a hope that may easily be shattered, a dream not possible in this world.

If this is the case, then a more sober subject for our attention might be not where peace begins, but where war begins. War, like charity, might actually begin at home in our thoughts and before that in our subconscious drives—fear, hate, and jealousy. War may begin with our tribal fears and narrow loyalties, with newspaper headlines, or with the emotional overtone of television news. War may begin in some rice paddy, in the State Department, or in the Kremlin. War no longer begins with a declaration of Congress. And finally, although a war may have an infinite number of causes, history will primarily record the proximate causes—a gunshot or a single military order.

But then peace also begins in these same places—in emotions of compassion and forgiveness and in thoughts of fair play and sympathetic understanding. So, too, peace can begin with newspaper articles and television programs. Peace gets a good chance in foreign embassies and in Congress. Peace may come from decisions in the Pentagon or the Soviet Foreign Office.

Both war and peace, then, are products of the same human nature and institutions. Whatever is human may be both good and bad. It is trite to say that man is eternally capable of peace and also of war.

But if ambiguous human nature is a slippery base for lasting world peace, the deep historical hatreds that divide mankind are even more dangerous. Some divisions are religious, some racial, some tribal, and some national. Consider just one or two chasms of contemporary friction and hatred. The Jews, tired of persecution, wanted to return to their homeland and, therefore, drove the Arabs from their homes in Palestine. Now the Arabs want to return to this same homeland, and war is brewing in the Near East. The Czechoslovakians wanted more freedom and the Russians were afraid of another build-up from the West, so another war is possible. America has vital interests in the Pacific Basin, and we are now involved in Vietnam. Conflicts also are found in Pakistan and India, in Cuba and in Central America. And the list goes on.

Perhaps none of these international situations is capable of solution. Who can solve the problem of the Middle East? Who can solve the situation in Vietnam, for that matter?

What then are we to do? If peace is a problem we cannot solve, can we live with these problems short of all-out war? If we are not sure about this fragile peace, or limited war, may we who are here today retreat to some smaller base? As a last-ditch stand, we might say that if a larger war comes, at least we in this room did not contribute to it. If all-out war does come, we can say that we added no weight to the scales that balanced ever so slightly on the side of a third world war. And perhaps we can do more. We might not only not contribute to another world war, we might even contribute some microscopic influence for peace. It is with this marginal optimism, namely, that each one of us may contribute ever so slightly toward peace, that I offer the following.

If peace begins with an individual of clear mind and good heart, and of broad loyalties and rational practices, then two specific requirements are also necessary. To win peace requires, first, a mind that is objective, and, second, a belief that is unshakable. Without objectivity, no one can begin to deal with the problem of world peace. And no successful movement toward peace is possible without a profound belief in the intrinsic worth of every human being on the face of the earth.

More specifically then, peace begins with the seeming contradictions of objectivity and belief. If objectivity is the goal of a university and belief the basis for good citizenship, how much more these requirements are necessary for a sound international life.

One difficulty in a democratic society is to believe that the individual viewpoint makes a difference at the national level. At the international level this belief or faith that an individual can make a difference and affect the outcome of some action is difficult to maintain when considering that there are three or four billion people on earth. Are we not, each one of us, mere chips of wood carried along by the huge river of international events? I do not know. I only know we do not talk as though it were so. This paper assumes that the individual is important at the international level – not very important, really, yet of some small importance.

It may help, in this discussion, if we use some imagination. Suppose when you leave this room today, somebody runs up and tells you there is a long-distance call for you. When you pick up the telephone, the operator tells you the White House is calling. You are then asked if you will be a delegate and represent this country at some international peace negotiation – for example, the Paris peace talks. You might be asked to represent the United States on an international commission to settle the Israeli-Arab dispute in the Middle East, or the individual calling says you are appointed ambassador to the Soviet Union or United States Ambassador to the United Nations.

The point I would like to make is that if a magnifying glass reveals you are not qualified for any of these assignments, it would also reveal that you are not too well qualified when you express your opinions privately about the Near East, the Soviet Union, or Vietnam – not in Paris, or Jerusalem, or New York, but while you are eating dinner this evening with a friend here in Logan.

Whether in Geneva, or Moscow, or Saigon, or Logan, what are the individual qualifications for effective discussion or successful negotiation leading to world peace? Realistically – not in some faraway city and not representing a powerful nation, but just as a student or a private citizen – would the beliefs and attitudes you hold, if magnified, advance or retard the peace of the world? And, unmagnified – believing that in a democracy a single individual makes at least a microscopic difference – would your individual difference weigh on the scales for peace or for war?

With this introduction, let us now turn to the subject for this occasion: "Where Peace Begins."

Could you be objective about your country if you represented it at the United Nations? Or would you be blinded by national self-interest? Would you fight for all you could get for your country without restraint as to what might be a fair share? Even more difficult, could you be objective about communism?

In all honesty, the answer must be negative. Objectivity is a noble dream never realized, especially where great human values are at stake. The answer then is not whether there is complete objectivity, but if there is partial objectivity. And this is possible if one searches out the causes of things, the causal factors that have created the present situation.

For example, for over a hundred years Russia has been invaded and slaughtered by soldiers from western Europe until the Russians are unalterably suspicious of every move from the West. In the Near East, who can dispense even-handed justice to both the Arabs and Israelis? But if not, then favorable judgment should go first to one side and then to the other with only one stipulation – the killing must stop.

Objectivity, while so very necessary, is a kind of North Star that guides but is never reached. But what about the second requirement – an unshakable belief – as a qualification for one dealing on an international level to establish a peaceful world? It is at this point that we touch the Christian ethic about agape. The ancient Christians understood the ethic of love not as a sentimental attachment to a person or group, but as a reverence for both the lovable and the unlovable, both friend and foe, both for those who helped and those who hurt. They believed every human being was intrinsically precious to God, regardless of merit. This was the basis of their faith. It would apply today if we loved the communists who vilify us at the peace table and who in Peking, the Kremlin, and Hanoi plot our downfall. Such a belief must be unshakable, even in limited Vietnam wars. But again, in all honesty, such a qualification is not wholly realizable. Our deepest beliefs, our total commitments, while they do not die in the heat of battle or the darkness of despair, only glimmer and sputter.

Where, then, does peace begin? It begins here on this campus with the person who has a clear mind and warm heart, and squarely faces the issues of peace and war and solves them by taking a middle-of-the-road position. This person, avoiding answers from the radical right or the radical left and walking and working on this highway toward a more peaceful world, is armed with two necessary qualifications – objectivity and an unshakable belief in the dignity of all men.

The Greatest Honor

Memory Grove, Salt Lake City
Memorial Day, 1969

□

Decoration Day is now a family day. Originally it was a day to commemorate those who had died in the service of our country. But now, as well as remembering our fallen servicemen, millions decorate the graves and recall memories of other loved ones gone ahead of us.

This particular service today is in honor of those who died while in uniform, those who took on the burden of their country in a very special way. All of us serve our country as good citizens, but here we gather to honor those who paid the supreme sacrifice for their country. Contemplating such an awesome and enormous sacrifice, we are reduced almost to silence. Scarcely any words, or even music, can express one's feelings.

I am simply one American, and in speaking to you today, I beg you to allow me to be what I am—a teacher. As such, I want to reason, reflect, and meditate with you about this Decoration Day and about our beloved America.

We have met here to pay honor and respect and express our love for those who could have lived longer but gave up years of their lives that we might be secure and free. The honor we now pay to them is both from our intellect and our emotions, both from our mind and our heart, both from our understanding and our love.

On the intellectual or understanding side of this honor, we assert the following propositions to be true:

> To live in our imperfect world can involve us in conflicts with others. Sometimes these conflicts result in war.
>
> American security – the safety and security for each one of us here today – is the primary purpose of military action.
>
> Before our atomic age, America fought two world wars. In each war we fought against powers that threatened our safety, our freedom, and the cherished values of our American way of life.
>
> Those who fought and those who died in these two world wars did so because we were in mortal danger. They died to save our freedom, our independence, and our pursuit of happiness.
>
> Since the second of these two world wars, America has fought limited wars, with limited objectives. The atomic bomb has made unlimited war unwise, unsafe, and even unthinkable. Yet limited wars, as in Korea and South Vietnam, are fought for the same purpose as the two world wars – that is, for our safety and our well-being.

Now, we ask the great question for all of us: Who is to say whether or not a combination of foreign powers would now, today, be able to successfully challenge our present security, our present freedoms, our American way of life without our struggles in Korea and South Vietnam? And who does not hope that through our sacrifices in Korea and South Vietnam, America, with credibility and bargaining strength, can now carefully, patiently, and wisely turn to the pathways of peace and lead the world in freedom and peace?

Even though we accept the present painful reality of limited wars with limited objectives, this can be changed. The past and even the present need not bind us. The future belongs to us. The future can be a brighter day in which there will be no more war.

The Greatest Honor

The single greatest honor, therefore, that we can pay to those who died for us, is for each one of us to make our own personal sacrifices for a future peaceful world.

Some of these personal sacrifices for peace begin with the ideas now in our minds. Some of the ideas are not compatible with peace. We cannot keep some of them and still have peace. Wars are made in the minds of men. Some of our minds need changing if we honor the dead as we should on this Decoration Day.

To repeat, some people have ideas they cannot continue to believe and still have peace. What are some of the ideas that must go? There are many, but some of the more dangerous are:

> That wars are inevitable because man is an aggressive and combative animal, and human nature cannot be changed.
>
> That wars are inevitable because sacred scriptures state that wars are inevitable.
>
> That wars will continue because of man's stupidity and ignorance, and in the future we will just stumble into war.
>
> That war will come because evil men, like communists, and evil nations, like communist nations, will try to take us over either peacefully or with war.

I do not believe that war is inevitable, and I believe it is morally wrong to believe war is inevitable. To say our future will be one with war is to edge us nearer to the likelihood of war. With such ideas and beliefs, we dishonor those who died for us in past wars, and we betray those now dying for us in Vietnam.

We must not so dishonor them. We must clear our heads of fatalistic ideas, base and unwarranted suspicions, and false concepts of our own superiority and righteousness. War as a means of settling disputes can be abolished, just as slavery and child labor were abolished.

Moreover, in addition to sacrificing and abolishing these fatalistic, false ideas, we must also change our hearts. It will not do for us to make a religion of anti-communism. We are all opposed to communism, but we must not let our hearts be filled with hostility, animosity, and hatred. Surely we can oppose communism better than that.

We want the FBI to identify and protect us from the communists in our midst, but we do not want the FBI to dictate the ideas and emotions to guide us in dealing with this difficult problem. We want the military to be strong if we fail in negotiation, but we do not want the military to influence us in our conferences. We want schools and churches to inform us about the tyranny of communism, but we do not want any teacher or minister to have the last word about how we should deal with it.

We need more humility and less dogmatism, more open-mindedness and less blind emotion. Above all, we want our political leaders to have this same humility and open-mindedness. It will not do for our country to act rashly from a pattern of ideas and emotions that belong to yesterday.

If war has been a necessary part of our past history, war need not be a necessary part of our future. The greatest honor we can pay those who died in uniform is to labor unceasingly to avoid future wars.

What, then, of the future? What, then, of the sacrifices we must make to avoid war – sacrifices both of the mind and of the heart?

We must discard many of our unwarranted anxieties and fears about the future, and even discard some of our neutral perplexities. Events abroad and at home have divided us into those who are nonplussed and those who are cocksure. It will not do to live in a mood of hesitation and doubt, nor can those be trusted who make snap judgments.

We must dig more deeply, search more carefully, and think more clearly about the timeless values and ideals of our democracy. We are not strangers to change and revolution. We must be calm before the extremists, the radicals, the revolutionaries. We must not be too upset when they accurately describe our failures. A premise of our democracy is that of continual progression from failures to corrections, wrongs to improvements.

Deep within America is the reality of change and experimentation. We did not allow our early revolution to freeze into tyranny as did the communists. We keep our revolution young and perpetual.

Just now we are involved in two long overdue revolutions—the black revolution and the youth revolution. Tomorrow we will confront other revolutions. Each will tell us something of our failures, and each will produce some of our successes.

Yet, with all our needed changes, there are some abiding values to guide us. Some of these values imbedded in our culture are: that each human being is a child of God; that each individual is to be respected for his differences; that each person is to be treated with dignity and respect.

Just now the two revolutions of the youths and the blacks are violating the rules of change. They are breaking the laws. They have great freedoms and channels of lawful protest, but some of them break these boundaries of fair play. And so they slip backward more than they go forward, they regress rather than progress. With their violence and lawbreaking they hurt more than they help. But they do not make us afraid. Our convictions about the sanctity of law, the sacredness of personality, the freedom to correct our failures gives us confidence in the midst of our present turmoil.

Nor are we afraid of peaceful competition with communism. Our free enterprise system, with its built-in self-corrections, its challenge of competition, and its incentives to produce well, will outstrip the social planning of any and all communist nations.

And we are not afraid of freedom, either to criticize or be criticized.

So on this beautiful Decoration Day, our hearts are filled with gratitude for all the past sacrifices of the men and women who died that we might live to make a future, better world. We will not disappoint them.

To use some of the words of Abraham Lincoln, we are still "a new nation, conceived in liberty, and dedicated to the proposition that all men are created equal." Brave men, both living and dead, lead us forward to a more peaceful and a happier world. And on this Decoration Day we dedicate ourselves again "to the unfinished work remaining before us. From our honored dead we take increased devotion to that cause for which they gave the last full measure of devotion – that we here highly resolve that these dead shall not have died in vain – that this nation, under God, shall have a new birth of freedom, and government of the people, by the people, for the people, shall not perish from the earth."

The Individual and the United Nations

Utah Association for the United Nations Banquet
October 24, 1978

☐

We have met on this twenty-fourth of October to celebrate the anniversary of the signing of the United Nations Charter just thirty-three years ago in San Francisco.

When the United Nations was founded I was greatly impressed with its possibilities. It was created for the single purpose of assuring a world at peace. As I look back now, like most Americans I was overly optimistic. The peace of the world has proven to be a problem of such enormity as to sweep many of us, from the side of over-optimism, to the side of over-pessimism.

The simple fact about the United Nations is that it must of necessity live in two contrasting worlds. One is the world of mankind's ideals, a world of peace with justice and freedom. This is the world speakers for the United Nations usually choose to talk about.

The other world is the world of harsh realities. It is our present world of poverty and ignorance and great suffering. I think no institution was ever created, or, one might say, ever condemned, to live with such sharp contrasts. And if our present world of poverty and suffering and ignorance were not enough, add to this a long list of human frailties – the love of power, the fear of change, greed, envy, and jealousy, all part of the world of human nature – with which the United Nations must deal. When these negative factors are added up, they make a staggering total. They are the forces that oppose the peace of mankind. Certainly, they make difficult the achievement of a world of peace with freedom and justice.

But I am an optimist. The development of our great natural resources will offset much of the world's poverty. Better medicine will relieve much human suffering. More and better places of learning will counter wide areas of ignorance. And as for our human frailties, they are counterbalanced by the good side of human nature. People love to give service. There is in human nature a joy in sharing, and there always will be the endless search for better justice.

Over thirty years ago I made a commitment to support the United Nations, and with modest time and means, I have kept that pledge.

Grace, my wife, and I have been partners in our support of the United Nations. Sometimes she traveled with me, and sometimes her part was to keep the home fires burning while I traipsed around the world as an American delegate to the plenary sessions of the World Federation of the United Nations Association.

One year we even made it a family affair. When our two daughters were of high school age, they went with me to Geneva, and made themselves useful by placing the countless resolutions, motions, amendments, and notes on the desks of delegates assembled there from so many countries of the world.

Looking back on those years, I think Utah has a good record in support of the United Nations. Among presidents of the Utah Association of the United Nations was the Episcopal Bishop of Utah, a state supreme court justice, a dean from the faculty of the University of Utah, the head of a prestigious law firm, the head of a large supermarket, and on our board was one of the General Authorities of the Church of Jesus Christ of Latter-day Saints.

I was never able to separate the United Nations from religion. But then, many good things cannot be separated from religion. I do know that the brotherhood of man is the very foundation of the United Nations.

The balance of what I want to say this evening relates to the problems of world peace—whether it can be won—and just one suggestion of how this may be possible. I caution that my suggestion is limited. It narrows down to a concept of the individual—a single, solitary, private individual. But then, our whole civilization is best described as one of individualism.

Someone has said that the greatest threat to world peace will be found in the individual of limited understanding and narrow sympathies. If this is true, then on the other hand there is great hope for a world of peace if the individual is one of *clear* mind and *broad sympathies*.

Most all of us, I suppose, spend much of our lives trying to emerge from our present limitations to a future of something larger and better. And nowhere are we more severely tested in this struggle than when we face the tremendous problem of world peace.

One way to state the problem of peace is to say that it is the tough issue of how free nations and communist nations can live on this planet, hopefully with some measure of goodwill toward each other. If there is a more difficult problem than this, I do not know what it is. And nowhere does the problem surface so sharply as in the United Nations organization in New York.

Here is what I think the message of the United Nations may be to each individual: If you relate your life and your hopes to the United Nations organization, you must be tough and durable, for your patience will be tried to the limit. The United Nations is no place for a mind with fixed ideas of ill will and deep prejudice. It is no place for a heart that is provincial and narrow in its sympathies.

In stressing this importance of the individual, it may be countered that single individuals, after all, cannot really affect the great issues of peace or war. One could well ask whether individuals are not more like pieces of cork or leaves floating along on the river of irreversible international events.

I do not choose to believe this, though it may be true. I choose to believe that the hope of the world is in a growing number of people, individuals, with clear minds and strong hearts. In our great democracy, a favorite reference is to "the grass-roots level." The United Nations also depends upon support at the grass-roots level – people, one by one, of deep personal convictions, independent, and with enough integrity to say: "I know my country needs a strong military defense, a good State Department, and an effective CIA and FBI, and I am glad to have them. But I want to do my thing, and my thing is to help my country by spreading sincere goodwill in the parts of the world where the people are communist, to extend to them a hand of patient understanding and warm friendship. I believe such an effort may be that small margin or increment that may result in peace rather than war."

One day, back in those chilly and suspicious days of the cold war, I received a telephone call, one of several I was accustomed to receiving, from an agent of the State Department in Washington. He asked me to host two VIP citizens from the Soviet Union, together with their interpreter. One was a former editor of *Pravda*, and the other was a friend I made at the United Nations meetings in Geneva.

I recall that as I drove to the airport to meet them, I hoped their visit to Salt Lake would be quiet and uneventful. Those were the days of strong emotion and broad suspicion. Against my hope for a quiet visit, the local newspapers had received word of their arrival, and in the hasty interview at the airport, one correspondent asked: "We understand your trip in America will be limited to visiting three cities. Why did you choose Salt Lake as one of them?" "Oh," came a warm and friendly reply from my Soviet friend, "I wanted to come to Salt Lake to see my good friend, Mr. Tanner." Sure enough, that reply was reproduced the next day in a very conspicuous place in the newspaper.

They stayed in our home that night and we had a friendly visit. The next morning Grace cooked them a wonderful breakfast and then we took a stroll in our gardens. A remarkable and surprising observation was made by the former editor of *Pravda*, at least it was a surprise to me. He observed rather casually: "I think, Mr. Tanner, that you have even more beautiful gardens than Mr. Eaton." In a flash I realized that I belonged to a narrow circle – one that scarcely any American would covet, but one that I prized, nevertheless. Cyrus Eaton, of Cleveland, was then widely known as one who favored trade and good relations with the Soviet Union, almost unheard of at that time. Standing with my Russian guests in my garden, I felt the triumph of a great victory. In those cold war days there were not many genuinely hospitable places in America for Russians to visit. And in those days I was aware that many of my fellow citizens would consider me suspect. But I was more certain that I was in harmony with the great Judeo-Christian tradition. Seen from this point of view, Karl Marx was a newcomer, and although his ideas had captured the minds in the country of my friends, centuries separated us. Marx favored violence and revolution; Christ asked for goodwill and kindness. Marx advocated the tyranny of a dictatorship; Plato favored the freedom of reason to solve our problems.

But for all this difference with my guests, I wanted to avoid the arrogance of feeling superior. I wanted to be a Christian, just that once; and to my deep satisfaction, I felt they wanted to be men of goodwill toward me.

Our Utah Association for the United Nations is but a small candle, yet it does devote itself to shedding the light of information about a great institution created to keep peace in the world. And if clear minds and warm hearts in all nations, communist and free, light enough candles for peace with freedom, then this earth, instead of spinning in nuclear silence, will be a habitation for human voices full of joy, love, and sadness–a place for human accomplishment.

II

TRUTH AND EDUCATION

Introduction

Chase Peterson

□

These lectures on truth and education come from a gentle capitalist of the lecture hall and the board room who argues for and has benefited from a rigorous pursuit of truth wherever his educated mind has taken him. Has there been a teacher-businessman-philanthropist to match Obert Tanner? Edwin Land, founder and inventor of Polaroid photography and part-time Harvard scholar, comes close. And there are probably others. But who else, while a full-time professor, developed a company that leads the world in its field and invested a large portion of its profits in projects to enhance civic beauty and intellectual excellence?

These lectures discuss education as the means to pursue Plato's ideals. They were written for public schoolteachers, university faculty, managers of organizations, and in fact could be primers for an MBA program as much as for a philosophy class. Obert Tanner created wealth by working hard and understanding human nature and its natural hunger for beauty and recognition. He escaped the bondage of wealth by exercising it in the pursuit

Dr. Peterson is President of the University of Utah.

73

of beauty. His inspiration has its roots in Bethlehem two millennia past and Athens 2,400 years ago. But the ideas are as fresh today as they were then and when he began to write his own interpretations thirty years ago.

The Teacher and America Today

Spring Institute of Salt Lake City Public School Teachers
May 16, 1958

□

Let us think for a few minutes about America, about her well-being, her safety, and her future. In doing so, let us be neither pessimistic nor optimistic but as objective and realistic as possible.

First, may I express the profound gratitude I feel for the freedom that is mine on this occasion. Your superintendent simply asked me to come; no suggestions, no instructions, and no limitations were imposed upon me. For this freedom I am deeply grateful. But I do feel one compulsion—it is to be as factual as I can. I shall attempt to state simply and accurately a few facts about our American life.

We all love America. We all want her safety and well-being. We want America to continue her free way of life for the generations to come.

Just now, in this year of 1958, America is in trouble. Two great problems are facing America. If either one of them is not solved very soon, America will be lost. One is the problem of world peace, of danger to America from without. The other is the problem of our schools, of danger to America from within. These two, peace and education, are the great failures of America. We are moving in the direction of war, and we are failing our schools.

75

All other problems in America are minor compared to these two. We can solve with some success juvenile delinquency, crime problems, unemployment, bad roads, and community health. But if we fail to prevent war, America will be a graveyard. If we do not do more than we are now doing for our schools, our great democracy is finished. The two, our schools and our foreign affairs, overarch all other concerns in American life. And here, we meet our two greatest failures.

Our present concern here today is the failure of America with her schools. What is this failure? It is that our business civilization, our free enterprise system, our wealth-minded nation will not sufficiently sacrifice for better schools. The whole atmosphere of American wealth-gathering and wealth-keeping is unfriendly to schools and to the teachers in our schools. We all say we want better schools, but we want more to keep the extra dollars which better schools would cost. We all say we respect the teachers of our children, but that is not wholly true. Both in their attitude and lack of generosity toward schools, Americans are now destroying their democracy.

If any institution can make America safe from war in the family of nations, if any institution can preserve our democracy at home, that institution is our free educational system for all the people. But America is not willing to pay the price. Americans individually are not sufficiently educated to help their country take a leading role in the family of nations. We claim our country is misunderstood, that other nations are ungrateful; but the truth is we are not educated. We do not know the facts of the world. We want world leadership to make others as free as we are free, but we do not know their languages, their histories, or their cultures. We lack sympathy. We have walls of prejudice and cannot reach other people. Our main concern is for ourselves. And so America stumbles along in foreign relations that risk war rather than build peace. Only our schools, if it is not too late, can educate us to take a proud place in the family of nations. But we do not have those schools. And so we are destined for a long time to come to walk the narrow line between war and peace, between life for a far-off better day or death in a vast thermonuclear explosion.

Leaving the foreign relations field, which is tragic enough, we turn to our domestic life. Here in America we want above all else to be free. As free men we can solve all problems with some measure of success and with a large measure of happiness. It makes all the difference in the world whether a problem is solved as free men do it in America, or whether conscripts of the state do it as in communist nations. This is the difference between America and Russia. Both solve their problems one way or another. But Russia does it by issuing the order, "Wanted: conscripts." We do it by saying, "Wanted: volunteers." Only a volunteer knows the joys of a freely chosen way of life. Only a volunteer knows the dignity and respect that make life glad, beautiful, and good.

How do men stay free? How is freedom maintained? There is only one answer: by education. Our schools have the final word on whether our democracy lives or dies.

When is freedom lost? When power is centralized. Freedom is lost when there is a combining of economic and political power, where the state owns and operates our economic life. Political power and economic power combined are a concentration of power so great and so final that they blot out the freedom of the individual. In socialism or communism there is no exaltation of private conscience and personal dignity; there is no free individual.

And our free enterprise system, regulated but not owned or controlled by the state, is the first line of defense for a true democracy. Teachers and preachers must see that businessmen, fighting off the encroachments of government, help to insure our academic and spiritual freedoms. If businessmen lose their fight for economic freedom, our intellectual freedoms will soon fall before a powerful state. This is the lesson learned from socialism and communism. Great centralized power leaves little ground for a free individual, and no ground at all for dissent of individual thought and private conscience.

But how do businessmen stay free? How does free enterprise survive? What prevents men from using the ballot box as a shortcut to socialism? There is only one answer – the free education of all the people. In schools each new generation has to learn from scratch the great values of democratic life. If these lessons are not learned well, demagogues take over, shortcuts are tried, freedoms are lost. Children can inherit property from their parents, but they cannot inherit an understanding and love for democracy. This must be taught by precept and example in our schools.

Thus, our schools perpetuate our democratic way of life. For example, they teach how complex and how difficult the free enterprise or capitalistic system is to maintain. The capitalistic system, like democracy itself, survives only because of critical self-examination; and through the criticism, the failures and shortcomings of capitalism are corrected, or at least modified and mitigated. Who teaches this wholesome criticism? Where are *all* institutions studied objectively? The answer is in our schools. Our schools study our economic system and appraise its justice or injustice, its fair or foul play. Corrections of unfair practices, abuses, or excessive greed, allow the free enterprise system to survive from generation to generation.

What if, in our schools, Americans were to learn mostly of the many failures of capitalism? Then capitalism is doomed, for it has many failures, as do all human institutions. One benefactor of clear thinking and good teaching about our capitalistic system is the businessman himself. But what if the businessman denies his support to better schools? What if his chamber of commerce spearheads a campaign against better schools? But worse, far worse, what if the business community imputes bad motives to the teaching profession? What if taxpayers resist increased taxation for schools because business organizations slander teachers?

I submit that businessmen who wound the pride of teachers, who offend their dignity, who hold them in thinly concealed contempt, are digging the grave of capitalism faster than creeping socialism or violent communism. For teachers will have the last say. Humiliated and belittled, they may retaliate in the classroom. There a teacher can weigh the many merits and the many demerits of capitalism. If that teacher has been humiliated, and sometimes even mortally offended, that classroom may become no defense for capitalism.

What if the teacher accurately points out the regular search of business for a profit, but does *not* point out the normal check on the extent of that profit in a standard competitive economy? What if the teacher talks of the goal of economic justice in socialism, but does *not* point out the loss of freedom to the individual in a social system where all power of business and government are combined? What if the teacher helps the student to see the vast inequities of income that business people sometimes gain by accident or cunning, while hard labor is meagerly rewarded, without pointing out that all economic systems including our capitalistic one have failures, but that the main value of any economic system is to keep men free?

Why can't businessmen see that their free private enterprise is best defended by teachers who possess sympathetic understanding of the problems of business life?

One reason is that some of these businessmen, themselves financially successful but without formal education, do not understand the underlying principles of a free enterprise system. Or, being people who see profit and loss in immediate transactions, they fail to comprehend the long-term conditions necessary for a free society. One of those conditions is a classroom teacher who is both well trained for his profession and well appreciated by all the community–especially by the business community. Has it never occurred to business people that teachers observe the silence of the chamber of commerce when the public is charged increased rates by businesses, such as the public utilities; and they also observe the strong protest against increased costs for any but other businesses? A public utility may need to raise its rates to render good services, but so too our schools cost more for good work.

It will be the end of freedom in America if businessmen are no longer free. Economic freedom is basic to other freedoms. Socialism concentrates power in the state, and a more powerful state means a more weakened individual. And this understanding is a matter of careful education. Economic freedom can only survive by free criticism of its abuses and failures. And this can only come by careful teaching from teachers who themselves are carefully trained. All this defense of a free economy is a matter for our schools.

Capitalism is a complex economic system. To understand its successes and its failures one must possess a knowledge of human psychology, sociology, economics, and political theory. But, above all these, capitalism requires a full awareness of the highest values in human life—values that are only possible to possess in a world of free men. And a world of free men results only when men are free in business.

So, America is in trouble! And the principal cause of her trouble is the failure of many businessmen to support better schools. Freedom is maintained by knowledge and understanding. It is lost through ignorance and irrational prejudices. He who opposes better schools, opposes America. He who belittles and humiliates the teaching profession thrusts a knife into the heart of our democracy. He who contributes poorly to education in America cuts the taproots of our democracy and bequeaths to his children and grandchildren an America that will no longer be free.

But there is another failure from mediocre schools. This failure is more serious than the gradual loss of our economic freedoms and even partial loss of our political and intellectual freedoms. This is the present failure of America within the family of nations. Beyond the loss of freedom at home there is the greater loss to America of her high standing in the society of nations because of an inadequately informed population. This failure could involve us eventually in war. It certainly will involve us in misunderstanding abroad, misspent money in foreign aid, and mistakes that are costly and unnecessary.

What is this world of 1958? It is a world divided between the free and the communist spheres. It is a world of 2,500 million, most of whom are illiterate and hungry. It is a world where masses of men are on the march to find a better life. It is a world of missile weapons, of power-hungry leaders, of freedom-loving people. It is a world of new science and old hatreds. It is a world of promise and danger.

What is to be America's role in this newly emerging, rapidly changing world? That will depend upon the quality of our schools. Will America understand other parts of the world, others' religions, others' history, others' cultural values? This depends upon the quality of our schools.

Suppose we as a people do not understand other peoples—their languages, their institutions, and their aspirations? Such ignorance on the part of our fathers made little difference to them. America was then secure, even without the facts of the world, and even without the sympathies of foreign peoples. But such ignorance in the smaller world in which we live today will either plunge us into war or, escaping that, relegate us to a position behind some other nation whose population is educated for world understanding and world leadership.

American schools need better scientific training, but even this training is not crucial to our security. Why? Because there is no longer any security through military strength. A country that is second in the number of guided missiles can still annihilate the stronger nation. Second-rate missiles can exterminate us quite as handily as first-rate missiles. Yet, our schools do need to be strengthened in science, even for the short-run security of our better missiles and our better military weapons.

In the *long run*, what America needs most from our schools are not *physical* scientists, but *social* scientists. America must prevent a war of her own extinction by preparing thousands and even millions of her people in the languages and customs of people all over the world. Herein, our schools may yet save us from a war of extermination. But our schools are not prepared to do this. Their funds are cut, their personnel is inadequate, and the teaching morale is low.

But not all the blame goes to those in the business community. In Utah, our schools began to slip downward in quality when a high government official started unbelievable public abuse of our teachers. This individual damaged our schools possibly for generations to come. So Utah schools started a downward course in personnel morale that has not yet been stopped.

How did all this happen so quickly? How did Utah lose her high position among the schools of America? Was it our financial penury or our inability to pay? Most of this tragic failure in our schools was not financial at all. It was psychological. It was a succession of blows that cut into the morale of our teaching profession. It was the open public statements of some political and business leaders that destroyed the personal dignity and public esteem of our teachers. Teachers, unlike people in the rough-and-tumble business or political life, are essentially missionaries at heart. They are sensitive, dedicated people. And when their pride is offended, their dignity outraged, and their humiliation complete, our schools are damaged beyond repair. Utah needs an apology for this public slander of a great profession. No other profession would have endured it. And never will Utah schools be healthy and strong again unless the public reverses this trend and the teacher is once more brought to a place of high respect in our public life.

Ladies and gentlemen, you who teach must be diligent about the quality of our schools. As each American proudly fights for the advancement of his own profession, his own vocation, his own standard of living, so you must unite and work as you are now doing for better schools. If you let down your fight for better schools you betray your profession, and in some real sense, you also betray America. America must have better schools if she is to survive. She must have better schools if she is to stay free.

This is your profession. If you slacken in your courage and hard effort for better schools, all of us are the losers. No other profession will champion your cause. Each profession must champion its own.

What I now say, I do so after careful reflection. It would be better that our schools did not open for a time than that they open to a profession of teachers who are beaten and discouraged, teachers whose work would most surely produce future Americans unable to maintain freedom at home and unable to survive in competition with other, better-educated nations.

America is no place for people who lack courage in a cause they know is right. If with unity of purpose and strength you do not lead this great country to standards of education necessary for survival and freedom, who else will do so? Your struggle has fairly started. You must stay unified in your purpose and in your efforts.

May I give you a suggestion of doubtful encouragement? Soon, next year or the next, our military will have a missile program so colossal and absolutely sufficient, that a push-button war could exterminate all our enemies. What then are we to do with the fifty billions of our annual taxes that go for the military? A state of saturation of absolute military sufficiency will come soon. Perhaps then we can turn more of our wealth to better schools. Americans are a tax-burdened and tax-weary people. Perhaps soon, their burden will be lightened and more will be available for our schools. There is just one catch to this possibility – the Russians will also soon possess power of absolute sufficiency to destroy America while we are destroying Russia.

But how will such a calamity as that be avoided? By our schools teaching the Russian language and history, teaching a sympathetic understanding of the Russian people, and at the same time teaching about the menace and the evil of communism. We can avoid an unspeakable tragedy for America by a greater appeal to reason in our schools and less appeal to emotions by our political leaders. We must communicate in every way possible with the people of Russia by exchanging teachers, businessmen, doctors, scientists, agriculturalists, students, government leaders, religious leaders, and every other conceivable exchange. While our military stays strong and keeps watch, our schools have important work to do – to instill in students decency, patience, and understanding for all the peoples of the world, including the communist nations, to the end that a war of our own destruction will never come to America. This can be done without any real risk of communist infiltration to our way of life. How? By way of good schools – schools that are far better than we now have.

For this reason alone, to prevent a future nuclear war, you teachers must demand and get better schools.

This, then, is the sum of the matter. America is in trouble today – deep trouble. Her trouble is caused by two gigantic failures – her schools and her foreign relations. The only single answer is American education – to improve its quality.

Is there any American who will not serve his country? Once it was a foot soldier who possibly gave the most. Today it is the good teacher who gives us adequate science, adequate international understanding, and adequate knowledge of the facts in our new world of 1958. A good teacher gives America her chance for continued freedom, and possibly the future freedom of all mankind. A good teacher gives America long-term survival, her future of peace through intelligent leadership.

I summarize by saying, America, be *proud* of your business people who supply the needs of our homes and our community with the highest standard of living the world has ever known. Be *proud* of their fight to stay free while also keeping themselves responsible to the rest of us.

But, America, be *not* proud of your businessmen who oppose the quality and the excellence of your schools. Be *not* proud of people who weaken this country, both within and without, by their opposition to better schools. Above all, be *not* proud of those who carelessly and tragically slander a great and revered profession.

America, you *are* your schools. You *are* your youth, and your youth are the America of tomorrow. Let no true American be proud of any defeat or loss the schools may suffer from any source whatever. Oh, America, be *not* proud when your teachers are careless of their profession, when they fail to give freely, when they could, but fail to achieve excellence. Be *not* proud if your noblest profession is discouraged and so performs with mediocrity.

But, America, be *proud* whenever your teachers cross the threshold of their classrooms with lifted hearts and eager spirits. Be *proud* whenever a teacher shares with joy and high spirit the learning and wisdom of the ages. Be *proud* whenever a teacher loves his profession. Within every classroom the love of that profession is what makes every teacher truly beloved. Be *proud*, America, for every teacher who is proud, for that teacher is the proud maker of whatever America is to be.

Plato's Trinity as Problem and Promise

Chapter of the American Association of University Professors,
Brigham Young University
October 9, 1961

□

Plato's three great ideals of goodness, truth, and beauty have been so universally accepted through the centuries by all men that one would never suspect them of being a source of trouble. As ideals they present no trouble. Everybody talks freely about them, firmly believes in them, and claims them for his own. These three particular ideals are like mathematical formulas that pass as a negotiable media of thought all over the world. They do not separate or divide individuals, nations, or religions. Everybody believes in goodness, truth, and beauty.

When, however, these great ideals are adopted within our daily lives, when they are taken from Plato's heaven of eternal forms and brought into our world of being, made flesh of our flesh and blood of our blood – then we involve ourselves in real trouble. Ideals and principles made incarnate produce the infinitely varying contrasts between our theory and our practice, between great principles and actual living, between professed faith and daily performance. Our trouble is not with our ideals. Our trouble starts with their humanization, both in our personal and institutional living.

One solution to the problem would be to turn our backs on these ideals and live on a lower plane of human existence. But man is so made that his eye repeatedly searches the heavens in quest of ideals that give direction and meaning to life. To live without ideals is impossible, and to live with them in successful daily practice is equally impossible. Indeed, it is to the glory of man that goodness, truth, and beauty—like magnets—draw with such power that in loyalty to them man willingly condemns himself to ultimate failure.

Another solution would be to deny that there is a real problem. We could, and sometimes do, maintain that our lives are altogether quite close to our ideals, and, while there are failures, there is really no great gap between our principles and practices. We call attention to our own comparative superiority and boast freely about daily accomplishments. Thoughtful people reject such pretense and self-righteousness. Human nature itself insures that daily practices are mixed with failures.

The only remaining solution is to face the problem as insolvable. We can never live by our ideals. We can use them each day for direction and be drawn toward them; but we can never reach them. It is well to face the problem and realize that the solution lies beyond our capacities. In so doing we reduce the dread chances of hollow pretense.

The fact is that Plato's trinity is at once both an insolvable problem and also a promise with infinite possibilities. Nowhere is this promise and problem felt more keenly and lived more fully than in a great university. Other institutions may follow the ideals of goodness, truth, and beauty, but specialization compels them to stress one above the others, as religion emphasizes goodness, science strives for truth, and the arts seek the beautiful. But a university may not be so specialized. The concern of a university is the universal—all of man's life. Neglect of any great theory or prominent practice in man's life denies the true function of a real university.

The second source of trouble concerning Plato's trinity occurs when one of the three assumes supremacy over the other two—when goodness dictates what truth shall be or what truth shall be taught, or when truth usurps the center of the stage, making goodness and beauty play minor roles in university life. On the other hand, the promise of this great trinity of values comes when there is a good balance between them, when each is important and none is neglected. The careful balance of these three great ideals is the challenge of any truly great university.

No proof is needed that universities today are primarily concerned with truth-seeking and truth-teaching, and that they neglect the ideals of goodness and beauty. Goodness must have been neglected somewhere, as witness our present world situation. Beauty has nearly always been slighted. The persistent question of today's university is not "is it good?" or "is it beautiful?" but, rather, "is it scientific?" It can be argued that the major concern of a university should be confined to discovering and teaching truth. If so, humanity will continue to stumble over barren wastes and edge its way along the narrow precipice between peace and war, and otherwise suffer great failures of goodness.

These past twenty-five centuries began with the Greeks believing beauty was man's supreme value; later centuries centered upon the good as supreme; and today we are expending most of our efforts on discovering and teaching truth.

The present imbalance of these three great ideals brings us to a great challenge facing Brigham Young University today. It is the challenge of maintaining a balance of each of Plato's trinity—of goodness, of truth, and of beauty. These three great disciplines do not overlap, and one should not dominate the others. Each ideal has a value-jurisdiction that the other two should not encroach upon. Each is autonomous and independent and free of dictation by the other two. Moreover, each ideal is practiced better if the other two receive careful and adequate attention.

Truth flourishes if goodness is a near and friendly neighbor. Beauty is more easily found if aided by truth and goodness. And goodness itself is helped if there be no lagging in the search for truth and encouragement in the creation of the beautiful.

Brigham Young University has a charter of strong emphasis upon goodness. Policies from the past up through today stress goodness that all can recognize. Thus, BYU might issue this challenge to her sister universities: "We intend no neglect of truth, but we do intend that our truth-seeking and teaching be balanced with goodness and with adequate attention to the beautiful."

Such a challenge from BYU would be heard around the world. Such an achievement would make BYU a mother institution, giving rise to better universities, a pattern for others to follow.

Nevertheless, there is one problem that must first be solved. Though it is a profound problem, it is not insuperable, not without hope of solution. This problem might be stated by the sister universities to BYU as follows: "You do stress goodness and beauty, but you do not balance these two values with an equal emphasis upon truth. Your goodness-value dominates your truth-value. When the two clash, it is goodness that reigns supreme and decides what truth shall be or what truth shall be taught."

This is a challenge Brigham Young University must answer, and try to answer successfully. It may take many years to do so.

Let us consider the conditions necessary for a future successful answer to this challenge. If a university is not to neglect its goal of seeking and teaching truth, then among others there are two basic preconditions: freedom and good method.

Consider first the indispensable requirement of freedom in any great university. Surely the basic requirements are met here at BYU in ample abundance: freedom of books in the new and magnificent library, freedom within beautiful classrooms, freedom of discussion, and freedom of a well-trained faculty. Surely truth is well-served where such fundamentals of freedom are met.

But all these great achievements do not completely satisfy. More is required. Great libraries, responsible teachers, and free classrooms are necessary but not sufficient for the freedom that truth requires in a great university. There is, in addition, the necessity of what might be called the delicate atmosphere and encouraging climate where the winds of freedom may blow gently, softly, and surely.

Freedom is a fragile plant that bends easily to every breeze of pressure. Freedom wilts before innuendos of power. Freedom disappears in the presence of absolutism. Freedom smothers with unfair argument. Freedom is destroyed with prying personal questions. Freedom is dead where men are afraid.

Our great libraries and classrooms are achievements for freedom, but they are not freedom's guarantee; for freedom is born of human life and subject to the frailties of human nature—jealousies, vanities, and the great satisfaction of exercising dominion, power, and authority over others. These aspects of human nature are the bullets that can kill freedom.

Freedom lives by confidence and trust. It is born in generosity, grows with tolerance, and flourishes with kindness and love. Surely, goodness is a life companion of truth, and truth can never bless humanity as well as it does by the sunshine of true goodness.

This is one great challenge before us: whether our goodness will be good enough to encourage freedom in truth-seeking, or whether our goodness will be mixed with the frailties of human nature—fears that new truth may endanger our peace of mind, jeopardize our place of importance, weaken our exercise of authority, challenge our place of exaltation—in short, upset our cherished and hard-won security. On the other hand, if goodness be kindness and patience, then the delicate breath of freedom will blow gently and surely across this campus from day to day, year to year, and generation to generation.

If someone feels discouraged about the reality of such freedom at BYU, may I add that such freedom is the great problem of all universities everywhere. Every campus has teachers, administrators, visiting speakers, and a public press – all too human – who are impatient with new ideas, made restless by lack of cooperation, fearful of criticism, and anxious to preserve the past. Indeed, such people outside the university are frequently strangers when they visit a campus. They are lost when they witness the life of a great university correctly performing its true function that so frequently involves reconstructing, recreating, and pioneering some new way heretofore untried and uncertain.

But freedom is only one prerequisite if truth is to flourish. Another requirement is good method. The ideal method of pursuing truth is the scientific method. The scientist, as scientist, is the true professional practitioner of the Christian virtue of humility. He holds all hypotheses, generalizations, theories, and laws with true modesty and mental reservations. He is open-minded and eager to hear a new modification, reservation, contrary fact, or even an outright contradiction. This ideal scientist – holding his beliefs with a provisional attitude, a tentative spirit, and a teachable mood – is also the type of scholar needed badly in the non-scientific disciplines, and in religion itself.

Mormonism at its core is a religion of progress – continuous revelation. But there never can be progress if emerging and exploratory ideas are halted by dogmatism. Ideally, Mormonism should experience none of the clashes common in other churches, such as that of reason versus revelation. There should be none of the heresy trials that judge ideas by standards of infallibility. Every gospel principle, every teaching, every ideal, according to the Mormon ideal of eternal progression, is subject to the enrichment that comes from wider experience in thoughtful and prayerful deliberations. Each gospel standard is enlarged and made more noble through probing for new possibilities, deeper insights, and more universal comprehension. Mormonism may progress statistically without such pioneering, but it never can make spiritual and intellectual progress without the humility of spirit or attitude that is tentative, provisional, expectant, searching, and awaiting new possibilities. Such progress enables us to receive revelation from God quite as much as we might say that scientific discoveries help us better read and understand the language of God.

Our gospel ideals are enriched as we think deeply and prayerfully. The last word has not yet been spoken on any Mormon ideal, principle, or practice. Our progress here must be eternal, but progress can be greatly halted by fearful, dogmatic, powerful men, or by men lacking in the deep humility that makes new discoveries possible.

Moreover, while the scientist's success is verification by observable fact, successful validation of religious principles is more broadly based, namely, a wider coherence between revelation and the reality we discover in our daily living. As faculty members we cannot afford to waste hard-earned wealth and countless years of otherwise productive lives by endlessly splitting hairs over propositions that are unreasonable and improbable. The old Mormon admonition to "stay out of the mysteries" is still good advice in order to avoid great wastefulness. We must follow the good methodology of dealing with high probabilities if we are to engage successfully with the truth ideal. Truth is the companion of those who look at God's handiwork as examples of the reasonable, the probable, the natural, and the common within our daily experiences.

Finally, the great ideal of a university is a careful consideration of goodness of itself, truth of itself, and beauty of itself, neglecting none of them and not permitting any one of the three to dominate the others. Such a challenge can only be met by the faculty members themselves. Administrators and policy boards can help, but the labors of each faculty member–free and courageous, prayerful and studious, kind and patient – are necessary to win the great challenge now facing BYU.

If someone is discouraged by this, let him remember that every great ideal is unattainable. The problem is that God has made us to live by our ideals in ways that are always imperfect. Such trouble is good trouble. Nowhere is it felt more keenly than in a university.

The hallmarks of a great university are, first, a people willing to give, not only of their material resources, but also of their great spiritual and intellectual resources. Such resources are the freedom given students and teachers to search for a greater good or larger truth and to create and appreciate the beautiful everywhere. Second, a great university is one whose individual faculty members are able to handle this freedom with careful responsibility, are devoted to good methods, and are courageous when freedom is threatened.

If BYU is to lead other universities as an example, it now faces the demand that truth be autonomous, not subject to goodness, but encouraged and supported by goodness. For while the gospel is essentially goodness – love of God and man – Latter-day Saints hold that the gospel also includes truth and beauty, and that a careful balance of goodness, truth, and beauty means a good life for man. To further these ideals equally is the great challenge now facing this wonderful university.

The Profession of Teaching

Davis County Professional Personnel, Bountiful, Utah
August 26, 1966

□

We have met in anticipation of the school year ahead. Specifically, this is an occasion to reflect upon our own lives as educators. We pause to think about the work we do, our personal involvement, our students, the community, our country, our cultural values, and even the world at large.

This is a time of beginning, and all new chapters in our lives deserve some meditation and reflection, some guessing and some planning, some hoping and some careful analyzing.

If it is true that each day of our lives is a hitherto unvisited country into which no man's foot has ever trod, this is also surely true of the first morning of a new school year. No moment in our professional lives can compare in excitement and sheer drama to that first glance at a new class of students – and the glance is exciting to them as well as to us. Some students are new and all of us are a bit older. Appearances may seem the same, but actually everyone has changed and we, too, are somewhat changed. Each one of us will soon enter a new world where no one can definitely say what will happen.

In this mood of anticipation and reflection, consider these three propositions:

1. That our teaching work may possibly be better than most other jobs and professions.

2. That our teaching work may also possibly be worse than most other jobs and professions.

3. That a teacher has one of the best chances for human happiness of all the various vocations and professions.

The case for the conclusion that our teaching may be near the top of all the different labors of man may be made for two reasons. The first is because the objects with which we work are human beings. Other professions and vocations also work with human beings, but most of them are not so directly confronted with people, so totally involved, so intimately related, or so personally sharing. With farmers, the objects are crops, and they are important. With doctors, it may be skillful surgery or accurate chemistry, and that is important. Lawyers are concerned with the rules for social living, and these rules are important. With manufacturing, the objects are things to meet our daily needs, and the objects are important.

But the objects of educators are whole human beings – physical, emotional, intellectual, and spiritual. They are concerned with the whole personality seeking maturity, emotional refinement, and intellectual comprehension. Our labors are not with the soil, or laws, or things, but with a whole human being, dozens and hundreds of them striving to become fully mature, integrated, successful, and happy. One of the most exciting things to witness is a human being trying for improvement, for control, for comprehension, and, above all, probing and pioneering for broader sympathies and better understanding of the people and the world in which we live.

This is your work. It is a noble labor with which to spend your lives. And there is a second reason for believing that teaching is perhaps the best of all professions.

Besides dealing directly with other people, we are also involved in dealing directly with ourselves – intimately and experimentally. Because teaching is direct confrontation with others, more than most other professions, it is also a direct confrontation with ourselves. A teacher brings his life into the classroom quite as much as each student must do. And nothing x-rays a human being like teaching a class of wide-eyed, wondering young people.

The specific challenge we face in such a professional fish bowl is to know our subject and not get ruffled while teaching it – else we fall on our face. Failures are common with every teacher. Sometimes a whole day is a failure, or sometimes just one class of one day. One sign of more prolonged failure, however, is a kind of scapegoat conversation that centers more and more on such topics as low salaries, dictatorial principals, indifferent parents, or problem students.

Teaching is no job for the squeamish, timid, and fearful. It deals directly with one's self, and this is something all of us prefer not to do. Imagine how difficult and, therefore, how rare it would be for a teacher to close the day with such thoughts as these: "I was wrong in what I said privately to Jim." "I had a poor eleven o'clock class today. I guess I just wasn't sufficiently prepared." "I've got to find some new way of teaching that sophomore class." "I hope I never blow my top again as I did today." "I must go back tomorrow and admit to the class that I was not too well prepared today."

The classroom is no place for personalities with emotional temperaments inclined to be authoritarian or dogmatic. Nor is it a place of escape for the lazy and slovenly. A classroom is a stage where poor performances are public knowledge.

So, teaching is more exciting and rewarding than most professions because of the human element. It is this fact that establishes our first proposition, namely, that teaching can be a better job than most other professions.

Our second general proposition is that teaching may possibly be worse than most other vocations.

Admitting that the good or bad in every kind of work depends upon the individual – his temperament, his training, his success – there are two facts about the teaching profession that cast a shadow over it, possibly more than most other professions. Teaching may have other negative aspects as a profession, but the following two are prominent.

First, teaching is extremely hard work. It draws heavily on the nervous system. Without limited classes and a long vacation, nobody can sustain himself or herself as an effective teacher. Compared to business, farming, legal work, writing, unskilled labor – all of which many of us have done – teaching is the hardest work of all. To teach means frazzled nerves, headaches, and weariness to the point of sleepless nights. Teaching is a tightrope where uncertain balance is maintained between the fresh beginning of the day and a dog-tired feeling at the end, between an eager forward leaning toward successful communication and a sudden backward slump of suddenly discovered weariness, between freshness and staleness within an hour, or a day, or a month, or a school year. The summit of good teaching comes quickly and is passed by unless there is adequate opportunity for rest and renewal.

A second cloud over the teaching profession, besides nervous exhaustion, is the room it offers for complacency. Teaching is, to some degree, a protected life. It is safe from many forms of harsh competition, and it is also difficult to observe excellence, sometimes so easily determined in other professions. Young people cannot render effectively the inexorable judgments of failure, such as those suffered in hospital operating rooms, in courts of law, on poorly managed farms, in business competition, or with unscientific experiments.

Poor teachers can get by. This cloud over the profession remains because nobody can tell exactly why, how, and where excellent teaching is done. Perhaps no other profession has a ceiling of excellence so high and difficult to reach and a floor so low and crowded. Teaching can be a difficult, uphill job or an easy drift downward.

Who is to judge? The students? The supervisors? The Board of Education? The parents? The answer is that all of them together may help in accurate judgments, but not any single one of them may be accurate. There is one source, however, of fairly accurate appraisal. This is the teacher himself. He knows when he is prepared, when he is fresh, when he has the class with him, when eyes brighten with comprehension or when brows furrow with doubt. The best judge of success or failure, of excellence or mediocrity, is the teacher himself.

To be sure, competence in scholarship is the indispensable element of a good teacher. And even mastery of one's field today may be out-of-date tomorrow. Competent scholarship means continual study. Thus, complacency is the darkest cloud over the teaching profession, because complacent teachers can get by.

Teaching is a journey with no arrival. Good teaching is an experiment never finished. Great teaching is a goal unattainable for any duration.

Who is a great teacher? The best answer is this: Since teachers are different, as students are different, certain teachers seem great to some students, but not to others. It is a good thing that teachers are different. Great teachers are probably as rare as great artists or great scientists. There is no sure pattern from which to judge.

As an illustration, I was educated as a child here in the Davis County schools, and for me there was one teacher who was greater than all the teachers I had or ever knew in universities. She was Miss Elizabeth Harding, who taught me in the fifth and sixth grades at Farmington. Another was G. Q. Knowlton, principal of that school. And there were other great teachers, two of whom were from Bountiful and taught in the high school at

Kaysville. They had the same last name. One was our teacher-principal, L. J. Muir, and the other was our history teacher, Frank B. Muir. For each different child there are different teachers, some of whom achieve the heights of greatness. To me, these were not only four teachers to whom I would give an "A" grade, they were more! They touched greatness, and I feel a reverence about the classroom memories I have of them.

Our work as teachers may possibly be one of the less attractive professions, then, because the work is such a drain on our energies and also because teaching so easily allows us to drift toward mediocrity.

The third proposition submitted for our reflection as teachers beginning a new school year is that a teacher has one of the best chances for human happiness of all other professions. Why? Because as teachers we can do so much to make others happy.

The greatest rule for all human happiness is that to be happy ourselves, we must make others happy. And because this is eternally true, our teaching profession gives us the best overall chance for the greatest happiness within our own lives.

The following are a few suggestions for making students happy. Get them to work. How? First, praise them without flattery, compliment them without shallowness, smile without routine, and nod affirmatively without habit. Second, help students see that your work, your subject, your field is at least as important as it really is. Help them to be sensitive whether they are facing a masterpiece in literature, science, politics, industry, music, painting, or invention. Tell them it is a masterpiece and why, so they never forget it. Third, be as kind to the slow as to the brilliant student; be patient with the troublemaker and the rebel. Seek out the discouraged, the embarrassed, the poor in attitude, and the unpopular.

You will be happy as you make others happy. And students will be happy if they work hard without too much drudgery and anxiety. They will work as they should if you motivate them to see the importance of your field, your masterpieces. A teacher cannot be all things to all students, but sometimes a good teacher can transform a whole life by generous approval or by compassion beyond the right of any student to expect.

In conclusion, I offer these comments in a general way on the future of the teaching profession:

My general observation is that, at last, the golden age of teaching has arrived. At long last, society is aware of the importance of education, good schools, and good teaching. If you doubt this, consider all that is expected of our schools. They are to save us from all our social ills. Everybody, more and more, looks to our schools and our teachers for life's best rewards. This profession is entering its golden age, and we are fortunate to have a chance to try our hand.

It may be true that humanity as a whole is ill prepared for the changes forced upon it in this twentieth century. But surely no profession tells us more about these changes and helps mankind toward more successful adjustment than does the pioneering work done by eager and able teachers.

Truth and Myth as Competitors for the Mind

Great Issues for Laymen in Contemporary Philosophy,
University of Utah
November 30, 1960

□

The truth and truth-claiming myths are the two great competitors for the mind of man. Both are very successful. They flourish together, not only within the culture of a people, but also within the mind of a single person.

To separate myth from truth is an enormous undertaking. It becomes a large part of the work done by a university. This effort to distinguish truth from myth is the primary element of progress in all the history of mankind. It is our contemporary problem as well, and it will occupy the attention of our descendants for many centuries to come. Progress depends on establishing truth and eliminating myth.

It is difficult to say, even today, which is the most successful, truth or myth. Which one of the two wins the greatest share of human loyalty? Which has the largest number of converts, which is the most powerful influence? I can't help wondering which has the largest domain within the lives of students on this campus, truth or myth.

While truth and myth can live peacefully side by side within both the collective life of a people and the life of a single person, they frequently do fight for control. Yet generally men and cultures quite conveniently accommodate themselves to their myths and their truths. They give loyalty to both as if there were no conflict. Quite frequently, however, a truth-claiming myth is challenged by truth itself, and then a struggle ensues. I think the greatest battlefield between truth and myth is on a university campus. Myth flourishes best off the campus. But, on the campus of a free university, the warfare between myth and truth is endless. Yet even here there is no clear-cut victory. If truth wins in one clash, myth survives to fight again; and if myth achieves a triumph, truth lives on to fight another day. Neither one can obtain the terms of an unconditional surrender, even on a university campus. While one or the other may win a battle, neither of the two can win the war.

But, this endless warfare has some compensation. If truth were to prevail over myth, the humanities and social science departments would just about go out of business. Myth keeps many of us going, pays our salaries, and generally makes life quite exciting. Myth is at once our friend and foe. Without it we would have to teach science or go into business—a horrible dilemma.

But why is myth such a successful competitor against truth? Why do men so often choose myth over truth? What are the sources of strength that myth possesses? Wherein lies its hardihood?

If truth is the description of whatever is the actual situation, the real state of affairs, the way things really are, and if myth is an explanation that is not factual, not real, not history, why should myth ever prevail over truth? If truth is the characteristic of a proposition that enables it to be verified by public observation, and myth can never be so verified at all, why the hardihood of myth? If truth is the correspondence between an idea in the mind and fact outside the mind while myth has no objective referent at all, nothing that corresponds to an idea, why then its flourishing success? In short, if truth is the reliable body of knowledge that enables man to make accurate predictions about the future while myth is born of the imagination and so fails every test of scientific investigation, why are myths probably more influential than truths? This is our problem.

This is no problem when myth merely expresses the esthetic experiences of mankind. Here the purpose is to entertain. Life would be impoverished indeed without the myths of the arts and literature. People cannot live by truth alone; we need relaxation and play. Man lives by his imagination as well as by truth. He also lives better when his myths effectively motivate his moral life, such as in the timeless parables, the purgation afforded by tragedy, or the vision of perfection. These myths mirror the universal aspects of human life. But why not accept them as mirrors? Why does mankind accept them as literally true? To be more specific, why is the population of this student body possessed of minds crammed full of explanatory and truth-claiming myths that will not hold up against scholarly investigation?

In summary, why does man deify and liberalize his myths? Whence comes the high prestige of truth-claiming myths, their large domain, their great power and authority over the life of man? Why, in effect, are myths not accepted for what they are, simply myths? How and why do they obtain the status of truth?

Four explanations are offered. First, truth-claiming myths are successful because of life's harsh realities. Second, truth-claiming myths are successful because they are useful to leaders of organizations in keeping their own power and authority over those who believe. Third, truth-claiming myths are successful against truth because they are an easy alternative to faith. Fourth, truth-claiming myths are successful against truth because they masquerade as ideals.

Returning to the first explanation for the success of truth-claiming myths, we find that many myths grow out of life's harsh realities. They try to explain the causes of suffering, they offer solutions to tragedies, they attempt reconciliation of mankind with a hostile environment, and they account for human injustices.

The early history of these explanatory myths is lost behind the curtain of recorded time. But through all history, to solve the problem of calamity, people have constructed the anthropomorphic myths of the gods opposing each other, of wars in heaven, of devils on earth, of evil spirits inhabiting bodies, and of personalized forces in nature seeking revenge, or dispensing justice, or recapturing lost pride. Mankind has created mythologies about heaven and hell and used them as forms of escape from present hardships and continual injustice. These myths win for man the victories denied him in the actual world. Suffering blows he cannot justify and seeing injustice he cannot rectify, man recreates the world with his imagination by means of myths that try to explain and reconcile. Science explains the world, but myth sometimes enables man to endure the world. It is no wonder that myth is so durable, so widespread, always so contemporary with the human life. Myth, like truth, is man's pillar of fire by night and his cloud by day. It sustains him in his upward reach. It gives him answers when all else is stony silence. Truth-claiming myth is man's helper of the way. Myths answer questions otherwise unanswerable. This is one source of the success of myth over truth. Truth-claiming myths will be with us for a long time to come.

The second reason for the success of truth-claiming myths over truth is their use by men to gain and keep power over others. If truth should prevail within the great political and religious power structures of our institutional life, most of these great organizations would crumble to dust. But myth and power flourish together. They sustain and support one another.

Why is this so? Because men who rule over others yield quite easily to those temptations that will strengthen and insure their power and authority. When facts are against leaders, as they so frequently are, myths are created, or existing ones modified, favorable to those in authority. Myths are not badgered by facts and need not be reconciled to truth. Myths can be shaped, turned, twisted, and formed to suit the situation. And always the pressing demand of institutional life is the problem of winning and keeping power. So, men at the top persuade men at the bottom that myths favorable to their own power and authority are true. Power structures see to it that books are written about such myths, councils are assembled, trials are held, and decisions made – always refining and clarifying a myth to the end that those in authority do not lose their power and glory. Hitler used the Aryan myth in his lust for power. Religious organizations draw upon myths in the Bible to persuade those daring to challenge authority. Economic systems use myths to sustain their prosperity, as the communists use the myth of promising a future classless society.

Wherever power is held by men at the top of a great organization, there myths will also be found. Power and myth are companions. Not always so are truth and power. Since myth is so frequently a tool that can be used on the side of existing power, myth will always be a successful competitor against truth.

Indeed, every power structure has two kinds of myth-defenders – the sincere and the insincere. The sincere myth-defenders may be the most effective, because they are persuasive and persistent. A sincere myth-defender has conviction, and in leadership possesses the bearing of one with authority and truth, thereby attracting many followers.

The insincere myth-defender is not as easily analyzed. There are, of course, shrewd, power-hungry leaders who simply use myths to win and keep their power. These are the lowest on the scale of moral character. But there are other insincere myth-defenders for whom a word of defense may be spoken – not a major defense, but yet a word or two. This is the myth-defender who suffers from a mean deal of the cards by society. This is the bright, capable, and well-educated man selected by a power structure for leadership, and who now in his new-found glory at the top realizes that he has been trapped into the necessity of defending the well-entrenched myths of the organization he leads. Now he faces the cruel dilemma of resigning his rewarding and glorious social exaltation or of propagating some truth-claiming myths. Few men caught in this situation will voluntarily surrender their glory. They turn to rationalizing—the vast good they can do in leadership compared to individual isolation, that the myth really isn't so bad and if interpreted rightly is nearly true, or as good as the truth, or even better than the truth. Long years of leadership by such well-educated men finally make of them the best defenders of myth the world has ever known. Their education gives them powers of myth refinements that amaze and warm the hearts of all their sincere myth-believing followers. Perhaps from this more doubting leadership myth has a stronger defense than it gets from the sturdy and rugged army of sincere believers. In any case, the conclusion is the same: myths will be with us for a long time to come.

A third reason for the success of truth-claiming myths in their competition against truth is that they give an easy alternative to the challenge of faith. While there are all degrees and types of faith, we might select a definition that faith is essentially the courage to believe and try without any guarantees. Successful myths come with guarantees attached. On the other hand, consider a great and defensible faith. It is a commitment to well-grounded ideals and the dedication of one's labors to their fulfillment. Such a faith is full of risks and inevitable failures. The common reference to such a faith as a leap in the dark is not without meaning. Uncertainty, insecurity, doubt, and dismay are the everyday companions of one who lives—and especially of one who works—by a noble faith. But why leap in the dark with all that risk if you can believe a myth that obviates such dangerous chances?

So, a college student, after a study of the methods of finding truth – for example, after examining authoritarianism, then mysticism, then rationalism, and finally empiricism – may conclude that there are limitations to all of these methods. He then may face two alternatives: to live by faith or adopt a myth that presumes in fact to certify, since none or any combination of these four methods can give a guarantee. Many college students, facing this choice, hold on to their myths. Why choose faith that at times appears no better than a broken stone for a pillow at night? A myth provides the comfort of eiderdown and the security and restoration that follows a long and refreshing sleep. Simply give in and accept the myth!

Truth-claiming myths will be with us for a long time to come.

A fourth reason for the victories of truth-claiming myths over truth is the capability of myths to masquerade as ideals. Ideals are best when loved for their own sake. Whatever the explanation of Plato's ideas or ideals, they do shine with their own light, and they are noblest when stated in the clearest possible language. But then myths are invented to express these ideals, and before long the myths replace them. Eventually, these myths masquerade as ideals; and as such they are given wide acceptance by the credulous. Nevertheless, myths thus masquerading as ideals generally downgrade those ideals. For example, the great and difficult ideal of vicarious sacrifice gets dressed up in a myth about disobedience that demands the death of a good man. The great and difficult ideal of universal fellowship gets dressed up in the myth about a chosen people who practice a local brotherhood.

The great and difficult ideal of justice becomes cloaked in the myth of man's forebears who disobeyed and thereby caused innocent descendants to pay the price of their own wrong-doing. The great and difficult ideal of learning masquerades in the costume of a myth that books are produced in heaven, or by other means, rather than through the patient labor of human effort. The great and difficult ideal of the life of reason becomes the myth of a deity who could offer salvation through the mystical experience of identifying with the Logos. The great problem of world peace gets dressed up in a myth of wars in heaven and a continuation of these wars on earth – with a personal devil as the principal troublemaker.

Thus, the noblest ideals of man are counterfeited by myths masquerading as ideals, offering escapes from facing up to challenges of great ideals. Great and true ideals themselves are demanding, and avenues of escape from facing up to them are readily taken. So, truth-claiming myths will be with us for a long time to come.

Myths involve the deepest desires of mankind – fears, hopes, passions, sentiments – some validating the social order, and range from expressions of artistry to sheer legalism. If myths were esthetic only – not explanatory and truth-claiming, not to be taken seriously – they might avoid their unworthy status as falsehoods and easy escapes from reality. But they do become truth-claiming. Their attraction and value are compelling, and their practical use for institutional survival too valuable to be discarded. Thus, truth and myth march side by side in our culture; they are so intertwined and woven together that frequently we fail to distinguish one from the other. Those who challenge a truth-claiming myth, either in the classroom or with a book or public address, can become quite unpopular.

But may there not be some defense for truth-claiming myths? Do they not justify themselves if, in believing them as true, a man can thereby soften the hard blows of adversity? If myths are mixed into the cement that holds power structures together, if successful institutions, with all the good they do, need myths to insure their durability, should the pursuit of truth be allowed to weaken or destroy them? Are not myths preferable to faith, if the risk might be no faith at all? May we not keep our myths if they express great ideals?

My answer is unfriendly to myths. There is no place for truth-claiming myths in a society sufficiently advanced to conceive and support free universities. A culture of greatness, whether it be in politics, religion, or economics, should constantly weed out truth-claiming myths. Truth-claiming myths spring from primitive explanations. It is better to face life as it is, thereby seeking for ways to improve it, than to use the escape of believing what is an untrue, unreal, or fictional interpretation of life.

It is better to disband power structures for possibly better ones than to preserve them by the aid of myths. It is, I think, wisdom to say: "Let truth be the thing it can be." It is better to live by a courageous faith than to live by dreams of the imagination.

In all the turmoil of separating truth from myth, I sometimes apply one or another of three methods. First, and the very best one, is an appeal to the scientist. And if the scientist has no answer, as may well be the case, then I try to use my own home-made scientific method, that of clarifying the meaning of a proposed truth-claim (hypothesis), testing it with future facts. Second, if that test is unsatisfactory, then I appeal to probability, and try to apply the highest probability—experience—and then accept or reject the truth-claim. Third, if scientific verification and high probability are not applicable or available to some truth-claim, I appeal to the test of what appears to be reasonable, at least what appears to be the more reasonable.

Verification first, probability second, and the reasonable third—these are my methods of disentangling truth from myth. As truth-claims go by in review, I would ask: Are you verifiable? And if not, are you probable? And if not, are you reasonable? Imagine all the casualties among truth-claims, all those that are unverifiable, improbable, and unreasonable.

Power Structures and Reason

Society of Utah School Superintendents,
Brian Head Summer Conference
July 18, 1973

☐

Power structures, the various ways human beings organize themselves politically, religiously, and economically, become both the servants and the masters of men. They are, therefore, both a blessing and a curse of human life.

To be sure, power structures are inevitable, necessary, and natural. But there is a scandal in the life of every power structure. No one, or very few, believes this scandal about the power structure to which he or she belongs. The scandal is not true about *our* political party, *our* church, *our* business, or *our* professional organization. And if we do have knowledge of this shame in our own power structure, we try our best to keep it a family secret, for we love our own power structure. The power structures of other people may be immoral, but not our own. How could our power structure be tainted with disgrace when we give to it our best – our time, our thoughts, our efforts, our money – and urge all right-thinking people to do the same? Our motives are good; indeed, they are almost pure. Our services are unselfish. What more could a power structure have than pure motive and unselfish action?

110

Nevertheless, there is a scandal in the life of every power structure on the face of the earth. It is that all power structures live a double life—they are a Dr. Jekyll and a Mr. Hyde. Duplicity and double-dealing are built-in factors of every power structure ever created or ever likely to be created.

The truth is that all power structures both generously give and selfishly take. They give man his social life, and they take away his individuality. They give purpose to life, and they outrage private conscience. They give security, and they impede progress. They give us great opportunities, yet they leave us greatly impoverished. They take the selfishness out of life, and they fill it with vanity and greed. They take the loneliness away from the individual, and they rob him of his integrity. They give freedoms, and they take them away.

One might say of power structures, with some change, the words spoken of deity in the sacred scriptures: "Power structures give, and power structures take away, blessed be the name, and also cursed be the name, of all power structures." Nothing on earth is so mixed with good and evil as are the various power structures of mankind. All of them lead a double life. We see this scandal in the power structures of others, but we deny or hush it up in our own.

Are there no purely good power structures? No. Are there any purely bad power structures? No, with the exception of those such as crime syndicates. All power structures are made up of human beings whose leaders and members have all the good and bad motives, all the frailties, and all the goodness of human nature.

Are some power structures better than others, and some power structures worse than others? Yes. Indeed, a meaningful discussion of power structures will not divide them between the good and the bad, for none are wholly good, and few are wholly bad. Rather, power structures are only relatively good and relatively bad.

How may one judge the good and the bad in all the varieties of power structures? There is but one single standard whereby one can distinguish all of the relatively better and all of the relatively worse power structures in the social life of mankind. This single standard is the meaning that a power structure gives to the life of its individual members.

And there is a single standard whereby one can determine whether the life of the individual has real meaning and significance. It is this: Does the individual possess more freedom because of the power structure to which he or she belongs, or is the individual more enslaved by the power structure?

And there is a single standard whereby one can identify this relative freedom or the relative enslavement of the individual. It is this: Does the power structure to which the person belongs encourage the individual to think for himself and draw his own personal conclusions? If so, it is one of the better power structures.

And there is a single standard whereby one can determine whether an individual is encouraged to think for himself. It is this: Does the power structure to which he belongs give opportunities or insist that facts and ideas be presented in a fair and impartial manner. Is there a "due process" of justice for ideas and facts in power structures as there is a due process for justice in courts of law? If power structures encourage a careful search for facts and the tolerant consideration of conflicting ideas, such power structures are of the better kind.

And there is a single standard whereby one can determine whether there is this "due process" or fair and impartial deliberation of new facts and new ideas. It is this: Does the existing power structure to which the individual belongs stay its hand and refuse to impose sanctions or punishment because of its respect for the dignity of its individual members whenever any of these members deliberate upon facts or ideas unfavorable to the power structure itself? If so, it is one of the better power structures.

Are power structures willing to allow their members to see the best and as far as they can, and then to say what they see? If so, they are among the better of the various power structures. This is the standard, the criteria, to distinguish between the better and the worse power structures, namely, the impact they have upon the life of the individual – whether such an individual may live reflectively and thoughtfully in freedom without fear or favor from his own or any other power structure upon the face of the earth.

Why should power structures be judged by their meaning for individuals? Why not have individuals judged by their meaning and significance for power structures? Why elevate the individual above his group? Many books and many philosophers have long disputed this issue. On the side of individual judgment as against corporate authority, on the side of individual conscience as against the controls of power structures, on the side of the lone individual who thinks for himself and draws his own conclusions, there is arrayed a galaxy of great heroes.

There was Socrates, both attacking and defending the state, but using his own reflective thought as the basis for his judgments. There was Jesus of Nazareth, who judged all institutions upon the single issue of whether they enriched or impoverished the life of the individual. There was Epicurus, perhaps the most individualistic of all. St. Paul was anxious above all else to establish the immortality of the individual human soul. Then came St. Augustine, and then night fell in human history when individual salvation became a concern not of this world but of a kingdom beyond this world. William of Occam, Abelard, and a few others were the only wakeful moments of this long slumber.

Descartes began the era of modern individualism. Protestant reformers made salvation a matter of personal conscience. Then came Locke and Berkeley and Hume and Rousseau. Finally there emerged the political philosophy of the founders of the American republic—Benjamin Franklin, Thomas Paine, John Adams, and Thomas Jefferson, among others. Above all came their opportunity to try this philosophy of individual freedom. America became the birthplace and the home of the largest grant of individual freedom ever known in man's long history. Later there were such heroes of individualism as Emerson, Thoreau, Whitman, Santayana, Howison, Bowne, James, Brightman, Flewelling, and a host of others.

However, this year of 1973 is witnessing a strange contradiction. America, the world's champion of individual freedom, recites the creed of our founding fathers—that the state is the servant of the people, meant to serve individuals. This is the philosophy of America. But our present practices deny our beliefs. We are rapidly collectivizing, merging, and enlarging power structures until America will soon be not the champion of individualism, not a country of infinite and varying degrees of small and less powerful structures, but a country of a few power structures so powerful that private conscience, personal judgment, and freedom to criticize will be no more. Modern science favors power structures. It favors the growing means of mass communication and the growing knowledge of psychological mass controls. We are rapidly shifting from a world of private free enterprise in economics, religion, and politics to a world of power enterprise and, consequently, to a world of slave enterprise.

What is the final destiny of our twentieth century? Will it be a dark night of Machiavellian power structures fighting each other, a world where all individuals will be stamped into corporate personalities? Will it be a final worship of Nietzchean supermen, where ordinary individuals are ground under the heel of tyrannical power structures? Will the world of tomorrow give up the philosophies of the individual? Will it be a world of socialism or communism for the state, of absolutism for religion, and of organization for business?

Are there any particular philosophies today that resist this inexorable drift toward the collectivism of larger and stronger power structures? There are two, personalism and existentialism. Consider first the philosophy of personal idealism. Here is a philosophy which attempts to take a stand for individualism on all the major battlefields of philosophic inquiry– metaphysics, epistemology, logic, esthetics, ethics, science, and religion.

In metaphysics, personalism makes the idealistic assumption that only persons are real, that all reality is in some sense personal, that personality is self-conscious and self-directive, and that there are essentially only persons and what they create. Religiously, God is a supreme creative intelligence, the source of all reality. Such a personal theism is opposed to pantheism and deism. Man is creative, eternal, and possesses an indestructible personality whose goal is to reach the highest self-expression through the fullest harmony with all other reality and through subjugating selfish personal interests to the supreme values of life.

Epistemologically, since the world of things comes from an intelligent source, it is intelligible to human minds, and our perceptions are true. Logically, our verbal symbols cannot adequately express the reality of life and the eternity of change. Therefore, we are compelled by the logic of pragmatism with its provisional acceptance of all intellectual formulae. Esthetically, art is a metaphysical form– there is a harmony between the person and things, and this makes it possible for the individual to intuit the forms of beauty, thereby finding pleasure and self-expression. Ethically, personalism opposes mechanistic and behavioristic assumptions. It holds people to be most real in their creative activity, in their reflective reasoning, in their critical thinking, and in their thoughtful living.

Personalism is the philosophy of freedom. Personality is the supreme value, and, therefore, power structures are evaluated in terms of whether they give to every person the best possible opportunity for self-development physically, mentally, and spiritually.

Now personalism may or may not be true. It certainly is not verifiable. But if we could have a choice among all the philosophies, most of us would wish that personalism were true. And if personalism is false, no one has good cause for rejoicing.

Yet personalism is not wishful thinking, even though it cannot be verified. Personalism has many reasons supporting it. And even if all the converging reasons favoring personalism do not adequately support its general hypothesis, it still remains one of humanity's enduring philosophies.

Besides the philosophy of personalism, there is today another philosophy of strong individual emphasis. It is that of existentialism. In this philosophy, the individual human being is the center of moral worth and the goal of action. Here the individual is absolutely free and has absolute responsibility. To exist is both to be free and also to create the world. This radically individualistic philosophy describes the existence of man as something like that of a finite and mortal God.

Existentialism holds that philosophers have put the cart before the horse in trying to know mankind in general, the universe in general, power structures in general, and then trying to apply to man in particular what it has thus learned from mankind in general, or the universe in general, or power structures in general. Rather, we should start with particular man, in a particular time, and at a particular place. Man's existence precedes his nature of essence. As a particular existence, man has particular problems. This is where we should begin. Existence is prior to the concept, the universal, the abstract, and the absolute. There is no general human nature, but only the subjectivity of one's inner life. Each person is rudderless and alone in a world which he little understands and in which nothing but death is certain. Each man makes his own nature by his own choices and actions. Even our environment becomes what our choices make of it. Each person's choices are wholly free and each is therefore responsible for his or her own world. This circumstance makes one's freedom awful.

Recognizing this responsibility for one's entire life, one experiences anguish and despair. For we are bounded in our existence by such situations and emotions as guilt, suffering, and death, and therefore the concerns of our lives are pointless and tedious. We should escape if we could. But we cannot. We can only choose anguish and despair. The choosing is what is important, not what is chosen.

Power structures have no meaning to the existentialist. The brute fact is our own subjectivity. As Henry Miller stated: "Like it or not, I was obliged to create a new life for myself. And this new life I feel is mine, absolutely mine, to use or to smash, as I see fit. In this life I am God, and like God I am indifferent to my own fate. I am everything there is—so why worry."

Having glanced at personalism and existentialism as two philosophic arguments on the side of the individual, we now return to a closer analysis of the very nature of all power structures.

Granted that power structures are necessary, that they give direction to the lives of individuals, and that they make our practical world better by infinite ways otherwise impossible for the individual to enjoy, why then is their price so high? Why do power structures shear away so many of our individual differences? Why do they hush our private conscience? Why do they obstruct so much original and creative thinking?

There are four reasons why all power structures, by their very nature, necessarily obstruct individual freedom and rational thought.

1. Power structures, like individual people, fight for survival, and therefore they obstruct any reasoning that could threaten their survival.

2. The dead hand of the past, present in all power structures, obstructs new ideas of the living present world.

3. The complexity and size of power structures make them slow to change and resistant to reason.

4. Human nature involved in power structures – the greed for power and the fear of losing it – crush dissent and disobedience.

The first, the struggle of power structures to survive, causes them to oppose things which threaten their survival, whether the threat is from an individual or from another power structure. Power structures fight in self-defense quite as individuals do, which means employing whatever tactics are necessary for survival, however brusque or even brutal.

When power structures fight each other they generally do so not by reason but by generating fears and emotional zeal on the part of their members. Institutional loyalty, duty, zeal, and sacrifice are the tragic weapons power structures use to survive. Such emotions blind people's reason. Of all human virtues, the easiest to win is that of institutional loyalty. Exploitation by power structures becomes both a sublime and tragic element of human life. Trading upon this noble and tragic virtue of loyalty, nations make war, churches make war, and businesses make war, and in these wars, both hot and cold, the individual or his new ideas are crushed.

Besides this struggle between power structures for survival, there is the struggle of power structures for existence when their individual members endanger or threaten their survival. In this battle the power structure uses reason if the danger is not too great. The universal policy of power structures is the simple formula of tolerantly allowing the dissent of reason if the use of this reason is insignificant. But, if the dissent of the individual's reasoning appears to be a potential danger to the well-being of the power structure, then the individual is crushed in proportion to the danger he or she presents. Herein lies the real curse of all power structures – the uneven fight of a giant against a single dissenting individual. Thus individuals are picked off, one by one, until all the dissenters, rebels, and liberals are silenced.

The second reason for power structures obstructing individualism is the dead hand of their regulations, creeds, and constitutions that rule over the present and the unknown future. There is a universal human weakness in men of authority to draw up codes and rules for those who are members, present and future. But our world of process and change is ever in defiance of those who would freeze life according to the ideas of particular men, of a particular time, and in a particular situation. Only the constitution or creed that allows for continual amendment is meaningful from one generation to the next.

Even when amendments are allowed, they are generally opposed by emotional zeal applied in the name of the founding fathers. Reason is thus opposed by emotion. Unfortunately, whenever reason is matched against emotion in a fight, emotion almost always wins the day. When creeds are outworn and life needs new breath, the name of deity is used, the emotion of fear is excited, the lure of rewards is held forth, and reason is always a casualty.

The third reason for power structures obstructing free individualism is their inertia, resulting from their size and complexity. Outside of physical objects, the greatest example of Newton's laws of motion is to be found in power structures – particularly the law that objects in motion tend to remain in motion. Power structures are habit structures. They are loath to change. Individuals can change, even against habit. But power structure habits stand like the pillars of Hercules in defiance of change, however pressing the reasons for change may be. Sometimes this inflexibility and inelasticity of power structures cause a revolution that destroys them. But a revolution is a rare exception. Primarily power structures rule and ruin unchallenged because dissenting reason is no match for their mass and complexity.

The fourth reason for power structures obstructing fresh reasoning is the human nature involved in all power structures. Human beings love power as they love almost nothing else on earth. Power gives them the expression of their ego. It expands their life and will over others. No honey is so sweet as the influence, authority, and dominion given to those who rule in power structures.

This story of human nature in power structures is simple and routine. It begins with all new leaders protesting humility and inadequacy, and pleading for help. But very soon vanity and pride begin to crowd their country cousin, humility. Eventually, human fallibility and frailty fade before the bright sunshine of joy in authority, in dominion, and in power and glory. (Any similarity between this awful thought and the school administrators in this audience is purely coincidental.)

When a person of authority in a power structure is challenged, and that challenge is a threat to the prestige or even the very power possessed by that leader, it is rare indeed that the challenge is examined by reason, objectively and fairly. Rather, emotions of survival come into play and color the reasoning used in reply. Thus, power structures object to dissent because power structure leaders are driven first to protect their position and prestige. They will surely oppose whatever might obstruct their power.

Since most of the great power structures are economic, political, and religious, what would be a description of the better types of power structures in business, government, and religion?

In business that power structure is best which says to each individual: "You may try your hand. Your business opportunities for success are not sealed off by vested interests. You need not be an 'organization' man. You may go into business for yourself. But above all, you may think and criticize whatever injustices you find in whatever economic power structure may affect your life."

In government, that power structure is best which says to every individual: "I am your servant. My power is given by you and may be taken away by you. My power is divided, limited, and some powers are forever denied to me. I will protect you from the tyranny of majorities as I would from the tyranny of a despot. Above all, each individual is free to criticize and dissent, and the test of this freedom will be the power of the individual to use all means of persuasion whereby the existing government may be changed or abolished in favor of new demands."

In religion, that power structure is best which says to each individual: "You are free to believe and also free not to believe. Your beliefs are so personal, private, and sacred to yourself that it shall never be permitted that you submit to questioning for heresy. All that you do in religion will be as a volunteer, freely given. Above all, you are free to think for yourself and to decide for yourself without fear and without favor."

In summary, those power structures weighed for their good and evil will be found to weigh on the better side if they live by the principle that their membership is composed not of conscripts, but of volunteers. And a volunteer is one who is free to think about the activities of his power structure, to criticize them without fear of consequence, and then, having enjoyed this freedom, still chooses to give it loyal support.

Power structures are thus good or evil as they encourage or obstruct the life of reason, as they allow each individual the widest margin of freedom to be, to say, and to reach his highest potential.

A University and the Adventure of Great Ideas

Phi Beta Kappa Address, University of Utah
June 10, 1977

□

As an introduction, I would ask each of you a rather large question. It is taken from one of George Bernard Shaw's plays where a situation is portrayed of God inviting His guest to see a play that reviewed the whole of creation, and as the curtain falls on all the history of mankind, God turns to His guest and asks: "Well, what did you make of it?"

Without presuming the slightest analogy, but with a little of the same curiosity, I would ask each of you, as the curtain falls on your undergraduate years: "Well, what did you make of it?"

I might narrow the question, that since the main business of a university is with the major ideas in various civilizations, including our own, which of all these ideas appealed to you most? Which of the great philosophers did you like best?

One meaning of Phi Beta Kappa is that it lies within the context, the frame of reference, we refer to as individualism. Indeed, all universities are mainly the nesting grounds of emerging individualism, places where students individually examine various competing ideas, trying personally to decide the truth or the value of various ideas. To a free individual in the sunrise of life, pondering which ideas to accept as true and valuable, a free univer-

122

sity is a great institution, perhaps the greatest you will know in your lifetime.

Almost all institutions created by man are power structures that advance those ideas and programs favorable to their own institutional success. Each institution wants to be successful in the purpose for which it was created. But a university has no single purpose to measure its success. It has no single policy or program by which to judge its failure or success.

A university is not a partisan of special ideas and value-judgments. It leaves each individual student to decide for himself or herself such claims and judgments. A free university does not try to indoctrinate, but leaves truth-claims to live or die within the mind of each student, and, likewise, every value-judgment to be preferred or rejected by each student.

So now, after your personal experience as a free individual in the freest of all institutions, especially at this moment of your well-earned distinction of graduation, I would ask the probing and sweeping question in Shaw's play: "What especially did you make of it?"

And you might turn the tables and ask me the same question. You might frame your question to me something like this: "Since we are at the beginning of life, with four years of university experience back of us, and your life's journey is almost over, tell us what you as a teacher have made of it."

I would reply that in dealing with great ideas in a university, at least four steps are important: their discovery, their harmony, their probability, and their priority.

About the first step of discovery, it can be said that as you entered the university, you would do better discovery work if your banners were checked at the gate. To be sure, nobody can completely check his or her banners at the gate. Psychologically, we necessarily take our preferences and prejudices with us as we enter a university. Our beliefs reflect a lifetime of social conditioning. But for all that, many students and teachers do achieve a large measure of impartiality, a high degree of objectivity. And yet, in the history of universities, nobody knows how many great ideas were neglected, undiscovered, or perished simply because students and teachers failed to check their banners at the gate.

To be sure, when university work is completed and we pass through the exit gates, as some of you will presently do, you will pick up your banners again, however altered they are sure to be. Some banners will be faded and some brighter, some shredded, some stronger, and some discarded. But whatever the case, the years in a university are not wasted if, in the inevitable clash of ideas, each idea is given a fair hearing.

Ideally, a university is no place for defense, but a place for offense, the adventure of an eager mind in search of new ideas and new values. Only when this takes place does a free university deserve to be called the greatest institution ever created by man.

My second observation about dealing with great ideas is to find some harmony among them, some compatibility. This is almost as difficult as finding a way to achieve harmony among people. Ideas, like people, disagree. They oppose and contradict.

Harmonizing one's own personal ideas is the labor of a lifetime. It is also some of the hardest labor of a university. For great ideas are no less great because they oppose each other. It is a major part of our work to expose their inconsistencies, their incompatibilities. This struggle for harmony and coherence is where the finest battles are fought, and where sometimes the remains of countless and once-cherished ideas are given up forever. As with much of life, so with great ideas, we cannot have our cake and eat it too; for while two ideas may both be true or both false, if they contradict each other, then if one may be true, the other is false.

I leave to other disciplines in the university their problems of harmonizing and reconciling. But turning to philosophy, there are some great ideas with premises that are so far apart, that in the name of simple logic one must say, for example: If mysticism, then not rationalism; if idealism, then not realism; if naturalism, then not supernaturalism; if matter only, then not the mind; if rigid determinism, then not indeterminism.

And, in methodology: If basically the scientific method, then not basically the intuitional method; if a priori assumptions, then not a posteriori; if analytic propositions only, then not the finality of the synthetic. And, in ethics: If private conscience only, then not public utilitarianism. And about our intellectual heroes: if Plato's assumptions, then not Aristotle's; if Spinoza, then not Hume; if Hegel, then not James.

Or, shifting to politics: If the practice of communism, then not the practice of a free democracy—certainly not the existence of a free university in the world of communism.

The books and classes and conversations that attempt to reconcile are legion in number. But the irreconcilable will not reconcile; the lion will not lie down with the lamb; and able students learn that in their adventure with great ideas in a university they cannot have their cake and eat it too. They cannot at the same time hold two completely incompatible and contradictory ideas.

One of life's incredible experiences is to observe how an individual—including perhaps each one of us—how one person can apparently live in peace with major ideas and assumptions that are so incompatible and contradictory.

Here I would make a confession. The confession is about my own lifetime of failure in trying to harmonize the major ideas of Jerusalem with the major ideas of Athens, the religion of ancient Palestine with the humanism of ancient Greece. From these two small countries come the two pillars of our present civilization.

Countless books and lectures have tried to harmonize them. But they will not harmonize. Yet both are important. So we accept them, one at a time, and give up the demand for consistency. Even so, reason and revelation cannot logically be reconciled.

Sometimes in a careless and ambiguous way, I escape the problem by shifting from propositions to people. However different they are, I love both Plato and the Galilean Carpenter. They are my two greatest heroes, especially when Plato has been tailored by his student, Aristotle. But even with people the contrasts and contradictions remain. One who is said to be our eternal contemporary is the Galilean Carpenter with his story of the Good Samaritan. Yet one wants also to feel at home with Socrates, discovering with him that what men claim to know, they really do not know.

My third observation about dealing with great ideas in a university is the discovery, sooner or later, that there are no absolutes, no finalities—just probabilities. Even the most tested ideas of the exact sciences do not go beyond probability. But then some probabilities are so high that we can build bridges with them, cure disease, and generally gain a mastery of nature that serves our human life.

One good result of the persistent and relentless study of great ideas is a university that may finally become a highway to the virtues of modesty and humility. Many freshmen—and for that matter seniors too—come to realize that their great ideas and their best defenses of great ideas must be qualified with first one reservation, then another, and another, ad infinitum. Upon this rather sober realization, many a good student has held a quiet and private memorial service to honor a great idea that he or she has finally come to see is not really so great anymore.

Thus learning leads to modesty; stated in philosophic terms, it means that a priori synthetic propositions are not possible, for synthetic propositions are only probable and analytic propositions are mere tautologies. I recall how stripped and poverty-stricken I felt when the final result had to be faced that mankind must wander on this earth with never more than empty analytic propositions, or only the probability of synthetic propositions.

But after these limitations, let no one put down mere probabilities. Probabilities are better than improbabilities; the reasonable is better than the unreasonable. And if this seems a rather small diet of satisfaction for a student searching for absolutes, one may be comforted in the awareness that there is still much work to do, for the likelihood is that countless beliefs of human beings on this planet are simply not true.

My fourth observation about dealing with great ideas is the adventure of deciding a priority among them. To which of the great ideas do you give top place? Granted, each may be important; but which rates just a little higher in your personal scale of values?

If my first question about what you have made of these past four years is a little personal, then the suggestion of arranging your priorities is even more so. But Plato did a lot of thinking about priorities, so we have a good precedent. Plato believed that all human values can be classified as a form of goodness, or truth, or beauty. To which of his trinity would you give the top place in your own life? Plato seemed to favor goodness, but at times, he gave priority to beauty. Which would you put first? Would it be goodness? To be and do all you can to improve yourself and help others? Or would your preference be truth? To discover and be faithful to your discoveries? Or do you give first place to beauty? To enjoy and create as much beauty as possible?

People like to hedge the question. They do so by claiming to choose all three – saying that in social relations, goodness comes first; in personal beliefs, truth comes first; and in life's everyday joys, beauty comes first. But all three cannot be in first place.

In my own years in a university, I began by placing goodness first. Then I decided that truth was the most important. Now I give beauty first place, and in doing so, have discovered a tranquility that compares to the beauty and serenity of a sunset. I wish you success and happiness in your future adventures with great ideas. I hope that your discoveries will be many, your harmonies logical, your probabilities high, and your priorities the most satisfying.

Freedom in Business and Freedom in the Classroom

Business, Industry and Education Day,
Brigham Young University
September 3, 1965

□

Present world history and current events in American life tell us a great deal about the meaning of freedom.

The purpose of my discussion is to establish the proposition that free classrooms and free business enterprise not only help each other to be more successful, each in its own daily work, but that both free classrooms and free business enterprise together are necessary for the broadest individual freedom.

More and more we realize that to make freedom live, the business world and the academic world need each other. They prosper together, and separately they fail. Alone, business gets into trouble. Alone, scholars are not as capable.

Teachers and businessmen have been separated in our American democracy for too long. Indeed, American history can partially be explained as a running contest between our cultural and our practical interests. Our national concern to satisfy material needs has often overwhelmed our cultural life. Pursuit of business success has frequently cost us the high price of cultural failures.

One way to explain and make clear this clash of the practical versus the cultural is to examine the contrasting attitudes of schoolteachers and businessmen. Conversations among teachers about businessmen and their business practices are frequently uncomplimentary. It is obvious to everybody that this negative critical attitude is passed on to students in the classrooms. Likewise, when businessmen have conversations about schoolteachers, their remarks are often uncomplimentary. And, likewise, it is obvious that this negative attitude is well known within the teaching profession.

Indeed, at times the business world and the academic world appear so far apart, so diverse in purpose, so unlike in attitudes, and so different in practice that one doubts if they really need each other. Further, one doubts if they help the other be more successful. Nevertheless, free classrooms aid our business prosperity, and free enterprise aids successful teaching. Together they form a bulwark of freedom for each individual.

With all our inevitable democratic turmoil and with all the present social upheavals across the face of the earth, nothing is clearer than this: Freedom needs both free classrooms and free business enterprise.

What follows is an attempt to spell out the basis for this mutual success – the philosophy, if you please, of how free business enterprise and free classrooms aid each other, help make each other more successful, and, above all, help insure freedom within our democracy.

It is encouraging to know that every business executive will be attentive to any suggestion regarding attaining greater success, and, likewise, teachers will be attentive to learning ways of doing their job in a better way. To this end of achieving greater success for both, the following propositions are submitted.

First, we must recognize that tensions between life in the

marketplace and life in classrooms are not only inevitable, they are healthy and wholesome for both.

The teacher and the businessman live in somewhat different worlds: one more involved with theory and one more with practice; one more objective and one more immediate and practical; one in the peace of the classroom security and one in the uncertainty of competition. Just because the climate and purpose of each is so different, this vocational contrast enables each to be a better critic of the other.

The practical man can prosper from the criticism of a theoretician. The teacher of theory can be checked best by those whose success is measured by actual results. These two widely separated disciplines of teaching and business will always live with each other in a climate of tension, but it is a tension that can be healthy and wholesome for both.

Every student of democracy knows that thoughtful criticism is necessary and good for every form of social life – in politics, in business, and in teaching. Indeed, constructive criticism is of great value for good homes and good churches. Every form of democracy is made more successful by thoughtful and responsible criticism. So it is a good thing for schools to be critical of business, and for business to be critical of schools. Tensions resulting from careful and factual criticisms mean greater success for both.

But we are interested in more than this value of criticism for its own sake. Our larger problem is to formulate the foundation of good criticism.

What is the basis of sound criticism? When are our inferences, conclusions, and judgments warranted and justified? When are they sound? When are they unsound? When is a comment or conclusion wholesome? When is it unwholesome? When is a business person's observation about education good, and when bad? When is a teacher's remark or teaching about business helpful or harmful?

The best and most basic answer is this: All comments, all judgments, all observations, and all conclusions made by both teachers about business and by businessmen about schools and schoolteachers are of value if they have a factual basis through stating what the actual situation is—in short, if they are judgments based upon the truth. Conversely, business and schools damage each other if their judgments about each other are not based upon fact.

This obvious need for opinions, beliefs, and judgments to have a factual foundation might appear unnecessary to emphasize or even to state. Yet it is at this point, the presence or absence of fact, that one can find the source of our social misunderstandings—indeed, of our social quarrels and conflicts, even of revolutions and bloodshed. One might even go so far as to say that the great majority of disputes—economic, political, religious, and educational—not only in America but in all lands and among all peoples could be settled peacefully and satisfactorily if both sides were in possession of the facts.

If somebody objects that facts are not easy to come by, that the facts may change from day to day, and that a biased selection of the facts can easily falsify the whole picture, all this and more must be granted. Nevertheless, man's greatest hope for the successful settlement of disputes, and, thereby, for satisfactory social and personal progress, can be achieved only if groups and individuals literally dig out the facts of the situation.

It hardly needs saying that businessmen and teachers, unarmed with facts and careless in their observations, can inflict immeasurable harm upon themselves and the whole community. Businessmen with disparaging attitudes toward schoolteachers wound our democracy at its very core. Teachers, unarmed with facts about free enterprise, can weaken the very pillars of our free democracy.

If freedom is to grow and not diminish, if business is to prosper freely and not be government controlled, and if classrooms are to remain free and teachers not suspect, teachers and businessmen must be careful in their critical judgments about each other.

To this end, not just to achieve better understanding but to help each profession toward greater success, the following drama is presented.

Let us imagine businessmen and teachers assembled together trying to state their purposes. A businessman and a teacher are called upon to open two separate meetings with prayer. The teacher might pray:

> O, Lord, help us teachers to represent to our students the way the world really is—no better and no worse. Give us a passionate desire to find the facts, and a strong dedication not to enlarge or diminish them. And with these facts, help us study and observe human psychology—all of its best and all of its worst. Especially now, as teachers and businessmen, make us aware, O Lord, of man's desperate struggle for bread and his deep fear of poverty. And because of this fear and struggle, help us understand man's temptations to win economic security as best he can, by means sometimes fair and sometimes foul. Help us teach the truth to our students so that when they leave our classrooms to compete in the economic world they may not say we misrepresented the world, teaching that it is worse than it is or teaching that it is better than they find it.

The businessman's prayer might be:

> O Lord, when we think of teachers and classrooms, help us realize that we are thinking about the very future of our beloved America. And if our words downgrade the teaching profession, then bring home to us that we are really downgrading the future of our American democracy. For if

teachers are discouraged with us and we with them, then new generations will emerge from our schools suspicious of economic freedom and impatient with our efforts to produce and distribute more goods for more people. If we are sensitive to the dedication of teachers, if we are sensitive to the cultural values of good schools, and if we want America to be free and strong morally, intellectually, and spiritually, then we must not only give more material needs to our schools, but far more–we must esteem more highly those who teach, for these teachers are teaching the people who will soon take our place.

Our first conclusion, then, about each profession helping the other to be more successful means that their constructive and responsible criticisms must have, so far as possible, a factual basis.

Our second proposition for greater teaching success and greater business prosperity is that both professions, but especially the teaching profession, must have a clear understanding of the principles of business competition. Few Americans, including businessmen and teachers, understand the principles that guide economic competition within our American democracy.

Our first proposition about competition is that all life is rooted deeply in competition; and every form of cooperation, however noble, necessary, and valuable, must ultimately submit to the test of competition.

Competition is the operational method of life, of survival, of success in all professions; indeed, it is the principle of excellence itself. Man is a competing animal, whether it be for food, pleasure, or glory. There is always the desire to win, to achieve, to climb, to have, and to keep. To be sure, man is also a cooperating animal. He shares, gives, and sacrifices. Whenever one supposes that cooperation can substantially replace competition, which is then played down, eliminated, or regulated out of existence, internal corruption and inefficiency result.

While competition operates in schools as it does in the marketplace, business competition is not too clearly understood, especially by the teaching profession. To illustrate, competition in the schools, while practiced in earnest, is not as desperate as competition in the marketplace. In business, competition is for keeps, the loser loses everything. Winning second or third place in business competition wins nothing. Competition in business is a severe and harsh taskmaster. In each competitive situation there is only one winner and generally many losers. Competition in business can be very wasteful of both economic and human resources. Not only may many lose, but even the winner's low bid may turn out to be a loss. And even if the reward is more money, it is often won at the price of lost sleep or ill health. Small wonder, then, that almost everybody tries every conceivable way to avoid business competition.

Schoolteachers, noting this waste of competition, this high price of the struggle to win, are likely to stress milder ways of cooperation by citing the community's cooperation in such fields as public health, recreation, and education. And businessmen also attempt to avoid costly competition by seeking mergers with competitors. Sometimes businesses are cited for trying to avoid competition by resorting to price-fixing or other conspiracies. Some of these practices violate the Sherman Anti-Trust law, the Fair Trade Practice Act, or some other government regulation or law designed to keep competition free, open, and fair.

Arguments are advanced that by avoiding competition, waste can be avoided, and, therefore, all will benefit. And we are often told that as giant corporations grow, great capital and large collective efforts are required and necessary, which is true enough, but there can also be the motive to weaken competition.

International cartels have both greater efficiencies and lesser competition. One might say that the world's greatest effort to eliminate competition is communism.

Nobody will deny that competition can be bypassed, and that cooperation operates with great success in our post office, schools, public health departments, and many other public enterprises. We are all glad that not all life is competitive and that much is cooperative, freely and voluntarily given and shared.

Nevertheless, every single effort of man to live by cooperation alone without the checks of competition always and ultimately faces a judgment day. And the judge is always the inexorable principle of competition – some new challenge, some new method, some unsuspected new possibility.

Every collective effort, whether public works, large corporation, or political system such as socialism or communism, will someday and somehow face competitors and competition. Every conceived system will be challenged and every power structure checked. Every method or system to bypass competitive challenge is doomed in the long run to failure.

It is no wonder that the principle of competition has a bad reputation in many places – especially among educators. They are themselves involved in a great and successful cooperative effort. While it is true that competition does exist among teachers and students, it is nothing like the severe competition of business.

The overall result of free competition in a free society is an economy that produces the highest standard of living for the largest number of people. In other economic systems, such as socialism and communism, both production figures and plain judgment make clear that they do not accomplish nearly so much for the consumer as do free businessmen with a profit incentive operating under the principle of fair competition.

A remark here might diminish some envy educators naturally feel when comparing their incomes with those of businessmen. If the comparative income is too inequitable, as it so often is, then competition may and usually does level at least some of the inequity. And if this does not do so well, the very high and almost unbelievable percentage of business failures may help ease the pain of jealousy. Not all who think they can provide a lower price, a finer service, or a better quality can do so. When the facts are faced, as they inevitably must be, not all succeed.

Let us now examine this principle of competition as it applies to American business life. Surely teachers cannot judge business-men and business practices without a clear understanding of the principle of competition as it applies to the practices of Ameri-can business. Briefly stated, business competition is based on the idea that the consumer is king. He can decide where, and how, and to whom his dollar will be paid. He decides this on the basis of the lowest price, best quality, finest service, or all three com-bined.

But, while the consumer is both judge and jury, he is not the one who determines that only the strongest competitor with the lowest price, best quality, and finest service will survive. Nor is competition practiced in our economy so that a strong com-petitor wins simply because he is the ablest and strongest.

In American business life, the principle of competition is not allowed to operate unchecked and with unbridled power. Open, free competition is not allowed to progress unimpeded to its logical result of success only to the most cunning or the most powerful. In America the principle of competition is joined with the principle of governmental regulation. For example, compa-nies cannot sell below cost for the purpose of eliminating com-petitors. Nor can companies raid the trained personnel of com-petitors for the purpose of weakening their competition. Many government regulations of business are designed to soften the harsh results of what might otherwise be success through sheer brutal competition.

We face here the very difficult question of how much gov-ernment should regulate business. When is government interference justified, when unjustified? If unregulated competition produces such harsh results as the strong becoming stronger and the weak becoming weaker, how much should competition itself be regulated?

Nobody knows the answer to this question. Nobody knows the right balance between government restrictions on the one hand and a completely free business on the other. This is a much-debated question in the schools, in legislatures, among business leaders, and, indeed, in various countries around the world. Some want total government control, as in communism. Some want as little as possible, as expressed in the policy statements of the National Association of Manufacturers, chambers of commerce, etc.

There is one principle applied with considerable success in our free democracy. It is that there will be no more government regulation than is necessary to produce an increased amount of freedom for the individual. The test is the freedom of the individual. The standard is the well-being of each individual.

To illustrate: Recently a clothing store closed its doors. Before it could have a close-out sale, it had to comply with the city government regulations. The regulations required that the close-out sale be limited to one month, an inventory of all the store's merchandise had to be filed, and no additional stock could be brought in from outside sources. These careful regulations prevented losses to other merchants that might result if the sale continued indefinitely with imports of inferior merchandise brought in to keep the sale going. Such a regulation protects not only other merchants but individuals who might otherwise be exploited. Such a city ordinance is weighed in terms of value to the individual. The rule is that restriction of competition is justified and the freedom of one man or one company is curtailed when the freedom and well-being of a larger number of individuals is at stake.

If such government regulation of business in the free enterprise system is taken for granted in our democracy, what about freedom in classrooms? Are there government regulations restricting freedom in classrooms? The answer is that there are almost no restrictions to the freedom of teaching and learning. The teacher moves in the realm of the mind, and our founding fathers wrote constitutional guarantees of intellectual and spiritual freedoms unsurpassed in all political history.

But with this almost unlimited freedom for teachers goes a heavy moral obligation. It is the heavy burden of teaching the truth, the facts, the actual situation, the real state of affairs, the way things are. A classroom is no place for emotional bias. It is a place for objective teaching, careful reasoning, and thoughtful conclusions based upon factual foundations.

American business practices can stand up well under such intellectual scrutiny, not because business people are outstandingly honest – though many are – but because the free enterprise system gives the most and the best at the lowest price to the consumer. Students in our schools need to know the principles and the limitations of free competition. They need to know not only because this knowledge helps free enterprise flourish for the benefit of the largest number of people, but for a far more important reason. More is at stake in free enterprise than the greatest possible prosperity.

There is a spiritual, moral, and intellectual stake in a free, competitive marketplace. It is the fact that if a nation's economy and political life are joined, as in socialism or communism, these two great powers of business and government will result in such massive power structures that they inevitably dominate the teaching and learning in the schools. If economic freedom is lost to government, intellectual freedoms are doomed. So the businessman, resisting unnecessary government encroachments on free enterprise, is fighting not only for business freedoms but also intellectual freedoms.

I conclude with the observation that business people and teachers will appreciate each other more if reliable information about the other is available to both. If this happens, the gain will be not only in greater prosperity, but also in a stronger freedom within our democracy.

III

RELIGION

Introduction

Carolyn Tanner Irish

☐

I am pleased to write a few words of introduction to this selection of my father's speeches on religion. I was a young girl when most of them were given, and I often went along to hear him speak. Those were occasions that influenced me deeply and gave me great pride.

Reading these speeches now, I am again touched by three distinctive contributions Obert makes to those who, like him, have taken the religious quest seriously: his independent perspective, his rational emphasis, and his kindness of manner.

These addresses share the independent reflections of one seeker with others; the categories of thought are all his own, and he does not patronize. " . . . In matters concerned with religion," Obert writes, "there are no special privileges, no aristocracy, no guarantees, and no assured salvation." Yet, this being a lifelong journey of discovery along ever new horizons of experience, culture, and history, all of us welcome those who with wisdom and hope can articulate difficult challenges freshly, as Obert so clearly does.

The Reverend Irish is an Episcopal Priest who has served in the dioceses of Michigan, Virginia, and Washington, D.C.

The rational element in religious life is difficult to maintain at best, and it always suffers in times of fear and change such as we have known in these post-war decades. Knowing full well that religious faith is not itself a function of intellect, Obert has courageously held out for "reasonable religion." In these talks, he opens out difficult questions for fresh inspection, often noting what has been fragmented, frozen, or forgotten in our habits of thought and piety, our orthodox or ideological schemes, our secure formulas and safe convictions. This is reason in the service of renewed vision, better hopes, and more practical solutions too. Any religion must offer that if it is to continue to claim our deepest loyalties.

Kindness is another quality that often goes by the boards in religious discussion, especially among the critics of religion—what Schleiermacher calls its "cultured despisers." I do think Obert is as good a critic as religion has (and all religion needs critics!), yet he is unusually kind about it. This is as much a product of his own gentle spirit as of principled restraint; but I may say I have always appreciated his sensitivity to the fact that any religious life that is more than sentimental fidelity or disinterested curiosity is profoundly *vulnerable*. We often become too defensive to hear otherwise good teachers and critics when they lack this sensitivity.

I am struck, finally, by the titles of this volume, *One Man's Search*, and of his soon to be published autobiography, *One Man's Journey*. Those titles convey a *dynamic* engagement with the deepest questions of life, and that engagement is still evident in Obert at the age of eighty-four. Those of us who have shared part of his own journey closely—or even briefly—have indeed been blessed by his capacity and his willingness to speak about it in open and public forums.

A New Religion for a New Age

General Interest Seminar, University of Utah
February 19, 1957

☐

Nearly every question about religion requires a clarification of what one means by religion. I will answer this question by making a distinction between two kinds of religion. The one kind or type I will call "fringe religion" because it borders religion and is marginal to the essence of religion. The other kind of religion I call "basic religion" because it pertains to that which I consider most important and fundamental to religion.

The terms "fringe religion" and "basic religion" are my creation and therefore quite arbitrary; yet such a distinction is helpful in deciding whether we may need a new religion for a new age. The conclusion of this paper may then be obvious, namely, that we will not need a new basic religion for a new age, but that fringe religion may change for a new fringe religion whenever the need may arise.

The burden now remains to make clear the distinction between fringe and basic religion and explain why one – basic religion – is adequate for any new age, and why the other – fringe religion – assumes constant revisions as new ages appear.

I do not say that fringe religion is unimportant; it is important, but is not basic. To use metaphors, the design of taillights

145

on new model cars is apparently very important to car sales, but is not basic as is the need of a red light for night driving. Fringe benefits to workers such as paid holidays, vacations, and over-time pay are important, but still are only fringes compared to actual wages. So fringe religion is important because it may lead to basic religion, but another fringe religion could also lead to basic religion, or some new fringe religion may yet be discovered. Moreover, no basic religion is found without the presence of fringe religion. And whenever fringe religion is found, basic religion is generally discoverable.

What is a fringe religion, or the fringes of basic religion? Doctrines and theologies, rituals and ceremonies, formalities and sacraments, these are of themselves the fringes of religion. They may effectively or ineffectively lead to basic religion. They certainly are subject to change with every new age. Sacraments and liturgies lead to basic religion, effectively or otherwise. Their varieties found in all religions and their changes made over time are sufficient evidence that they change with any and all new ages.

All types of religious organizations are a fringe to basic religion. As a means to basic religion, some religious organizations are more effective than others. But the history of organized religions reveals that every organization changes from time to time, sometimes becoming extinct, while the purpose for which the organization came into being, basic religion, abides independent of the vicissitudes of any or all organizations.

In substance, if we define man as a symbol-making creature, the symbols he makes in religion are its fringes, and the experiences these fringes lead to may or may not be basic religion.

There is one observation to be made about fringe religion. When it is stressed for its own sake, when doctrines, sacraments, and organizations are considered as ends rather than as means, the result is a poverty religion. This is not fatal to religion, for people are widely adjusted to poverty in religion. It is probably true that most people mistake fringe religion for basic religion. And it is also true that since it is fringe religion that produces the best statistical records for all organized religions, religious leaders frequently stress the elements of fringe religion over basic religion. Indeed, it is a wonder that with the high prevalence of fringe religion and the poverty resulting therefrom, that basic religion survives at all.

What is basic religion? And why will it be adequate to any new age?

Basic religion has two aspects—one is the love of man, and the other is the love of God. What is meant by the love of man? The early Christians used the Greek word "agape" which means a passionate, non-self-centered, unqualified concern for the well-being of a neighbor, expressed by care and support. It means to recognize actively the sanctity and claim of selfhood in all persons alike. Agape means love for another self not because of any lovable qualities which he or she may possess, but purely and entirely because it is a self capable of experiencing happiness and misery and endowed with the power to choose between good and evil. The love of man is thus more than a feeling, it is a state of the will. To love one's neighbor means to reverence human life everywhere and under all conditions. And this includes even our enemies. Agape is an attitude that separates people from their evil deeds. One may hate what a man does, but not hate the doer, as we may dislike and disown our own deeds, but do not generally dislike ourselves. That is, we may hate evil acts while desiring the real good of the self who commits them. This law of brotherhood is the essence of basic religion and is found in the scriptures of all major religions.

Buddha said: "Let your light so shine forth that having left the world to enter in to so well taught a doctrine and discipline, you may be respectful, affectionate and hospitable to all men."

Confucius declared: "In seeking a foothold for self, love

finds a foothold for others; seeking a light for itself, it enlightens others also."

Mohammed said: "Give unto the poor and the orphan and the bondman for His sake, saying 'We feed you for God's sake only; from you we require no recompense nor any thanks.' "

And Lao-tzu, founder of Taoism stated: "For the holy man there are no outcast people."

In Christianity, the word "love" is not an emotional sentiment or feeling, nor a romantic attraction seeking love in return, nor an intellectual attitude, "but an inward turning of the will of the self in devotion to the neighbor, as the reflection of the love of God to man and in imitation of Christ's love for his chosen disciples."

The question before us now is will this basic ingredient of all religions, the love of man, be replaced by something new? It has endured through more than twenty centuries of successively new ages. What foreseeable new age may replace it?

Near a mural of the figure of Christ on a building in New York City is this answer to our question: "Man's ultimate destiny depends not upon whether he can learn new lessons or make new discoveries and conquests, but on his acceptance of the lessons taught by him two thousand years ago."

If we call our atomic age a new age, is there any present need of mankind more desperate than the religion of love? And if we get by our present international crises and emerge into a new age of international cooperation, will it not also be based upon the ethic of love? Can there be a better world within our imagination than one of goodwill, exercised toward all persons, good and bad, grateful and ungrateful, friendly and hostile—a world that acknowledges no boundaries of race, nation, sex, or economic status?

The second basic concept of religion is the love of God. Will some new age discard the idea of God?

Now we are on less empirical ground. The arguments from reason, the cosmological, teleological, and ontological arguments for God's existence are no longer as compelling as they were in the past. Doubts are created as science reveals the vastness of our universe, the evolution of life, the history of the Bible, and the new psychology of man. All optimism flees before man's inhumanities. Tragedy and evil stalk the earth, stamping out the faith of millions who reply to the poet Robert Browning that maybe God is not in his heaven, after all, and even if he is, all is certainly not right with the world.

Finally, man has turned from a religion which once promised to satisfy most of his wishes. Once men prayed for rain, now they harness rivers. Once men were dependent upon heaven for good crops, large families, and freedom from pestilence. Now science is religion's competitor in giving man what he wants. The great issue between science and religion is not intellectual, sharp though that issue has been; it is that men are giving up religion in favor of science because of what science can do for them. As someone asked: "Is God becoming progressively less essential?"

Is it at this point that we ask: Will this present age replace the religion of theism with the religion of humanism?

One answer is that many have already done so. That much theism exists today among 900 million communists is doubtful. China had almost none before communism came. The churches of Europe are attended primarily by women and children. Yet there is a present widespread revival of religion.

Our question is whether some new religion may be needed, either by ourselves in this new atomic age or by some age yet to come. My reply is that the second basic essential to religion, a faith in God, will endure through whatever new ages may appear.

Three reasons are given for this conclusion. First, man's intellectual search, while insufficient to answer the question of God's existence, offers reasons for, as well as against, the existence of God.

We have classified doctrine and theology as belonging to fringe religion, but we also said that fringe religion was important—not basic, yet important. The reason theology and philosophy of religion pertain to the fringes of religion is that their doctrines and ideas change with the new ages, new discoveries, and new thoughts of man. But, while the ideas about God may appear to change, the experience of God appears to abide with men in all ages.

Like scientific hypotheses that are continually subject to progressive corrections, so man's ideas about God will change with future experience. They are valid only within a limited historical epoch. Religious experience changes, and so all theology is hypothetical and likely to be changed or modified in the light of new experience. Theology and religious doctrines therefore should be as tentative as are scientific hypotheses. It is for this reason that theology and religious doctrines are only the fringes of religion, though important fringes to be sure.

The second thing to be said about man's intellectual search to prove God's existence is that while a good negative case can be made, a good positive case can be made also. The cosmological argument does offer one explanation for a world now in existence. The teleological argument does give one explanation for the orderly and purposeful process of life and especially of the mind. The ontological argument is yet the best definition of God—that he is that Being than which none greater can be conceived. The argument from moral experience remains one of the best insights into the possible nature of God as well as our esthetic experience. While no one of these arguments may be sufficient, all of them together converge upon a theistic hypothesis.

A basic reason for accepting a theistic interpretation – one that will live through whatever new ages may come – is the nature of religious experience itself. Here is a fact, yet one which defies intellectual analysis. It is a strange thing that an experience so decisive as to influence a person's total life and commitment should yet be described as ineffable, unutterable, indescribable, and unexpressible. It is no wonder that universities find religion a difficult problem, for it seems to defy or escape our intellectual categories. It is, therefore, also inevitable that universities are unable to deal with more than fringe religion – the ideas about religion, not the personal and private experience of religion. It is no wonder that churches and free universities are respectful but reserved toward each other. The university attempts to explain what is inexplicable, while the churches believe that they do explain the inexplicable.

Religious experience means that, for the individual, God is not a matter of belief or opinion, but is a genuine, experienced fact, an inescapable reality. It means there is a difference between saying "I believe in God the Father Almighty," (which is simply a belief or perhaps only an opinion), and saying, "Enter into thy inner chamber, and having shut thy door, pray to thy father who is in secret" – that is, finding God real. At least God here is not mentioned to end an argument. The argument from religious experience is that just as friendship is not a matter of proof but rather of experience, so too is beauty a matter of experience, also love and goodness, and so also is the experience of God. It is a deeper matter explained by the poet: "Earth's crammed with heaven, and every common bush afire with God: But only he who sees, takes off his shoes."

People can change some aspects of their environment, their architecture, medicine, and automobiles, but they cannot greatly change themselves. Each human being starts from scratch. Each begins evenly with all others, and in matters concerned with religion there are no special privileges, no aristocracy, no guarantees, and no assured salvation. Everywhere and always men struggle with the same basic problems that are of special concern to religion: bad tempers, overweening ambitions, lustful drives, and tragic failures. No one is exempt. No one is sure. Failure is everywhere.

With hopes and dreams people have looked out upon the universe and wondered if it is friendly or hostile. They will likely do so for a long time to come. Whether the universe sponsors man's highest values is the paramount question of all man's religions. Because the answer is so important, but not final, man's attachment to religious affirmation will endure for a long time to come.

No university can change human nature or answer our questions about ultimate meaning, purpose, or destiny of human life. College students, like all other young people, fight a hard battle for self-control, and their attitude is altered perhaps only slightly because they are in college. College students, like all other young people, look out in wonderment upon the world. They in part draw their answers from books and lectures, but there is no great margin of certainty over non-formally educated people as to whether this universe will guarantee their finest hopes.

A university needs religion quite as much as a coal mining town, communist community, New York, or Salt Lake City. The same problems of life and alternative answers prevail everywhere. It may be, then, that if God is left out of some new religion in a new age, this would be true: that man the sinner would lose his strongest help; that man the sufferer would lose his securest refuge; that man the thinker would lose his greatest thought; that man the worker would lose his greatest motive; that man the lover would lose his fairest vision; and that man the mortal would lose his only hope.

Is Religion an Aid to International Understanding?

Great Issues in Religion, University of Utah
February 23, 1955

□

This evening we are to examine religion as it affects our international understanding. The issue is whether religion is an aid or an obstacle to our international understanding, whether religion is a social force that essentially unites, or divides, the peoples of the world. Is religion a substantial influence in favor of peace and international brotherhood?

The question calls for a factual answer, but the facts are not easily determined. So we answer with a few facts, some general experiences, and much that is mere opinion. Even then, most of this discussion will be in the realm of value and hope – should religion aid our international understanding? What hopes are justified that it will?

The original question is so broad that it needs some narrowing. It might be qualified by asking: Is religion, for the most part, an aid to our international understanding? Obviously some of religion is an aid, and some of religion is an obstacle. But, for the most part, is religion an aid or is it an obstacle to the international understanding between the peoples of the world? That is, when the scales are evenly balanced and we then add religion, does the needle of the scale point in the direction of better international understanding? Or does the pointer indicate that religion has made the difference in the direction of international mistrust and general misunderstanding?

I would divide my answer into a judgment of the past and a hope about the future. In history, religion for the most part—both in theory and in practice—has been a divisive and alienating factor in human international life. Each religion has demanded unconditional surrender of all other religions, and of all other nations and peoples. Salvation was for all men; but salvation was Christian, or Mohammedan, or Hindu, or Buddhist. The truth was for all men; but the truth was Catholic, or Quaker, or Jewish, or Baptist. Religious vocabularies made frequent use of such words as "gentile," "heathen," "unbeliever," and "the damned."

Religion generates deep convictions and strong loyalties, while international understanding calls for something else—it requires calm reasoning and a willingness to compromise. The present condition in Palestine, India, Holland, and here in America, multiplied many times, forms a great deal of religious history, including some religious wars. It is probably true that no prejudice, even racial prejudice, is as prevalent or runs as deep as religious prejudice. It endures through the centuries and defies the closest proximity, so that some students feel that until religion is made impotent there can never be much hope for international goodwill and understanding. Such a conclusion may be reached with observations about the Near East.

However, let us not dwell on the bleak picture of religious failures. All institutions have their share of failures. In political life it is the tragic failure of unbridled nationalism; in economic life it is the universal failure of justice. In other forms of social life the failures make a staggering total. Even science has its common failure of immodesty—refusing to admit with sufficient frequency that there are many areas of human behavior that science cannot touch.

But religion is not static. There is a great ferment now taking place in the world's religions. It may be compared to another Reformation. Religion is examining itself. The present world upheaval has forced religion to change. A new world with greater religious vitality is in the making.

This evening we examine this religious reformation only as it affects the possibility of a better international understanding. There are three facts about our contemporary world that affect the present participation of religion in man's international life. The first fact is a new world that science has made into one community. The second is the struggle between communism and the free nations. The third is the revolt of the masses for a better life.

These three facts have compelled religion to make two fundamental changes. One is the disentangling of its great universal and primary principles from peculiarities that are local and secondary. The other is an emphasis of those principles characteristic of a mature religion.

Our question then, of whether religion is an aid to international understanding, can be answered affirmatively because the major facts in the present world upheaval have elicited from religion several changes that are so fundamental as to be characteristic of a religious reformation.

We turn now to the first of these dominant facts, namely, the new world that science has made into one community:

The dominant fact of the twentieth century is that the entire population of the earth is now included within a single community. There are no more ocean barriers, no mountain barriers, no barriers of the north and south poles, no barriers of any kind. There is only one race now – it is the human race. The old ideas of nationalism and isolationism are as dead as feudalism. We are all dependent on one another, every one of us on the earth. The hard lesson of the twentieth century is that we cannot make a heaven in our own country and leave a hell outside. We are members of one family, the human family – 3500 million of us. The borders and barriers between us have fallen away. Psychological barriers remain, but they are tumbling by the hour. Any future war will be a civil war. Peace is indivisible. Peace does not exist for any nation if there is a war in any other place on our planet. The world is one. The human family is one. The entire population of this earth shares a common fate – for good or ill – in war or peace. We all share it together. Any war started now is started not against another country, but against humanity.

The unity of mankind was approaching rapidly in the nineteenth century. It has come in the twentieth century more rapidly than was expected. It has been forced upon us before we are prepared for it. Various traditions, diverse environments, and incompatible ways of life are colliding with each other in rapid succession all over the face of the earth. Peoples are being pushed together and rubbing elbows whether they like it or not. Some will face and recognize what is happening, but most people are neither sufficiently informed nor emotionally prepared to accept this new world of one community.

The result may be summed up in this way: humanity is in a precarious balance between the forces of violence and the forces of peace. It is by no means clear at this time which of these forces will prevail. We do ask, however, whether religion will now become an aid to the forces of peace and cooperation.

The second fact impinging on man's religious life is the present struggle between communism and democracy. Politically, our present situation is a world population roughly divided into three parts: one-third communist, one-third democratic, and one-third what someone has described as "an uneasy camp of watchful waiters." In this present political division can religion be an aid to better understanding?

The third fact is the revolt of the masses, particularly in Asia and Africa. They are restless for freedom and bread. In their hunger, poverty, and ignorance will they be won to communism or to a partnership with the free nations? Can religion make a substantial contribution to the necessary international understanding called for by their revolt?

Let us turn first to the struggle with communism. What does religion say? Can religion offer a better chance for humanity to edge its way along the precipice and finally emerge into some future world of peace and understanding?

The answer is affirmative.

In the first place, religion does not identify itself with communism or capitalism. It criticizes both. In capitalist countries, the churches have courageously criticized the abuses of absolute economic individualism. Sometimes, of course, they have identified themselves with the current economic system, but more and more they are demanding that our economic life stand under the judgment of high religion – of fair play, equality of opportunity, and the denial of exploitation. And the result? Our free enterprise has corrected some of its own excesses and injustices. Religion has not done all of this, but it has helped to create a nobler character in mankind; it has helped to create a social conscience, so that class and wealth distinction have not sharpened to the point of producing a totally corrupt society.

Much remains to be done. But this much is true: the charges made by the communists against our Western economic system are essentially false. And they were made false in part because religion has courageously demanded that our economic life stand under the judgment of moral laws – under the judgment of the prophets and of Christ.

What is religion doing behind the Iron Curtain? It certainly is not criticizing the economic system. To the extent that it is unable to do so, religion fails in one of its most important functions. But we cannot say that all religion behind the Iron Curtain is a failure. Sometimes there is great vitality of religion in underground faith, and strong resistance is made on the non-political level. We are reminded that when all others knuckled under to Hitler—even the universities—some men of religion held fast. They are also holding fast today in many parts of the totalitarian world. Evidence has been received of a religious revival now taking place in Hungary.

In the second place, concerning the struggle between communism and the West, religion is stating forcefully the meaning and the danger of a political totalitarian society. Religious literature and men of religion are helping man understand that the real conflict is fateful, not on the economic level, but on the cultural and spiritual levels. Religion marshals the churches of the world to oppose political totalitarianism as a deadly threat to the political, spiritual, and cultural freedoms of all the nations of the world. The issue needs to be sharpened in our minds; as Professor Bennet of the Union Theological Seminary states: "In the communist state the absolute teachers are absolute rulers—a combination that leaves no space in which the human spirit can breathe."

The religions of the world have a stake in this international conflict. They see the struggle not as a power struggle between Russia and the United States, but as a mortal danger to the freedom of men and women. The churches, therefore, support the opposition of the free world to further communist expansion.

Even so, however, the churches, as expressed in their international councils, are uneasy about an overemphasis of the military approach. We need military strength as a necessary counterweight to the military power of Russia. This military strength of America is a service to the freedom of all non-communist nations. Religion has become realistic about human nature, our self-centeredness, pride, and struggle for power. But while accepting this necessity of military strength as a realistic protection against the expansion of Russian communism, the churches are aware that the importance of military power can be overrated.

Of greater importance are the roles of ideas and constructive programs. In the final analysis, the struggle of religion with communism is due to the claim of communism to have the only solution to the problem of human life. Communism accepts no judgment from outside itself. It has become "an idolatrous substitute for God." It closes the mind to anything beyond itself so that when the individual faces the power of the state, there is no mercy. Contrast this absolutism of the communist state with the place of the individual in our free world. Here the individual has a standing before God, and regardless of political belief or lack of conformity – and even in opposition to the state – no society may cancel the standing of that person.

And so the aid of religion in this great struggle with communism is to point out the need of social reform in the various countries, to teach mankind the moral and spiritual issues involved in the struggle against totalitarianism, and to stand firmly with the rights of the individual against the state. But even in this role the churches must guard against some of our forms of anti-communism that threaten freedom of the mind and freedom of institutions.

Anti-communism has been necessary, but it has also taken a heavy toll, especially here in America. We have created a fear of dissent. We have standardized many minds. And, of most immediate danger, we have caused millions of Americans to take lightly the risk of war as long as the war was against communism. This has now reached such a danger that the Atomic Energy Commission last week released the information that one hydrogen bomb could destroy eleven million people between New York and Washington. It was believed necessary to release this information to the American public since the Russians also have the hydrogen bomb, and we need to pause for reflection.

The second aid of religion to the contemporary scene of international relations relates to the present world revolution, which might be called the revolt of the masses in their struggle for a better life. What has religion to say? The answer is important because peace will never come to a world where the causes of war continue to flourish. These causes are poverty, hunger, ignorance, fear, disease, chronic anxiety, and oppression. The situation is best described by saying that the world is in a ferment, a state of unrest, an upheaval, a revolution—especially the masses of Asia, Africa, and South America. As one writer described it, "The stirring peoples are going places—the only question is, where." One aspect of this ferment is called "the rise of the dependent peoples." Since the war ended, of the 800 million dependent peoples, 600 million have attained their independence. These countries are: the Philippines, India, Pakistan, Burma, Ceylon, Jordan, Israel, Korea, and Indonesia—one-fourth of the people of the world. They want bread and liberty. The fact we face is this: if we want peace, we must not only guard against overt aggression, we must help these peoples improve their standards of living. Communism makes an alluring appeal to the hungry, the sick, and the oppressed. But people of the vast underdeveloped areas of the earth can be won as working partners in a genuinely free world.

What has religion to say? One answer has always been clear: that our obligations go beyond the family, community, and nation. Religion holds that men are bound together in a single community, under one God, "whose moral purpose undergirds and overreaches the entire world." High religion has always transcended national boundaries. At its best, it makes its adherents worldminded. Its message has been that, as God is one, man is one. In this revolt of the underprivileged, religion offers hope and practical encouragement, especially from men of high religion now living in the more privileged areas of the earth.

The total effect of these three great changes in our present world has produced several kinds of religious reformations. On the international level two of them are the disentangling of religion's great universal principles from that part of religion that is local and secondary; and the emphasis of principles characteristic of a high and mature religion.

Concerning religion's great universal principles, it can accurately be said that men of religion were pioneers in seeing the world as one. But they were few and their followers far fewer. Now humanity desperately needs aid in finding universal ideals that will produce a unified world culture. The proposals for unification are legion. One of them is the well-known slogan "Workers of the world, unite." Another banner is "democracy," others are "humanism," "existentialism," and "liberalism."

What has religion to offer for unification? In the face of the sobering statement by Dr. Albert Einstein that "any future war would indubitably spell the annihilation of all civilized humanity," will it be said that religion, before such a challenge, is helpless and a failure? In the face of this crisis, what religious hopes are justified?

Two developments of great promise are taking place. They give cause for hope that religion will help to unite mankind in the necessary task of building a worldwide culture.

First, while the religious leaders of the world have formerly, and with some hesitation, sought to find areas of agreement, they are now being literally pushed to find common grounds that unite men. They are seeking out the universal principles found in all religions that might form a basis for unity and better understanding between nations. Such an effort, known as the ecumenical movement, is long overdue, and may not even now achieve the necessary results in time.

This search for agreement is not intended to find religious unanimity nor establish a universal faith, but to find common areas of agreement where mutual understanding is possible. It seeks to make of religions everywhere a force for unity and international brotherhood. Each religion would retain its own special insights, its own rituals, its own government. The question squarely before the churches and all religions is whether they will help deeply religious men and women to understand one another across the borders of their own separate histories, doctrines, and organizations. If people of religion are themselves not able to understand and appreciate the basic good and value in each other's work, what hope is there that religion will do other than stand aside while the human family plunges from one catastrophe to another?

Education—especially the humanities and the social sciences—together with religion are the two great institutions whereby mankind may pioneer an ever-expanding worldwide culture. If religion is not to fail in its part, each church and each faith must disentangle those universal ingredients from matters that are local and individual. They must find brotherhood and unity, or be annihilated with the humanity they presumed to save.

At a recent world conference of religions, the various faiths assembled and agreed that all religions had these ten points in common:

1. The Unity of All Life.

2. The Interdependence and Brotherhood of All Men.

3. Love and Service to Fellow Man; Not Domination or Attempted Power over Him.

4. Non-Violence and Non-Injury: No More War or Killing.

5. Help—Not Exploitation of the Weak and Backward.

6. Purity of Life and Motive.

7. Simplicity and Few Possessions. True Riches and True Happiness Are Within.

8. The Worth of Individual Man and the Ability of Every Man to Achieve High Status in Life.

9. The Immortality of the Soul.

10. The Union of Man with God: Which is the Final Truth of Every Religion.

Perhaps a shorter and certainly a universal creed of all religions is the love of God as the purest being, and a love for man. In the present religious ferment, there are many conferences and councils of religious leaders and laymen, all striving to achieve a brotherhood on which it may be possible to build a worldwide culture.

In the second place, there is another change that is taking place in religion, giving evidence that it will be an aid to man's international understanding. This is an emphasis on those matters that are characteristic of a mature religion.

Aristotle said that a proper description of anything was only possible when the description related to its highest function. This would be true when we describe or define religion. We must see religion in its maturity if we are to understand it. Failure to do this is common in universities, even in this Great Issues Forum. Frequently when reference is made to religion, what is actually referred to is immature religion. There is a failure common among students, and even teachers, to confuse an immature religion with a mature, developed religion. It will not do to confuse astrology and astronomy, or alchemy with chemistry. Neither is one talking about religion when he is confusing it with what is immaturity in religion.

We are careful to distinguish immaturity in art and in literature, but not so careful to qualify our references to religion by saying: "I now mean low or immature religion." What is mature religion? Professor T. M. Greene of Yale gives this description:

> A religion can be said to be "low" or "primitive" in
> proportion as its beliefs are superstitious, its ritualistic
> practices magical, its basic orientation egocentric and
> anthropocentric rather than theocentric, its social pre-
> cepts directed to conventional correctness rather than
> to inner spiritual righteousness, and its prevailing atti-
> tude arbitrarily authoritarian and dogmatic.

It is altogether clear that immature religion will be of no aid to
international understanding. Rather, immaturity in religion will
always be a block to world culture.

What, then, are those characteristics of high and mature
religion, especially in that area capable of giving aid to international understanding? Professor Burchard, dean of humanities at
M.I.T., gives this restatement of a very old commandment: "We
must seek for everyone else in the world exactly what we seek for
ourselves, no more and no less." And Professor Burchard is striking at an old enemy of international understanding, self-
righteousness, when he writes:

> We need desperately, and from childhood, to know
> other peoples through their own eyes and not only
> through our own. Then we will learn that: There is no
> fundamentally greater good in one race or people than
> in any other.
>
> Certain people may have achieved certain kinds
> of progress. It is their duty to share the progress as fast
> as possible with all other peoples who want it but never
> in a paternalistic way, and never primarily for the profit
> of the one who has already attained it. (All the high
> points of progress have not, by the way, been achieved
> by the Western world and certainly not by the people
> of the United States.)

If we bear these basic principles steadily in mind and are persistent in our own beliefs, we shall prevail. We shall need in America to be zealous in preservation of our internal liberties, zealous in extending the freedom of education to young Negroes and young Navajo Indians, zealous in insistence upon a consistent morality in our statecraft, zealous in seeing to it that the *manner* of our quest for immediate objectives does not turn them into dross when they are attained.

What *is* mature religion, particularly on an international level? It is this immortal mandate from Leviticus: "Thou shalt love thy neighbor as thyself." But to love our neighbor, we must first know him. Difficult as this may be, many opportunities are present. Knowledge about the United Nations, of its work, problems, and membership will help us to know our neighbor.

The great religious ideal of peace on earth compels all religions to support the United Nations. This is mandatory, for no machinery for peace can succeed except it be based upon the faith and confidence of people. The United Nations is not self-sustaining. It may well be true that whether the United Nations succeeds or fails will depend to a marked degree on whether the churches support it. Professor Justin Wroe Nixon, professor of Christian Theology and Ethics at Colgate-Rochester Divinity School, makes this observation:

> In the 18th century the founders of our country were challenged to dig channels through which the tides of desire for individual freedom and national independence could flow. . . . If we fail now to construct great institutional sluiceways—such as the United Nations—through which the concern for the common interests of mankind can flow, the tides of human feeling that are moving toward world cooperation will turn into

raging torrents of frustrated desire, and change the fair fields of human hope into swamps of brackish despair. . . . This is the task of this century. There is little doubt that the historian of the future will judge us according to our success in accomplishing it.

Many qualities could be named about a high and mature religion, but of this we may be sure – it will take universal ideals shared by all religions, namely, the worth and dignity of man, the moral postulates as timeless imperatives, and the unity of man as the purpose of God to rise above the levels of class, nation, and race, to the high level of humanity.

Religion Today in America

Great Issues Forum, University of Utah
April 29, 1959

□

What is the meaning of America's present turn to religion? What basis does it have? How may one explain it?

The meaning of this widespread interest in religion may be explained both in theory and in practice. My purpose will be to explain it according to present religious practices. This distinction of theory and practice is impossible to maintain, and actually, I shall use theory to explain practice in this discussion.

No one theory or concept is adequate to explain America's present turn to religion. Religion is infinitely complex, as is America and all her people. Nevertheless, like the scientist, we search for some formula that will account for the largest number of facts. My own choice of a basic concept to use in explaining America's religion today is to borrow a phrase from Professor Gilbert Murray. It is the famous concept he used to characterize the philosophy of the Stoics and Epicureans, which he described as the philosophy of the "loss of nerve."

I choose this phrase, "loss of nerve," to explain America's present religious emphasis. It is not adequate. Much of the present religion in America today is religion of strong nerves and strong minds. But even so, a great deal of religion in America today, and

167

perhaps most of its new emphasis, is the loss-of-nerve kind of religion.

A loss of nerve is the condition that exists when a man or society loses faith in himself or itself, when man loses faith in his capacity to shape or determine his own destiny. This is the situation in America today. It might otherwise be called the decline of liberal religion and the rise to supremacy of orthodoxies, both new and old.

What factors in America today have produced this loss of nerve? There are many. The usual formula is to call this twentieth century a time of revolution, then cite the world wars, the depressions, the march of men for freedom and bread, the struggle for power, and finally the discovery of nuclear energy.

All these factors have contributed to some alteration of present religion in America. And there are other factors, such as our rush for wealth, our loss of wealth, and the realization that wealth is not as satisfying as expected. There is the desire for pleasure, and the realization that recreation and pleasure are satisfactions of short duration. There is the drive for power, and the resulting emptiness of honor and glory.

Our values are up for question. But if this suspicion does not produce a new search in religion, life's present tragedies, coupled with impending ones, will shake its present foundations.

The truth is that most Americans are frightened. The term "anxiety" does not quite cover the situation. We are frightened of a nuclear war. We are frightened of communism. We lack faith in the United Nations. We are uncertain of our allies, and almost certain we cannot survive as "fortress America."

But most of all, contemporary America has lost its nerve because it has no real plan for the future. There are no solid workable plans to prevent a nuclear war. There can be no solid plans to win a nuclear war. There are no solid workable plans of how to live as good neighbors with those communist nations that contain a billion people. There are no solid workable plans to create a future world of peace, justice, and progress.

America today has only one solid workable plan. It is to be superior in military power. And because a child can see that inferior missiles are quite adequate to do the same job as a superior missile, and because nuclear weapons are not our exclusive possession, it is no wonder that there is a general loss of nerve by peoples both in America and elsewhere. There is no security through superior military power. A nation whose economy depends upon $50 billion annual outlay for war power has a right to some anxiety.

A good barometer of this anxiety and loss of nerve may be found in a nation's religious practices. What do American religious practices tell us about the nature of the religion to which America is now turning? The answer may be found if we classify America's present religious emphasis into types.

There are three kinds of religion, or expressions of religion, being stressed in America today. They are not new, but their emphasis makes them appear almost new. We will give them artificial names, which, nevertheless, partly describe them. They are, (1) fringe religion, (2) success religion, and (3) a new orthodox religion. These three types or expressions of religion are not all that is going on in American religion. As a matter of fact, most Americans are probably not aware of any basic change or shift of emphasis in their own religion. But these three types now receiving strong emphasis do tell us much about the present so-called turn to religion. And the common factor about all three is that they reveal a loss of nerve.

What is a religion without a loss of nerve? Perhaps there is none, or should be none. But what is a religion of strong nerve? We will attempt to describe such a religion at the conclusion of this paper.

Returning to these new, or newly emphasized expressions of religion characterized by a loss of nerve, we will first consider "fringe religion."

Fringe religion has a total membership in America of about six million people. These are divided into approximately a hundred different sects, each bearing a different name. There are fourteen million adherents to this type of religion outside the United States. Fringe religion includes the revivalists, puritanical preachers of doomsday, jazzy gospel singers, faith healers, emotional pentecostals, snake handlers, spiritual mediums, speakers in tongues, and spiritists. It is said that there are two million spiritists in Catholic Brazil who combine Catholicism with voodooism, primitive animism, and general sorcery. According to President Van Dusen of Union Seminary, this spiritism in Brazil is the most amazing and fastest growing religious prodigy on earth today.

It is difficult to determine where fringe religion and real religion join, but it is possible to define religion as fringe religion when it centers upon emotions aroused by shouting, belief in magic, and sorcery. It is not so easy to define fringe religion when it is based, as many are, on a literal interpretation of the Bible, the promise of a life-transforming experience, a strong group fellowship, and/or emphasis upon the Holy Spirit. And it is even more difficult when it includes a strong missionary spirit that seeks out the lonely and the forgotten.

In any case, this fringe religion is the fastest growing Christian movement in America today, now numbering six million followers. It finds its converts among the uneducated whose faith in reason and common sense is undeveloped and whose confidence in one's self and one's control of destiny is expressed with magic, animism, or voodooism, mixed with references to Christianity— some true and some false.

The second type of religious expression in America today is

"success religion." Paul Hutchinson, editor of the *Christian Century*, calls this the "religion of reassurance." Mr. Hutchinson, in an article in *Life* of April 11, 1955, writes that Americans may be divided into religious high brows, low brows, and middle brows. High brows understand the religion of Niebulov, Tillich, and Maritain. Low brows belong to what we have described as fringe religion. Middle brows go for success in religion. Undoubtedly success religion, or the cult of reassurance, accounts for most of the turn to religion in America.

It would take a long list to include all the expressions of success religion. Americans take it very seriously because Americans worship success. It is, therefore, no wonder that this success religion has produced most of the present boom in religion. The high priest of this type of religion is Norman Vincent Peale, though one must hasten to add Bishop Fulton J. Sheen and Rabbi Joshua L. Liebman.

In substance, this success religion attempts to tell men how to live a happy, satisfying life. It is the application of psychology for the cure of souls. It seeks to relieve tension by combining Freudian psychology with religious faith. It tries to correct the psychological dislocations of people. In seminaries it is the department of pastoral counseling. It is related to the confessional in the Catholic church, namely, to relieve men and women from a sense of guilt and restore self-confidence. Some of it is profound, and much of it is successful.

On the other hand, it is interesting to see how far it goes in its "win psychology." At the extreme end, its practice will lead to the opening of football games in the Southwest Conference by prayer. In Dallas, a bathing beauty queen was selected after a word of prayer. Printed forms of grace are on the tables of some railroad dining cars. Public gatherings of a secular nature are more and more adopting the practice of prayer for any occasion. Recently a layman's committee got the Advertising Council of America to give them $6 million worth of free advertising in newspapers, radio, television, and billboards as part of their campaign for "Religion in American Life." Some think the most impressive success has been the capture of the juke box where millions listen to sensuous love songs interspersed with religious hit numbers, such as "Have You Talked with the Man Upstairs?" "Mother, Home, and Heaven," "It's No Secret What God Can Do."

This secular emphasis of success in the everyday world began with the social gospel movement and now takes on the form of positive thinking. In effect it says, follow these rules and you will win a salary increase, have more friends, and be a good parent. One church advertises: "Come to church so you can see your friends." Another appeals to American win psychology by advertising "Come to the world's largest Sunday School–attendance last Sunday, 5,240."

The turn to religion in America is a phenomenon of major proportions. From 1925 to 1957 church membership in the United States increased 85 percent, whereas the population increase was 42 percent.

Are these the only forms of religion in American contemporary life, which in my opinion have the common factor of possessing a loss of nerve? Is this all there is to be said about religion in America today? By no means. There is another type of religion in America, religious liberalism. Religious liberalism has almost vanished from America, but not quite.

What is religious liberalism? Before saying what it is, let us say what it is not. Liberalism is not necessarily opposed to conservatism. It depends upon what is being conserved. Sometimes conservatives are radical in what they want to conserve. We meet radical conservatives in religion when they want to return to a literal interpretation of Bible stories, some of which are patent nonsense. We meet conservative radicals in politics who want to return to George Washington's concept of fortress America. We meet conservative radicals in economics who want to return to a concept of freedom for themselves regardless of what they do to other people.

A liberal may be a conservative in holding such an old notion that every man should have his own freedom of belief. Liberals may be as anxious to conserve as are conservatives. Liberalism is not necessarily opposed to conservatism, though a liberal is generally much more willing to break with the past than is a conservative.

A liberal is not opposed to religion because he is a liberal, any more than a conservative favors religion because he is a conservative. A liberal is not any more optimistic than the facts warrant. To say that liberalism means optimism is true, but to say that liberalism means *shallow* optimism is merely name-calling.

The sum of the matter is that there are all kinds of conservatives and all kinds of liberals – yet not quite. It is possible to say three things about liberalism that are almost universally true of all liberals, aside from a general willingness to break with the past.

First, a liberal believes in freedom of belief, but in a particular way. He believes that freedom involves inevitable disagreements, and that such disagreements can indicate a healthy situation. The reason for this belief is the liberal's suspicion of absolutes, and, therefore, his unwillingness to give or receive the last word on any subject. The liberal takes a note from the scientist and allows his ideas, like scientific hypotheses, free play of the facts which often results in their frequent alteration or occasional discard. But such progress results only from a wide tolerance of differences.

The second generally accepted characteristic of a liberal is the opposite of the loss of nerve. A liberal believes in man. Recently someone said that the twentieth century made him feel ashamed he was a member of the human race. The liberal does not think so. Some things make him ashamed, but not all. On the balance sheet of human failure and human success, the liberal looks at both sides and retains a lot of respect for the record of humanity.

Some of the optimism of the liberal is due to the following: people have allowed narrow nationalisms to lead them into one war after another, but they have also created the United Nations organization; people have exploited other human beings for wealth and plundered nature's resources, but they have also adopted rules of fair competition, social security, and conservation programs; people have tyrannized and enslaved others, but have also abolished slavery and emancipated women; they have denied equal opportunity, but they have also created a Supreme Court for thoughtful justice to which they have sworn obedience; people have discovered America and produced great wealth, but Americans have also shared it with less fortunate nations; people have lived in ignorance yet created public schools, lived in superstition yet established seminaries, and suffered in squalor yet erected beautiful homes.

The liberal sees both sides. Because he believes in man he is not stampeded by the fear and anger of war, depression, and tyranny. He does not think his belief in man will save him from war, tyranny, or depression; but he believes man has a good chance of avoiding or overcoming them. The liberal always works close to reality for modification of the present situation. He does not believe in cure-alls, nor will be surrender to the status quo. He gains by compromise and arbitration. He lives in a world of give and take, sometimes winning and sometimes losing.

In summary, the liberal is proud of man's record. Many gains in human life are so recent that it was only yesterday there was ignorance, slavery, and poverty. Today the liberal is content to say there is less ignorance, less slavery, and less poverty. Tomorrow, by great faith and effort, there will be less. The present record is not very good, but neither is it a record of shame.

The third characteristic of a liberal is that he is not any less religious because he is a liberal. In religion, the liberal loves the truth with his mind, his heart, and his soul. But, regarding his love of truth, the liberal is like all others in that he does not love truth enough to die for it. It is his temperament to retreat and live to fight another day.

What is the *religion* of the liberal? The varieties are infinite – theistic, agnostic, humanistic, pantheistic, pietistic. But there is possibly one common denominator of all religious liberals. It is their faith in human reason. The liberal will not surrender his reason to claims of faith. He may go beyond his reason to a strong religious faith, but he does not willingly go against his reason for the sake of religious faith. Whatever religion the liberal possesses, he wants it to be harmonious with reason.

What has happened to the liberal in American religion? Some have grown tired and silent. Some have fought their way to excommunication. Some have been converted to orthodoxy. Some have been converted to humanism. Some have gone underground and are waiting for a brighter day.

It is clear that the conservative element of American religion has won a clear victory over the religious liberal. Orthodoxy has fought the liberal for what he is – one who would challenge a religious belief if he thought the truth were at stake. Such liberals are dangerous to organized religion. With the aid of our tragic times, the orthodox have had a field day against the liberals. Crisis theology has replaced natural theology. The Bible has become immune from criticism. Authority is preferred to free inquiry.

Driving the liberal from their ranks with charges of shallowness, the orthodox have claimed a depth of insight unknown to the liberal. Pointing to liberalism as falsely appraising man's goodness, the orthodox have cast themselves upon the grace and mercy of God. The end result is a religion for America best characterized as a religion with a loss of nerve. There is great faith in God, but little faith in man.

This victory of the orthodox over the liberal is achieved at a great price. With the liberal gone, pessimism takes over. Man no longer thinks of ways to avoid war, but prepares for eternity. Man does not face communism with faith in democracy; he is as afraid of communism as early Christians were afraid of the devil. With the liberal gone from American religion, the churches have turned to an emphasis of personal salvation of individual souls, neglecting the social salvation of freedom from war, want, and ignorance.

So, in America, the fringe religion of revivalism, animism, and sorcery prevails over the moral religion of the Hebrew prophets. The success religion of win-psychology prevails over the profound insight of Christ that religion is not success but sacrifice, that "he who would gain his life must lose it." The orthodox religion of pessimism and other-worldliness prevails over the optimism of faith in man and his possibilities to win a free and friendly world.

My own conclusion is that nothing ever will be healthy about the religion of America until the liberal returns. Religion divorced from reason takes the risk of becoming just plain nonsense. Religion divorced from faith in man takes the risk of giving comfort while man blows himself to hell or heaven. And religion divorced from facing man's social problems takes the risk of deserting man, at least in this twentieth century, which is perhaps his greatest hour of need.

Seven Minutes About Brotherhood

Utah Chapter, National Conference of Christians and Jews,
Hotel Utah
May 25, 1971

□

I was asked to speak seven minutes, and I can better safeguard that time limit if I read my part.

All of us have met this evening to celebrate a great ideal in our democracy, the ideal of brotherhood. The simple fact about brotherhood is that, in practice, it is hard to win and easy to lose. For every example of brotherhood, another example of its failure can be found.

Brotherhood may begin within a family, then be transplanted to the more severe climate of the neighborhood, then to the community, and thence to a nation. If maturity continues, brotherhood of heart and mind may expand to include all of our species on this planet.

Likewise, the failure of brotherhood can begin within a family, fail within a community, fail in love and devotion to one's country, and finally result in war.

Both brotherhood and its failure are based on human nature. Put very simply, human nature is both good and bad. Each of us is a mixture of the selfish and the unselfish, the mean and the tender, the rough and the merciful.

Perhaps the clearest and deepest meaning of brotherhood is the ability to imagine yourself in the other person's position, and then treat that person as if you were him. This form of brotherhood takes a lot of imagination, a great deal of sympathy, and a tremendous amount of understanding.

Some of the landmark teachings about brotherhood include: the prophet Micah saying that God wants us to be just, love mercy, and walk humbly; Saint Paul reminding us that if brotherhood is lacking, we are no better than sounding brass and tinkling cymbals; and Saint Anselm asking that we think of God as that Being than whom none greater can be conceived. The Book of Mormon scriptures state the timeless appeal that "the Lord inviteth all men to come unto him, black and white, bond and free, male and female; and he remembereth the heathen; and all are alike unto God, both Jew and Gentile." Then there is that ultimate and most difficult test of brotherhood, declared to us by Jesus of Nazareth: "I say unto you, love your enemies."

In the final analysis, brotherhood is the result of our personal experiences in our homes, schools, churches, travels, employment, and now through television and other methods of communication.

I have been wondering lately about experiences that help or hurt, succeed or fail in the practice of brotherhood. As most people do, I prefer to hide my failures—downgrade them, explain them, excuse them, and cover them with good words. It would disturb all of us if a psychiatrist were to probe the hinterlands of our motives. For myself, even on the positive side, the margins of brotherhood, the victories were not of myself but of the people I've loved, the philosophers I've admired, and the poets and prophets who have given comfort, hope, and inspiration to my effort to be more brotherly.

Here then, are just a few, a very few, who greatly helped me along the way—my mother, first and of great importance; Miss Elizabeth Harding, my sixth grade teacher; L. J. Muir, my high school principal; E. E. Ericksen, a philosophy teacher; Adam S. Bennion and David O. McKay; and, most important, the girl I married and our children.

My favorite philosophers were Socrates, Plato, Aristotle, Benedict Spinoza, Immanuel Kant, David Hume, William James, John Dewey, and C. I. Lewis. A few of the many colleagues I've respected, loved, and admired are Sterling M. McMurrin, O. Meredith Wilson, Waldemer P. Read, Jack Adamson, M. Lynn Bennion, Daryl Chase, and C. Jay Parkinson. My political favorites, as for most of us, were Thomas Jefferson and Abraham Lincoln.

My political loyalty, for the safety of our country and for the future success of America within the family of nations, is for the United Nations. Some bright future day we will avoid the heartbreaks of Korea and Vietnam as we strengthen and better support this great organization for world peace.

My favorite president of the United States is generally the man presently in office, and I am proud of President Richard Nixon for pioneering a cautious and sincere pathway for us in reaching the hearts of the millions of wonderful people of mainland China. Brotherhood is for our allies, but it is also for those difficult to deal with. The highest quality of brotherhood is expressed when we reach out to those who have the least right to expect anything from us.

My favorite church is the one into which I was born, and which I can never repay for its help.

Here in Utah are countless examples of brotherhood. We are inclined to be modest, and our failures are painful. Yet families in Utah would probably lead the nation in giving of themselves to the families of the American Indian. In humane practice, in our day-to-day respectful treatment of black people, we rank high. And when we fail on that precious side – the priceless climate of human dignity – we are at least partly conscious of our failures and we do make progress.

Brotherhood is tested in so many ways. One of them is the relationship of employer–employee. The struggle for bread is a desperate one. Yet I have discovered here loyalties that silence me with awe and wonder.

Finally, brotherhood must surmount life's tragedies, such as the loss of loved ones, personal failures, injustices suffered, and opportunities lost. In his poem entitled "If This Were Faith," Robert Louis Stevenson put it this way:

> To go on for ever and fail and go on again
> And be mauled to the earth and arise,
> And contend for the shade of a word and a thing not
>   seen with the eyes:
> With the half of a broken hope for a pillow at night
> That somehow the right is the right
> And the smooth shall bloom from the rough:
>   Lord, if that were enough?

In the country churchyard of Stoke-Poges, Thomas Gray wrote his famous poem, "Elegy Written in a Country Churchyard." My favorite lines are these:

> Perhaps in this neglected spot is laid
>   Some heart once pregnant with celestial fire;
> Hands, that the rod of empire might have swayed,
>   Or waked to ecstasy the living lyre:
>
> . . . .
>
> Here rests his head upon the lap of earth,
>   A youth, to fortune and to fame unknown;
> Fair science frown'd not on his humble birth,
>   And melancholy mark'd him for her own.

In my earlier years, I thought the supreme value in life was brotherhood. I wrote books about it. Then, in my restless way, I turned to philosophy in a search for truth. I taught philosophy for thirty years. When I became restless again, I turned to the search for beauty. I love each of this trinity from Plato—Goodness, Truth, and Beauty. But just now, in these sunset years, I find myself trying to leave the earth a little more beautiful than I found it. I still ask "Is it good?" and "Is it true?" But even more persistently, I now ask, "Could it possibly be made to be more beautiful?" Surely, beauty and brotherhood must somehow go together.

I realize, at last, that I shall never create anything of lasting value or greatness, and so I find consolation in these lines from "Cleon" by Robert Browning.

> I have not chanted verse like Homer, no—
> Nor swept string like Terpander, no—nor carved
> And painted men like Phidias and his friend:
> I am not great as they are, point by point.
> But I have entered into sympathy
> With these four, running these into one soul,
> Who, separate, ignored each other's art.
> Say, is it nothing that I know them all?

Brotherhood at its best is positive and life-affirming. An unknown poet has given us these lines to live by:

> He who would bind to himself a joy
>   Does the winged angel destroy
> But he who kisses a joy as it flies
>   Lives in eternity's sunrise.

IV

FREEDOM AND DEMOCRACY

Introduction

Warren E. Burger

□

Every human being created by God is unique, but some are rare. Unlike the lowly ant–which has not changed for 65 million years–there are a rare few human beings who help the human race move slowly upward in the spiral of time.

Obert Tanner is one of those rare people. In his life he has combined the highest values along with qualities and achievements Americans especially admire. His life reveals great professional and material success as well as constant concern for others. It reveals a lifelong focus on the values that have evolved over the centuries, since people came out of the caves and down from crude tree dwellings. He has been a public leader as well as a patron of the arts, of music, and of literature. He is a creative thinker and writer who has always acknowledged the importance of the supreme values of freedom and democracy.

Perhaps most important are his many contributions that help human beings understand themselves, their purposes and values,

Mr. Burger, Chief Justice of the United States from 1969–1986, is presently Chairman of the Commission on the Bicentennial of the United States Constitution.

185

and the responsibilities of freedom. In our time we sometimes call such rare individuals "role models." Whether as a teacher, a businessman, a man of the law, a civic and community leader, or simply as a person, Obert Tanner's life makes him a model to be emulated by all.

The Supreme Values of Democracy

American Institute of Chemical Engineers
August 19, 1974

□

It is a great honor to address a convention of American scientists. Even though this paper is far afield from your science of chemistry, it is nevertheless about the life all of us share in our democracy. All of us have been disturbed by recent events in our political life; but the future is no less a challenge. We have currently a whole bundle of difficult problems. Sometimes they are called revolutions – the youth revolution, the black revolution, woman's liberation revolution, and something like a revolution involving the executive branch of our government. Besides the category of revolutions, there is the category of crisis, the crises of energy, education, welfare, environment, and the greatest crisis of all, inflation.

All these problems plus others unmentioned add up to a staggering total; but at least for the moment, we do not have the towering problem of war, hot or cold. Indeed, if we can live successfully within the family of nations, we can probably handle our domestic problems, even if we do so with a large mixture of both successes and failures.

The emotional impact of recent times has provided motivation for this paper. Yet, the look backward at recent events is not

187

intended here. The intent of this paper concerns the future. In summary, this discussion will be an examination of the resources, the capabilities of democracy to solve difficult problems, problems of revolution, if you please, and the problems of one crisis after another.

In the crunch of a crisis, being driven to the wall, we look at ourselves, ponder the future, and then sometimes dig down to see if we can find some bedrock foundations of our society, some solid base of our civilization itself. In essence, we are like the scientist who is constantly adjusting a hypothesis to account for new facts; and, indeed, as scientists search for a formula that may account for the largest possible number of facts, so we are here searching for the largest possible concepts, ultimate ideas, and basic values so that with them we may clear our minds of at least some of our contemporary contradictions and calm our emotions concerning some of our current confusion.

This paper then is one of large ambition, if not immodest intent. But at least the difficulties involved, like the difficulties of science, need not deter or discourage. The broad outline of this paper, therefore, will be a definition of our democracy, what we are, and what we are not. Then a digging down, if you please, in search of our bedrock foundations, if we have any. And finally, a careful look at what we commonly think are the supreme values of democracy.

The Definition of Democracy

What is democracy?

Democracy is problem-solving—no more, no less. Democracy is solving one problem after another, with both success and failure, then solving the problems created by the most recent solutions, especially those solutions that turn out to be failures or partial failures. Democracy is a process, and though we stop for a moment with some present solution, as in the historical event of installing a new president of the United States, yet this pause is momentary, for democracy never sleeps, never takes a vacation.

It is important, in looking over our resources for solving problems, to realize that democracy gives no guarantee of reaching good solutions. Sometimes the solutions of democracy are bad solutions, and sometimes they become bad with changing circumstances.

The Genius and Nature of Democracy

But there is one element in democracy that is its very genius, its priceless quality, its claim to greatness. This is the principle of self-correction. Democracy corrects its own mistakes. Failures are not permanent. Possibly the best definition of democracy is to say that it is a state of perpetual potential revolution.

In reflection, in thinking about the nature of democracy and seeking a description of democracy, there is a close analogy of democracy with the situation of a young couple on their wedding day. On their wedding day a couple are saying to each other that they now face life together, solve problems together, and face the future together, whatever may come. So it is with democracy: together people solve their problems for better or worse. But if for worse, then the worse can be corrected.

Another analogy that comes near to the heart of the meaning of democracy is the old maxim that, "He who wears the shoe, knows best where it pinches." Democracy says that whoever feels the pain of some pinch, just these people in pain are the ones who should be free to talk and do something about it, since they are the ones who can best tell if the pain is in fact relieved.

If those who worked out our constitution two centuries ago had just one thing they could tell us, they might say something like this: "We do not even know the problems of the future, much less the solutions to the problems arising 200 years from now. But we give this Constitution and in this Constitution we preserve for you, we insure for you, the necessary freedom to talk, to write, to assemble and to act on your problems, believing as we do that you, our descendants, will solve your problems with reason and with compassion so that life, liberty, and the pursuit of happiness for the greatest number of people, over the longest period of time, will be the destiny of this nation."

All this is well enough, that democracy can solve problems and correct its own mistakes, but a very large question still remains, namely, the question of the best way of solving problems. People everywhere solve their problems – in China, in Africa, in England, and in Russia. They may not have so much freedom, but in the largest sense, man everywhere is a problem-solving animal.

The Issue of Democracy

The issue is quality, the better or the best way to solve a problem. While we hold generally to Bentham's utilitarian standard of solving a problem for the greatest good of the greatest number over the longest period of time, still, we would like to have the assurance that there is some better or best way to go about the problem-solving process itself. Then, if the solution is not so good, at least the procedure was the best procedure, the best method. Negatively stated, a poor procedure, a bad method, will almost certainly mean a bad solution.

To find the best procedure for solving a problem in our democracy we may do well to seek the wisdom of the ages, scan the centuries for a lighthouse along the rocky shoreline, some North Star to give direction, some light from the past to guide our way into the future.

A Preliminary Reservation

One preliminary reservation about this discussion should be made in deference to you as scientists. We will now be involved with the broad field of human values and, as you know, unlike the highly successful method of scientific verification, a discussion of human values involves general terms and sweeping generalizations that are quite beyond the reach of verification.

Nevertheless, the field of human values is a subject with a history of more than twenty-five centuries. In these centuries values have been identified and discussed by the best and wisest of the human race. Moreover, some of the conclusions of these scholars and teachers appear as durable as the most probable of scientific hypotheses.

The Wellsprings of Our Democracy

Exploring now for the best ways to solve our problems, we will x-ray our western civilization to find the very core of its being, the central meaning it has for finding the good life, the most satisfactory life, not only in centuries past but in this century, in this present year of this twentieth century.

Our civilization is quite accurately named a Greco-Christian civilization. It is like a river with two tributaries: one tributary has its wellsprings in the ancient land of Palestine, and the other tributary has its fountainhead in the ancient land of Greece. Palestine gave to us the primacy of the ethic of love. Greece gave us the primacy of reason. These two great human values of reason and love are the taproots, the wellsprings, indeed, the very foundation and the pillars of our present civilization.

What is civilization? Professor Stace of Princeton University defines a civilization as "an attempt to express in institutions what a people living in a certain area or age think to be the good life."

So in our civilization today, we think the good life is more likely to result if we solve our problems with reason and love. This is no small undertaking. Reason and love are impossibly high standards. We simply cannot bring to our problems the unmarred qualities of both reason and compassion. Bias and prejudice mar our reasoning, and emotions cloud our compassion. Nevertheless, if social problems are difficult to solve with clear reasoning and humaneness, one thing is clear, and that is that no solution is likely to be a good one if error and animosity are applied to a solution.

The Main Difficulty of Democracy

Consider for a moment the difficulty of solving a political problem. In science, objectivity is almost a necessity for solving a problem; the facts must speak for themselves. But in politics, objectivity is lost in the whole field of human values and human desires. And one of those human values and desires, as all of us know, is the love of power. Next to food, drink, and sex, man loves power more than anything else. Everybody likes approval, and there are few who do not enjoy acclaim and influence, and also having authority, dominion, control, the last word. Being honored, praised, and elevated are satisfactions that few can disclaim. While this fact of human psychology, the love of power, can motivate accomplishment, it can also motivate tyranny. One can frequently be led to greater oppression struggling to keep power than in the struggle to gain the power in the first place. So, our two-party system, with all its high cost in nonobjectivity, even its times of animosity and bad reasoning, nevertheless is one effective way to level power, so that those who wear a shoe with the pinch of tyranny can themselves relieve the pain.

Even so, power could be dissolved more effectively if better reasoning and more goodwill were brought to the task. Many recent events have involved our democracy in an excess of bad reasoning and an excess of ill will. For example, in recent times the news media has become extremely powerful. Modern technology has placed in the hands of a few the awesome power of easily conditioning the thoughts and emotions of millions of people. News gathering and news reporting, under private ownership control, are sometimes saturated with bias and prejudgments. Small wonder these days have been days of emotional living. But with all these recent failures, the news media has brought a balance of positive values. We see more clearly and firsthand on television those who reason poorly and those who reason well, those whose emotions are born of prejudgments and those who appear determined to play fair. Democracy depends upon self-discipline, and for all their recent failures, the news media will likely be more self-disciplined in the future, rather than submit to the coercions of government control.

What is failure, and what is success? Failure can result from application of a poor, even a bad, method. Success can result from the application of a good, even a superior, method. Now we are back to those bedrock foundations of our civilization mentioned earlier, namely, goodwill and good reasoning.

The Meaning of Reason

Examine for a moment the meaning of reason. The value of reason was given its classical statement in Plato's *Republic*. Plato established the primacy of reason upon the idea of proper function, that the proper function of reason is to govern and control the psychological elements of appetite, sensation, desire, and emotion. He reasoned with enduring persuasion that just as the organs of the body have a proper function, the heart to pump blood, etc., so the proper function of reason is to rule the whole man. Such a control by reason gives to man the kind of life that is most satisfactory; and the failure of reason to govern and control results in a life that is unsatisfactory.

Establishing reason as the basis for the good life and the good society, ancient Greece became possibly the highest civilization in all man's history. It was a civilization where reason produced the satisfaction of good balance, harmony, and moderation. Negatively stated, the failure of reason was found in excess or the lack of moderation.

In modern times we more narrowly define reason as the

method by which to find the truth. That is, with good reasoning we can determine the way things are, the actual state of affairs, or at least the highest degree of probability. Such a high standard of truth-finding is the goal of science. It should be the goal of all life, but alas! man is mostly emotional. And in political life, when the issue is who gets the power, truth is of less concern than it should be. But, one thing is very sure: nothing in politics or outside politics can ever be lasting in value if it is based upon the falsehoods of unwarranted conclusions, the fallacies of hasty conclusions, snap judgments, innuendos, guilt by association, and all the rest. A democracy living by errors and bad reasoning is a democracy in bad health, in deep trouble.

On the positive side, consider two examples of reason at its best. These examples are the scientific method and English common law. Ancient Greece, for all its primacy of reason, did not fully discover and practice the scientific method. They preferred conversation – brilliant conversation to be sure – but they preferred much talk over the arduous labor of verifying their hypotheses. Not until Galileo, in modern times, was the greatest discovery of the human race – the scientific method – discovered and fully practiced. Needless to add, this scientific method has transformed human life on this planet, and not the least of human accomplishments, by this great method, is found in the science of chemistry.

It is important for democracy to know that the scientific method is applicable beyond the fields of the exact sciences. Our political life could be enriched, enhanced, and even ennobled by more frequent checking of statements with the facts, the probabilities; and where such good evidence is lacking, the scientific method is at least a good guide to the more reasonable.

The other great example of reason is English common law, the foundation of justice in our courts. For many centuries the common law has been reason applied to life, the classic and most important concept being the "due process" clause in our constitution. Rendering justice, to every man his due – this is the cement that holds our civilization together.

The Meaning of the Ethic of Love

Turn next to that other foundation of our democracy, that other condition for solving problems well, the ethic of love. The classical example of this ethic is the parable of the Good Samaritan. This Judeo-Christian ethic is not so much philosophically defended in ancient literature as it is simply affirmed, affirmed in parables, stories, history, and especially in the life of the Galilean Carpenter – where love is affirmed as the mainspring of human action. The founder of Christianity gave a single message that can be summarized in a single sentence, namely, that human personality is sacred and that to harm any personality is wrong and to help any personality is right.

The term "love" has many synonyms. Some of them are "compassion," "selflessness," "sympathy," "humaneness," "kindness," and "goodwill." In modern times we sometimes speak of the ethic of love as the Golden Rule. Today we hear much of the word "ambiguity." Ambiguity is admissible in the life of reason, but in the ethic of love there can be no ambiguity. Love is never ambiguous. In life's vicissitudes, and particularly in the difficult problems of politics, we either have or have not goodwill, we either have or have not compassion, we either have or have not humaneness, we either have or have not charity.

Mature men in politics, the finest men in politics, have many qualities, and one quality is the ability to see the other side of a problem, indeed, the several sides of a complex problem. To find good solutions to difficult problems, great men in political life remain friendly with their adversaries, they possess undiscourageable goodwill in the heat of controversy. They are compassionate with the failures of others.

Nothing ever will be completely healthy in our democracy

without the element of kindness, deeply felt and widely practiced. Our civilization and our democracy depend upon this ethic of love. No extremely difficult problem can be solved without it; and, with humaneness, all problems are better and more easily solved.

To be sure, the crunch of a crisis brings out both the good and bad of human nature. But without a crisis, a vast amount of goodness is evident just in everyday life, in the work-a-day world. In democracy some of this goodness finds expression in volunteerism, in voluntariness. Beyond self-interest there is the public interest or social interest that needs volunteers who love enough to help, share, and give without thought of self and without care of public notice. Dictatorship calls for conscripts, our democracy asks for volunteers.

The Glory of Democracy

Indeed, if one were to name the highest achievement of man on this planet, the very highest watermark of quality and excellence, it would be a free man who was socially minded, a free individual dedicated to the public good, an independent person voluntarily sharing, giving, and helping others find their own highest potential. For if one word were to accurately distinguish our culture, that word might be individualism. Individualism is based on the ideal of the infinite value of the individual, and on this ideal our own civilization is measured. Individualism means that each person is to have the right to rule his or her own life, the right to think, to speak, and to act so long as this does not infringe on the same right of others. But such a precious ideal carries a high price tag: the price of a strong voluntary life, the willingness of an individual to respond to the public good, to love his fellowman.

The conclusion, then, is that in order to solve its problems, democracy depends upon the fusion, the blending, of reason and compassion. Democracy depends upon individuals – one by one – of goodwill and good minds, of reason and humaneness, of intelligence and sympathy, and of good thinking and high motives. Such people are the foundation and the pillars of our civilization and of our own American democracy.

Home Democracy: Difference, Tolerance and Cooperation

National Conference on Family Relations, University of Utah
1961

☐

When Plato considered the great trinity of goodness, truth, and beauty, he did so with something like the respect and awe for their timeless value that we today might feel in considering this modern trinity of difference, tolerance, and cooperation. For the concepts of difference, tolerance, and cooperation are three terms that spell out a single ideal, the ideal of freedom for the individual. Individual freedom is the single value around which nearly all contemporary history is now turning. The challenge of communism has taught us many things, not the least of which is that we more carefully search out the deeper meaning of freedom. There is a present urgency for us to do so, and there are no concepts today that spell out this meaning of personal liberty as does this modern trinity of difference, tolerance, and cooperation. Just now our concern is the achievement of better family relations through an analysis of difference, tolerance, and cooperation.

These great concepts aid us not only in family life, but also in the success of our democracy and, finally, in the success of

198

present and urgent international affairs. Indeed, the very quality of life itself is enriched by thoughtful consideration of the meaning of difference, the meaning of tolerance, and the meaning of cooperation.

Referring to Plato again, one can easily imagine that in some dialogue he might personalize this modern trinity, referring to difference as the problem-child of the human family and tolerance and cooperation as wise counselors. The counselors try to keep difference on the path of promise rather than allow it to drift into chaos, such as the breakup of a marriage, the failure of democracy, or, finally, a third and last world war.

In search of a better understanding of the meaning of these three great concepts, we observe first of all that the fact of difference – variety, novelty, plurality, change – is not only the great problem of human life but is also its great promise. As a problem, difference compels us to face the unexpected and make adjustments – some easy, but many very difficult. But then difference is also a promise. If we fail one time in solving a problem, this world of endless differences offers us yet another chance, a new opportunity for correction and improvement. It gives us undying hope for ultimate progress.

The meaning of difference is made clear in the light of its contrary concept, sameness. Both sameness and difference are very great human values. Sameness gives life security and stability. Difference gives life adventure and progress. Yet sameness, like difference, can also be a problem. As a problem, sameness can mean endless routine, weary monotony, and harsh tyranny. But as promise, sameness can also mean personal security and social stability. It is interesting to speculate that most people probably prefer the value of sameness over the value of difference. Sameness promises peace of mind, while difference means unrest. Sameness promises unity, while difference means division. Sameness means certainty, while difference means guesswork. Sameness means living by habit, while difference means facing a problem.

Perhaps we here today would evenly divide on which of these two values is superior. Some of us would think of sameness as preferable, while others would favor the value of difference. But then, whole civilizations disagree on this point. The Orient and the Occident have long disagreed over the supremacy of these two values. Oriental civilization inclines to the basic value of sameness, stressing values favorable to it such as peace of mind, imperturbability, serenity, tranquility, and oneness. On the other hand, our occidental civilization inclines toward the basic value of difference, and so we are generally friendly to problem-solving, worldly progress, activity, individualism, and experiment. This split over the choice of a supreme value, whether it be the value of difference or the value of sameness, runs through all of life. It divides men into liberals and conservatives—liberals favor difference and change; conservatives favor sameness and the status quo.

In religion, men are divided as to whether they favor the prophetic tradition of change or the priestly tradition of sameness. The prophetic tradition has always faced life's differences with eagerness to choose and to change, while the priestly tradition would disallow many differences in favor of sameness, asserting that commandments are the same yesterday, today, and forever.

In the area of economics, men of success generally favor sameness, while hungry men inevitably search for difference.

Independent of the choice of one value or the other, it is important to face squarely the enormous and overwhelming fact of difference. It is the great fact of life. Our world is peopled by those who daily use and abuse their differences. Difference is a two-way street of progress and regress. It is of first importance for us to be realistic about a universe where change is king and difference is abiding.

Just now our world is being torn apart by its differences. A list of them would be innumerable, but one of the major ones is the three-pole split within the family of nations—between the communists, the free, and the neutral. There are also differences between the affluent and the poor, the literate and the illiterate, the black and the white, the nationalists and the internationalists, the Orient and the Occident. Within each of these major divisions, the variety of differences multiplies. There are different religions, different economic systems, different educational theories, and different social practices, not to mention the countless varieties of institutions, each one demanding from its members loyalties and sacrifices that make up so much of life's sublimity and tragedy and so much of goodness and wickedness in the lives of men.

Finally, we come to the most important and most profound difference of all, the one that creates so many of our problems as students of family relations. This is the difference of each individual.

The differences between members of any one family are truly staggering. In the beginning, two people, almost strangers, each with a different history, personality, and preferences join in marriage. From this union of differences come children so unlike as to make parents incredulous. For all the bridges a family builds to cope with differences, for all the common needs and sought-for satisfactions unobtainable outside the family circle, and for all the sameness of unity that the power of discipline and the art of persuasion can produce in family solidarity, the overpowering fact emerges that each member of a family is wholly unique, vastly different, and therefore a major problem to each of the others. Each individual is not only a problem to others of the same family, but a problem to others in society, and indeed, a problem to organized institutional life itself, just as society, family, and economic, political, and religious organizations are in their turn a problem to free and independent individuals.

Having faced the fact and also the problem of difference, we turn to possible solutions. The problem of difference is generally solved in one of three ways. First, one difference seeks to abolish another difference and if unsuccessful, at least to dominate it. This is the solution of tyranny. Surely this group has met this solution over and over again in the breakup or lost happiness of otherwise promising marriages.

Second, two differences unable to dominate one another come into endless conflict. This is the solution of continuous conflict without even the benefit of an armistice or temporary truce. Some marriages are like that, or nearly so. Perhaps this is also an accurate description of the two blocs of nations, the communist and the free. We would like to ask of these two blocs if there ever is to be a diminution of our vast differences and nerve-wracking tensions.

The third solution to the problem of difference renounces the first of tyranny and the second of constant battle. This solution takes a humble view of the asserted superiority of its difference. Whatever the difference may be, its hallmark of greatness is modesty, and superior claims are held with misgivings, always tentative and always provisional. Then, without the blinding emotional zeal that always goes with asserted superiority, one difference thoughtfully considers another difference with an open mind, seeking some common ground for peace, or at least a truce. But this solution goes much farther. Possessing a generous hospitality, it considers that the opposing difference might have a quality worth borrowing and, even more, the possibility that perhaps the two opposing differences might supplement each other for mutual gain and reciprocal benefit, resulting in a greater good than either alone could achieve. Above all, humanity will always suffer whenever one difference maintains itself by engendering hatred, ill will, or animosity against another.

This third solution, that differences may have some common ground and that each may possess a value worth sharing so that the two supplement and improve one another, is apparently the theme of your conference.

A good family is void of tyranny – the first solution. It is not one where father rules, or mother dictates, or the youngest continually gets his way. A good family is void of permanent and perpetual conflict – the second solution. The ideal family's security and peace may be dimmed from time to time by the inevitable differences that arise between free and independent personalities, but still this family is able to make home a haven of security and, above all, a place of understanding while jealously protecting the independent judgment and personal integrity of each member. A good family at its very best is one of profound respect for differences, for freedom of choice, and for individual responsibility. But even more, it is one where differences grow and thrive, and where they borrow, share, and supplement each other with abiding modesty for their own difference and kindly tolerance for the difference of others.

Why is the third solution of difference so difficult and rare? Granted that family life is not mainly a tyranny or conflict, still, why is the achievement of home democracy so full of obstacles? While most homes are not really places of tyranny and constant quarreling, why isn't there a much larger share of the positive achievements of tolerance and cooperation? Negatively stated, why is there such a much greater amount of tyranny and conflict in our homes than is necessary? Why such an excessive amount of bossing and bickering?

One answer, among others, lies deep within human nature itself. Without careful accuracy for psychological terminology, let us refer now to one facet of human nature that causes so much of the trouble between human differences. This is the inclination, indeed the basic drive, of people to boss others–to rule, to dominate, to give orders, to be at the top of Bunker Hill–in short, the basic human need to win over differences. It may be true, as some claim, that next to the basic drives for food, drink, sex, and association, power is the value most cherished and sought for in all human relationships. In observing human social life, including family life, the deep satisfaction people obtain through exercising authority, presiding, ruling, being obeyed, having the last say, overriding objections, trampling dissent, or, in short, being as near as one can climb to the top in social authority and prestige, is the drive that frequently makes the words "tolerance" and "humility" sound like brass and tinkling cymbals. Small wonder then that there is so little true democracy in the home, in society, and in the world at large.

Human nature has numerous altruistic qualities that help provide good solutions to the problems of difference. But human nature also has within it powerful opponents to good family life, real democracy, and world peace. And even though this drive for power can be defended as a source of leadership and service, it does in fact also make for the elbowing of one's way past and over others, thereby crushing the best chances for solving problems of difference.

I would not offend the loyal members of our great and near-great institutions that are here today, but I would remind you that leaders themselves are subject to this human frailty, quite as much as the rest of us. Therefore, be realists and expect them to fight unremittingly for the security of their exalted positions and for the power, glory, and dominion of the institutions they lead. If there are some who think this basic desire to rule over others is overstated, one will find a key to its understanding in the fact that when man proffers to divinity what he thinks his God would most prefer, he is revealing a great deal about his own preferences–universally, men say to their divinities, "Thine is the power and glory forever and ever."

But is there no real solution to this great problem of difference? Do power structures and our own desire for wider influence have the final say in all or most of our social differences? Some would answer affirmatively. That power and might make right is a discouraging answer. It is discouraging even if one believes that benevolence and sharing can partly counterbalance it, because the countless obstacles to right, to fair play, to deep respect for differences are ever present both in ourselves and also in the institutions we create, and, I might say, in the institutions that create us.

Let us now consider the two suggested solutions proposed in the agenda of this national council—the solution of the problem of differences here proposed by the two terms "tolerance" and "cooperation."

What is the meaning of tolerance? It is a word used for many purposes. For the mistrusting true believer, it can lead to heresy. For the political dictator, it is another word for treason. For the arbitrary parent whose favorite word is obedience, tolerance is a strange word and even if understood, is quite unacceptable, especially where family success and discipline are intertwined and considered synonymous. For a person of private and secret racial prejudice, tolerance is a word he publicly claims for himself. For many vocations and professions with lax ethical standards, tolerance is a word that is used frequently to ease the conscience. In the public mind, generally, tolerance is a word that means live and let live.

Granted that definitions may be arbitrary, neither true nor false but only useful, there is one definition of tolerance that is particularly useful and meaningful to professional individuals in the area of family relations. This definition is one of several in *Hastings Encyclopedia of Religion and Ethics*. It reads: "Tolerance assumes the existence of an authority which might have been coercive, but which for reasons of its own is not pushed to extremes. It implies a voluntary inaction." This is the meaning of tolerance in the highest quality of family living, namely, "authority which might have been coercive." As differences inevitably arise between husband and wife, parent and child, and between children themselves, there is in the finest homes a forbearance in the use of coercion. Instead, there is a profound reliance upon persuasion. Using only two terms, one could say that the problem of difference is generally solved by coercion, or by persuasion, or by a combination of both. Most families use both persuasion and coercion. Few families rely on coercion alone or persuasion alone. But that family is best which considers coercion only as a last resort.

Success in family life can be measured by the degree it diminishes the area of compulsion in favor of the area of persuasion until children mature to the point where their controls and compulsions come from within. Our problem with coercion is not that it may sometimes be necessary, but with the use of it when it is not necessary. It is the excessive use of coercion, psychological coercion even more than physical, that so frequently diminishes the quality of family life.

No one will deny that coercion, sometimes physical, is necessary as a last resort. Therefore, we pay tribute to an efficient police force and to our armed forces. In doing so we always hope, however, that their total effect weighs heavily on the side of peace and justice so that persuasion prevails and becomes stronger in the life of individual families, and also within the entire family of nations.

Granted that juvenile delinquency results all too frequently from lack of discipline in the home, the truth may be that excessive family discipline, actual family tyranny, is practiced on a scale so gigantic as to beggar imagination. Sometimes the dictator is father, sometimes mother, sometimes older brother, or even and frequently, youngest sister. But always and in every family the drive is present and pressing for some to play the boss and smother opposing differences. In parents this takes the form of psychologically attempting to make their children carbon copies of themselves. Rare indeed is the home of true democracy where there is individual freedom of choice, individual expression of ideas, and profound respect for what is singular and different in each member of the family.

My single point is that nowhere does the ideal of tolerance meet a foe so implacable as it does in another's ego, another's demand for obedience, another's insistence upon power, another's joy in exercising authority.

In the scale of a half-million years, it was only a moment ago that the ideal of tolerance came timidly on the stage of man's social life. The faces of coercion – physical and psychological – are many, and the two forms comprise the solution for problems of difference used frequently by family members in many homes of otherwise great quality. A home of tolerance is a home of voluntary inaction in the use of coercion; it encourages each child and, indeed, each husband and wife to be independently himself or herself – unique, creative, and free.

We commonly say that the institutions of persuasion are the home, the school, and the church. Other political and economic institutions also depend to a degree upon persuasion, but they also possess brute power whenever persuasion fails. However, the great reliance of the home, the school, and the church is not ultimately upon coercion, but rather upon persuasion.

Even so, the excessive amount of psychological coercion that intimidates the independent thought and free speech of each individual in our schools and in organized religion is enormously large. Tender, frail tolerance, so recently a newcomer to man's social life, faces the fact that while the leaders of these institutions of persuasion are often good men of selfless dedication, they are also subject to the frailties of human vanities and the universal human concern for power and authority. The result is that these great and good institutions of persuasion are now deeply colored by the evil of excessive psychological coercion and by a woeful lack of genuine tolerance toward their own internal differences.

Finally, there is the second requirement for successful living with our differences. It is the ideal of voluntary cooperation. Cooperation, like tolerance, is a word of many meanings. Our concern now is with cooperation that is voluntary. Granted that life is mostly coercion, that free will is debatable, and that compulsions are the road signs of life's highways, still we do not lose faith that some of life is voluntary. If persuasion is meaningful, democracy justifiably calls for and reasonably expects us to be volunteers. If persuasion is not meaningful, then the communists win and the only call that is meaningful is for conscripts. We either handle our differences as volunteers or as conscripts. Either as free citizens we voluntarily assume the cooperation necessary to handle our differences with friendly tolerance, or as state citizens we are coerced to cooperate without the dignity of personal independence.

A good home is a home of volunteers, a bad home is a home of conscripts. A good home waits patiently in the presence of unwilling cooperation until the choice to cooperate is freely and willingly made. Sometimes it takes years for a child to grow in the quality of voluntary cooperation. Forced decisions in family life may be efficient and effective, but they have little place in the life of real quality. So, too, in a democratic society, vocations and professions must have large areas of voluntariness. Doctors remain men of great dignity only if they voluntarily assume the problem of a healthy populace. Lawyers walk in the steps of great men only if they voluntarily cooperate to keep society one of equal justice under the law. Businessmen make "free enterprise" a great ideal only if they voluntarily cooperate in making the business standards of the community honest and fair for everyone.

A good husband and a good wife try to out-volunteer each other in what they think the other would like. Good homemakers are always volunteering to go the second mile. The birthplace of the voluntary spirit is a good home. Encouragement, compliments, praise, and recognition are the wellsprings of a child's strong life of freely cooperating.

Now it is well to state that the problems of our differences should be handled by the ideals of tolerance and cooperation, but as we have indicated, the practice of this ideal – the realization of tolerance and cooperation – is quite another matter. Lest anyone think this is some easy road, let us formulate the problem again. The problem of difference is the problem of freedom, and the problem of freedom is never solved. Our founding fathers understood this when they coined the phrase, "eternal vigilance." How, for example, can a person different from all other people, different even from every other member in the same family, maintain the freedom necessary for his or her unique and individual personality to express itself and at the same time modify some of this precious individualism in favor of the persistent and necessary demands of the family as a whole? How can a free and independent personality remain free and independent while also bound to the loyalties of family life that require so much selfless love and costly sacrifice? For example, how can the father of a family exercise some special and rare talent he may possess if he risks the family economy by changing his work? How can a mother take time for personal development if the labors of each day leave no time and, most of all, no energy? She might have read more widely, written and spoken more wisely, created unbelievably, but the cares of a family never allowed her special genius to be uncovered. How can a boy of real talent within a family of great economic need get the chance to become a great scientist? How can a girl of promise realize the freedom of her special abilities when the demands of a family budget or family labors deny her even a chance?

These are the practical difficulties. Greater than these, however, are those referred to as psychological—the willful smothering of personal differences by a dominating member of the family, or by an institutional leader who is afraid of individual expression, or by a society that puts a premium on conformity while paying only lip service to individual freedom.

Nevertheless, we are not discouraged. We are committed to three propositions: first, the greatest of all problems within the family is that of difference; second, after love the greatest of all virtues within the family is tolerance; and third, the greatest practical achievement in family living is voluntary cooperation.

If this ideal of family greatness exceeds our grasp and eludes our efforts, we are not dismayed. We squarely face the fact that the way we handle our differences comprises the greatest challenge of life. It is the continuous challenge of a good home. We are unyielding in our faith that the best home is the one which allows each individual member the fullest possible exercise of personal differences. And the best school, or church, or society is the one which checks its own inclinations to erase those precious differences in its members, since God has so created us and therefore intends that we so remain.

Western Civilization and Utah

Governor's Prayer Breakfast
March 21, 1978

□

I feel very humble in being asked to say a few words on this occasion. This is a moment of humility and self-examination for all of us, and we seek help in our effort to do better.

No burden is as great or more keenly felt as that when we assume responsibility for other people. Parents feel this burden in their family responsibilities. Though not so directly responsible, political leaders sometimes more than others feel the need of divine guidance – as do all of us. Public life is problem-solving, and some of our solutions greatly affect the lives of our fellow citizens. It is good, therefore, that the President of the United States and the Governor of our state feel the need and the value of such an occasion as this.

Our purpose is to find perspective. We search in public life for a larger view of our role, whether that role be political, economic, religious, or educational. We seek wisdom and understanding concerning the highest values of our culture in order to see more clearly the great landmarks of our civilization.

Sometimes, we must admit, absorbed as we are in the pressures of daily tasks, our directions become faulty, and, like mariners in a storm at sea, we wish we might see the North Star for some reassurance. So our purpose today is not to discover some totally new direction, but to remind ourselves of truths and values we already know well, but may have neglected. We wish to reflect upon our basic ideas and ideals, and feel assured that we may not have strayed too far. With this desire for perspective, for the larger view of our daily work, I have chosen the rather large subject, "Western Civilization and Utah."

If I can, I would like to first state the meaning of our great western civilization, and with this meaning appraise and judge the success and failure of life here in Utah, the quality of our culture today, and the values of our contemporary civilization. Such a large purpose can include no more than a few glances, like a few glimpses of the stars at night, one might say. Hopefully, we may see the North Star and determine whether we are on course and in harmony with the highest and best we know for human life on this planet.

The Meaning of Western Civilization

First, I want to define or explain the meaning of the word "civilization," and then present an explanation of our western civilization, the origin and meaning of its major ideals. The word "civilization" may be defined as organized goodness, the whole complex structure that includes knowledge, belief, art, morals, law, and customs. I like the definition of my teacher, W. T. Stace, who said that civilization is goodness expressed in the institutions and customs of a society, more specifically, the good life is one which people themselves feel to be good, healthy, satisfactory, and happy.

The goodness and expression of a satisfactory and healthy life in western civilization as we have known it in Europe and America have their roots in the two small countries of Greece and Palestine. Ours is a Greco-Christian civilization. From ancient Greece we inherited the ideal of the primacy of reason. From Palestine we inherited the ideal of the primacy of love, sometimes called the ethic of selflessness. Together, these two values, reason and love, became the pillars of our western civilization.

The Greeks expanded their belief in the primacy of reason to become an ethic of moderation, and, possibly more important, from this primacy of reason emerged their aesthetic value of balance and harmony. In doing so, ancient Greece seems to have placed beauty as the supreme value of a satisfactory life.

The other pillar of our western civilization is the Judeo-Christian ethic of love, or selflessness. These two, reason and love, one from ancient Greece and one from ancient Palestine, are the cornerstones of what we know as western civilization.

The Infinite Value of the Individual

From both reason and love has emerged an idea which is the foundation of the democratic way of life, namely, the infinite value of the individual. All our democratic institutions are based upon the premise that individuals are of absolute value. Each individual is intrinsically unique, never to be treated as a means only, but as an end, and so of ultimate and absolute value.

Some of you may remember the classical formulation of the great philosopher, Immanuel Kant. His expression is the best summary of the foundation of democracy, indeed, the best perhaps to be found in all literature. He said, "So act as to treat humanity, whether in thine own person or in that of another, in every case as an end withal, never as a means only." This was his famous categorical imperative—every person is an end value, not just a finite or means value, and therefore of infinite value.

In totalitarian governments the individual is a means, an instrument to serve the state. Our idea of the absolute value of the individual postulates that the state is the means, an instrument to serve the individual. From this idea of the infinite value of the individual have emerged three fundamentals of our democratic way of life—freedom, equality, and individualism.

Freedom

First, consider freedom. There are two kinds of freedom in a democracy, one is personal, the other political. Political freedom is representational government, where sovereignty resides in the people. Personal freedoms are freedom of speech, of the press, of worship, of teaching and learning, of assembly, among others. Political freedom involves discussion and compromise on public issues. Personal freedoms – those of speech, press, and worship – are never compromised except in very special circumstances.

While freedom is sometimes considered the supreme value in life, it is not an end in itself. Political freedom may be used to put an end to tyranny and oppression. It is freedom from something, but far more important than that, freedom is *for* something. Freedom is to be used for some good cause that serves the public interest so that individuals may be helped in finding a good life, a life with satisfactions that make for a healthy personality. Personal freedom should be used to achieve one's fullest potential, making one's personal life glad, beautiful, and good.

Equality

Second, consider equality as one of the fundamentals of a healthy democracy. The North Star that has guided the course of our democracy for two hundred years was expressed in our Declaration of Independence with these immortal words: "We hold these truths to be self evident, that all men are created equal." This ideal came from the Hebrew prophets and the Christian Messiah, and when combined with the Greek primacy of reason gave us the rock foundation of our present democracy, namely, the idea of the infinite value of the individual.

But are all men created equal? Indeed they are not. Some are bright and some stupid, some morally good and some bad, some useful to society and some useless, some strong and some weak. No two men, and today we add no two women, are created equal. No two persons were ever created exactly alike. Our founding fathers knew this inequality quite as well as we, but what they meant was that men are intrinsically equal, and as end values men are equal. Men are equal because each one has a value that is infinite.

In religion we say that God loves each and every human being as though there were but a single human being to love. We say in our democracy that every single person is equal before the law. And a good society is one that affords equal opportunity to each individual. However diverse the results of these opportunities may be – for each person will turn out differently – there must always remain equal dignity for every man, woman, and child.

Also in business, each employee is different in capacity, yet every employee is a center of consciousness with feelings and purposes the same as an employer. Therefore an employee deserves to be treated with as much respect as an employer wants for himself. Each is equal to the other in dignity and basic human rights.

Individualism

Individualism is the third fundamental of a healthy democracy. There are two kinds of individualism, one good and one bad. Bad individualism is expressed as "Every man for himself." Sometimes called "rugged individualism" in practice, this kind of individualism is selfish and shows a disregard for the welfare of others. Good individualism is the use of free agency to become the best one can be by developing one's power and capacities to better serve one's self, neighbor, community, and, if possible, all of mankind.

Utah

These, then, are the fundamentals of the world's western civilization. From ancient Palestine came the ethic of love and compassion, of sympathy and selflessness. From ancient Greece came the primacy of reason, the value of moderation, the ideal of balance and harmony. These two ideals merged in European history to become the principle of the infinite value of the individual, and from this ideal emerged the three fundamentals of our democracy – freedom, equality, and individualism.

In this hour of meditation, prayer, and reflection, we cannot help wondering, by these immortal standards, how well we are doing in the culture of our beloved state of Utah. No doubt some of us are optimistic, and some of us are pessimistic. One thing is quite certain, however; a meeting of supplication, such as this, is a time for complete honesty with ourselves and our fellow citizens.

My own view is that we make a mistake, we fail, if we are overly optimistic. We know our freedoms are abused, our equality is partial, and our precious individualism is used as an excuse by many who exploit others while themselves barely staying within the law. But we also make a mistake, we fail, if we are overly pessimistic. To the pessimists I say try to remember that in two costly world wars we were fighting for the very life of our civilization, and the price came high.

This twentieth century is very unlike the previous century. This century has witnessed one cataclysmic event after another: World War I, the Great Depression, World War II, the atom bomb, and the cold war. It has been a world of such rapid and great changes that they have been called revolutions – the black revolution, the youth revolution, and the sex revolution. There has been a series of social upheavals challenging the values of our culture and our very civilization. We all know, or should know, that revolutions frequently, if not generally, create greater human misery than they correct. Yet my favorite description of democracy is that "the one who wears the shoe knows best where it pinches." More than that, the one who wears the shoe has a right to ease the pain and is the best judge of whether the pain has, in fact, been relieved. Our so-called revolutions have been caused by some pinch that cried for relief. However bad were some of the social consequences of these so-called revolutions, some needed good may have been accomplished.

My own view is one of optimism. It is that the candles of our western civilization burn brightly here in Utah. They are especially brilliant in our daily living. First, in Utah we respond well to the ancient ideal of thinking and reasoning our way through life – in our schools, in our homes, in our politics, in our businesses, and in our social relationships. We try to be rational, to listen, to discuss, and then to find some balance and harmony. This great university has helped us immeasurably in living a good life through reasoning.

Utah also gives great emphasis to Judeo-Christian ideals. Religion is a vital part of our culture. The ethics of kindness, tolerance, and sharing are strong forces in the state of Utah. Let no one underestimate this influence in our daily living.

I am optimistic, yet I think realistic, when I say that we have a tendency to underrate our great culture in Utah. I think it is better than most of us realize. We have a long way to go, but we build firmly on the foundations of our western civilization. The quality of life here in Utah is too easily taken for granted. It is far better than many judge it to be.

Conclusion

There is one measure of our culture I have left for my conclusion. In my earlier years, I did not think Utah did very well in its devotion to the great ideal of the beautiful. I felt little was done to preserve the beauty of God's out-of-doors and to support the efforts of artists to create and render our lives richer with song and dance, painting and sculpture, and music.

I have changed my mind. I now think that Utah may be at the threshold of a renaissance in the arts. And very important, we are also at last awake and preserving the great natural beauties of our state, not just with parks but the highways and byways of our daily travel.

On this occasion of prayer, I close with the creed of many in our state – godliness is helped by loveliness, and nothing is ever right until it is beautiful.

If Free Men Stay Free

Governor's Appreciation Dinner
April 28, 1972

□

Occasions such as this make one thing clear: The words of our language are inadequate. A sincere "Thank you" is sufficient most of the time. But in the presence of great happiness and deep appreciation, the words "Thank you" simply do not cover the situation. I think Grace and I prefer the words, "We love you. We love the people of our state. We love this good earth, and the beautiful skies that are Utah."

I confess I've worried about this evening. Particularly, I've worried for fear my emotions might show. Fearing this, I decided to write and then hide behind these few words. I would like to think about the meaning of this occasion for all of us. Surely there is a deeper meaning than honor for just two people.

My search for this deeper meaning is as follows. The governor of our state must think a good deal about the well-being of all of the people. In doing so, he must frequently contemplate the current successes and failures of our democracy. Perhaps these reflections have had something to do with these kind and thoughtful appreciation dinners.

Each honored citizen comes from a different background and a different profession. My background is student of philosophy and businessman. In keeping, then, with that which I am sure is the governor's larger interests for a sound and healthy state community, I will, as the character in literature, "sing for my supper." I will not really sing, fortunately, but I will "sing for my supper" by thinking with you about philosophy and business.

How do these two disciplines, philosophy and business, relate to the governor's concern for a more successful democracy? My answer is to relate them to the greatest value of our civilization, freedom. Philosophy and business have a big part to play on the side of man's freedom.

Consider philosophy first, the psychology involved in the study of philosophy. Studying philosophy, one both gains and loses peace of mind. Just when some viewpoint or conclusion looks acceptable and sound, the practice of philosophic inquiry raises new questions and suggests new possibilities. Peace of mind in philosophy is always temporary, provisional, and tentative; it is never final or complete. Truth, to the student of philosophy, never appears better than just high probability. Thus, philosophic inquiry can disturb one's peace of mind, unless, of course, one is satisfied with conclusions that are no better than just a little more reasonable or a little more probable, but never final or absolute.

On the more positive side, philosophic inquiry can put a lot of things together, help us see things as a whole, and find some harmonizing principle, even though later on every harmonizing principle may need to be modified or enlarged.

So, the study of philosophy is considered by many as dangerous, both for the stability of the individual and the security of society. They see this restless search for truth as confusion and relativism. Others see it as an application of a religious ideal, namely, the Law of Eternal Progression. In any case, no argument is needed to show that in our contemporary world of so many new ideas and new values, our open, philosophic turn of mind can be a priceless asset.

My own conclusion, Mr. Governor, can be put this way. Citizens are better citizens if, while holding firm to their well-tested convictions, they can say to themselves in open-eyed wonder, "By the grace of God, I may be wrong." Philosophy, as with science and religion, is a search for truth. The Great Master said that truth would make us free. And truth can free us from enslavement to the past, free us from the tyrannies of the present, and free us from irrelevant ideas. Far more important, truth makes us free not only *from* something but *for* something—free to create and, possibly even more important, free for newer and finer loyalties.

Each student, each citizen, all of us, Mr. Governor, tend to settle down in our lifetime with a few solid conclusions and a few deeply held personal convictions toward which we feel a warm and satisfying loyalty. I now give one of my own, one of my deepest loyalties. It is my loyalty to a method for finding truth. Known as the scientific method, the wonderful thing about it is that it is so successful outside of the sciences. It applies to all truth-claims—political, religious, economic, etc. This method means the eternal changing from one principle to possibly a greater principle, and then the testing of this new possibility, new hypothesis, or new generalization by whatever new facts or better evidence is available. So the search goes on for what may be the more reasonable, the more probable, or the more truthful. Some call the application of this great method of truth-finding the search for wisdom.

What does business contribute to man's freedom? Here is my conclusion, and by the grace of God I may be wrong; yet I think not.

I believe that the free enterprise system, with all its failures, is the solid front-line defense of mankind's most precious freedoms. These are our political and intellectual freedoms. Political freedom is our free choice of leaders who hold great power over us. Intellectual freedoms—the hallmarks of our civilization—are the freedoms of speech, religion, learning, and so on. The great lesson of socialism and communism is that no society can keep its precious intellectual and political freedoms when the state owns and operates the means of production and distribution.

To be sure, our free enterprise system freely accepts government regulation. Government, for example, can help to maintain free and fair competition, oppose economic exploitation, etc. But always the most important freedom must prevail, which is that every person have an equal opportunity to try his hand and thus be enabled to live freely and strongly.

One other observation about the business world is that of all the freedoms of free enterprise, the greatest of them all is the freedom to be generous. Stockholders can hardly be expected to petition corporate officers to give away even a small fraction of their dividends. However, corporate officers may convince stockholders and, indeed, convince themselves as well, that unless they give away five percent of net earnings to good causes (actually only two and one-half percent is given, since the government in its generosity will excuse the other two and one-half percent in taxes) for philanthropic purposes, the free enterprise system will become deeply tarnished. Such a weakness or failure of freedom could someday mean that men will no longer be free to be either generous or selfish. This greatest freedom of free enterprise, to be generous, is priceless when used and could be costly when neglected.

Every businessman knows, or should know, that the most successful rule in every phase of business is the Golden Rule. Most businessmen are aware, or should be aware, that freedom in business, free enterprise, has no guarantees for tomorrow. What many businessmen do not know, and what many stockholders do not know, is that unless business freedom is used with generosity, some pied piper with a campaign collectivist song will lead people to the destruction of the entire free enterprise system.

Mr. Governor, the two ideals of an open mind and a generous heart leave all of us as failures. We close our minds and our purses when we really should keep them a little more open. Yet we are not complete failures. We maintain great universities, and we do give generously. Nevertheless, both scholars and businessmen are on trial every day. The jury of the people observes well our failures, and we must therefore give them solid evidence that we possess inquiring minds and generous hearts. So it must be if free men are to stay free.

I do have one more idea I would like to express, but this one is so deep within me that I cannot bear to think I may be wrong. The greatest joy in life is a love of the beautiful. Mr. Governor, no blessing is greater, and none more needed, than a citizenry with passionate devotion to things beautiful.

Aesthetic experience is not just an art-gallery experience. Everyday experiences—the places where we work, the things we make, the people we see, our buildings, our streets and parks, the pitch of our voice, a smile, mountains and deserts, music and furniture, water and snow—mean that godliness is helped by loveliness. When we say that man is that he might have joy, one avenue is the lovely and the beautiful.

The businessman in me will out, and so I propose that far more private philanthropy go, not so greatly to education, for the taxpayer will provide this, and not so greatly to health, for the taxpayer will also provide this, but to a search to find the more beautiful. This should encompass experimentation in architecture, landscaping, ballet, theatre, the wilderness, and, above all, great music.

Mr. Governor, appreciation is a two-way street where nearly all the traffic flows one way—from the individual's thankful heart to parents, to brothers and sisters, to relatives, to classmates, to teachers, to colleagues, to customers and friends, and above all, to the partner of one's life.

To be sure, much of life cannot be appreciated. Life is more than downhill coasting. There are family brothers who pin your ears back, classmates who are better, teachers who are unfair, customers who complain, competitors who win, and friends who depart. Alas! there is also adversity which no one expects and no one avoids. Tragedy stalks our path in the farewell of loved ones.

Even so, Grace and I find, on balance, more beauty than ugliness by a million times, more truth than falsehood, more kindness than we deserve, and possibly, just possibly, more goodness than tragedy. This evening our prayer is expressed by James Whitcomb Riley who wrote: "And with all the needy, oh divide, I pray, this vast measure of content that is mine today."

Freedom's Best Fight

Utah Academy of Arts, Sciences, and Letters
April 17, 1964

□

Freedom's best fight takes place in a free university.

Where and when freedom wins its greatest victories are difficult questions. Against totalitarianism, the victory might be military. Against economic exploitation, the victory might be in free competition. Against invasions of privacy, the courts successfully defend private judgment and personal independence. A case can be made, however, that freedom's best fight takes place in a free university.

Freedom and tyranny take many forms in a free society. The wins and the losses of both are uncountable. Every person each day experiences now freedom and now some form of tyranny. Both freedom and tyranny wash over our lives leaving their marks of hurt and help. Which wins most of the battles, freedom or tyranny, is an open question.

Yet of this we can be sure: Freedom at its best is not won by force or in the marketplace; but, rather, the greatest freedom is won in the world of ideas, in the mind where decisions are made about what to believe and how to live, where we have freedom to think and search for better ideas, for new possibilities. It is our thesis that the institution most friendly and helpful in fair and thoughtful consideration of various explanations is a college or university. To foster the life of adventure with new ideas is the main work of a great university. Other institutions face the demands of being successful by meeting practical needs. New ideas or possibly unfriendly ideas rank far below financial or membership goals. In higher education, the ideal is to consider an idea with objectivity. The symbol of a university is individualism, a solitary student in a library or classroom, or two students in thoughtful conversation about some new idea. The ultimate symbol is a student reflecting upon the evidence or reasonableness of an idea, and privately deciding which idea to accept as true, and which idea to reject as false, or probably false.

What is freedom?

The question is difficult to answer. For our purpose in considering mankind's endless struggle against tyranny, we can say that freedom requires independence. Free universities satisfy this requirement. College work at its best is an independent and courageous student searching for *truth*. Tyranny can generally be overcome if truth can be established. Truth is tyranny's mortal enemy. Truth does make us free.

What is truth?

Broadly speaking, we may describe truth as whatever may be the actual situation, the existing state of affairs, the way things are, the world as it really is, the facts. Some of this truth is verifiable through science. Some is yet to be discovered. Much of what the truth may be is yet quite unknowable. More narrowly, we may define truth as the correspondence between a person's idea and the external factual situation. When an idea in the mind corresponds to an outward fact, we say the idea is true. When an idea in the mind does not correspond to a fact, we say the idea is false. Stated another way, truth is characteristic of a proposition, namely, the verification or non-verification of what the proposition asserts by checking this assertion with sensory observation. This is the scientific method.

Beyond such a general description of truth lies the whole world of the unknown, some of which is our world of faith and hope, some of which may be true and some false.

A university's very life is this search for truth. Science and the scientific method give us our greatest success in establishing truth. But scientific verification is not available in much of our search for truth. Beyond the sensory tests of science, a university may have to seek truth by the test of what is reasonable, or probable. In this search for truth, what is reasonable may depend upon what is presently known about similar experiences. Truth will probably cohere and fit together with facts and experiences already known.

So much for definitions or descriptions of freedom and truth. Let us turn now to the fight that freedom has in a university. The fight centers upon discovering and distinguishing between truth and error. Our concern now is a possible conflict of truth with a community's powerful institutions – economic, political, or religious. Almost all forms of human oppression prosper in powerful institutions.

Many of the issues in a university are concerned with truth-claims made by religious leaders, by business executives, and by elected government officials. Even more, the issue of truth-claims in a university may originate with ideas taught in the home, ideas expressed by friends, or even conclusions reached by an individual himself or herself.

Tyranny, oppression, coercion, and subtle pressures are inevitably involved in all of mankind's organized social living. All institutions in a free society, including a free university itself, are scrutinized for their freedoms or tyrannies. Institutions serve our practical needs, but they may also necessarily dictate policies that tyrannize over private conscience. An institution can be mankind's servant and master at the same time. It is this attempt of institutions to master people that produces tyranny. So, a free

society commits itself to curbing the inevitable tyrannies within
its free institutions. And nowhere in a free society is this endless
labor of purging our lives from institutional tyrannies done as
well as it is in a free university.

A university has the two qualifications for this difficult and
sometimes painful task. First, it fearlessly examines the truth-
claims of the community's powerful institutions. Second, it lives
by individualism in its highest form. Each student is free to make
his or her own decision of what the truth may be. In a very real
sense, a university is a judgment seat of society's powerful institutions. Small wonder, then, that these institutions are sensitive
about what goes on in a university. For if institutional truth-
claims are successfully challenged, the choice of such an institution is either to change or to commit greater tyranny.

It is not too much to say that the great wellsprings of a free
society are thus found in its institutions of higher learning. Universities are fundamentally involved in purifying and purging the
community's institutions of their false claims so that men can
escape enslavement and live in freedom. Consider what free universities might do in communist countries. But then universities
and colleges have more than enough to do here at home.

Consider now the second qualification of a university in the
fight for freedom – its high quality of individualism. A university
is not collective in its work, not highly organized, and not unified
in policy or practice. It is highly individualistic and pluralistic. A
university is little more than a gathering of autonomous and independent individuals. Any form of institutional life in a university
is secondary and even unimportant compared to the great purpose of encouraging each individual to decide what to believe
and what to disbelieve, which ideas to accept or reject. Scrutiniz-
ing ideas is the very life of a university.

In the span of a person's life, the childhood years of inex-
perience cannot allow for much freedom. But college age is the

emerging period of freedom and independence. In college, mature men and women freely examine all the good and bad of society. In rare moments they even achieve that high degree of objectivity whereby they scrutinize themselves as a product of a singular inherited pattern, the product of some twenty years of social conditioning. It is in these years from eighteen to twenty-two, or from twenty to thirty, that, involved in university work, freedom's best fights are won.

After the college years, men and women change from a life of free inquiry and a mood of challenge to a life filled with social responsibilities. Thus, after college, people change from asking questions to answering them. They shift from challenge to defense and from doubt to certitude. Important as defense may be, valuable as the ability to answer some questions may be, and as satisfying as psychological certitude can be, these functions are not humanity's claim to greatness, nor are they the highways to enlarging freedom.

This period of free inquiry within a university, granted to emerging citizens, is the greatest single gift a free society can bestow on its members. For in our free society, life can be imagined as though we were on a long and disciplined march with only this one chance to break ranks, one time to get out of uniform, one parenthesis of great freedom. This is the meaning of a university.

Prior to the college years, one's life is being conditioned. After one's college years, one faces the necessity of trying to condition others. The golden years of freedom are in this brief span in college when life's burdens are held in abeyance while each student independently asks penetrating questions and freely suggests and weighs new possibilities. After these few brief years in college, the love of truth meets a serious challenge – that of achieving personal or institutional success. After college, wholesome doubt faces the fear of insecurity, and personal convictions are challenged by institutional policies. In college, duty can be clear, and truth may win. After college, duty may be compromise, and truth may become secondary.

These college years of freedom are the wellsprings of a free society. This fresh look at society's failures by eager and courageous men and women heavily favor freedom's battles against tyranny. Such victories are not easily won. Great personal battles are fought on every campus.

The peaceful atmosphere of academic life is misleading. Intellectual storms of varying intensities are sometimes beginning, sometimes raging, or sometimes subsiding on every free campus. These battles of individual minds begin at waking, continue in classrooms, and go on at lunch, in libraries, in conversations, and when studying far into the night. On campus, individualism and freedom are lived at their best. On campus, tyranny suffers its greatest defeats. On campus, freedom fights its best fight.

The Constitution and Freedom

Archives, Washington, D.C.
March 17, 1986

□

I am honored to be a member of the Commission for the Bicentennial of our Constitution. We are all honored that we can relate to a document that is unparalleled in the history of mankind. It is arguably true that the three documents most influential in our twentieth century are: the Bible, Plato's *Republic*, and the Constitution of the United States.

In the bicentennial year, we will be trying to better understand the greatness of our Constitution. Imbedded in it are the basic values of our western civilization. These values influenced the men who wrote and ratified the Constitution.

In essence, the Constitution is a procedural document, a method whereby a government is created to establish a free democracy. As such, the Constitution is a means to an end. The end is a free people who have "inalienable rights to life, liberty, and the pursuit of happiness."

But the Constitution is more than a framework for a government. In our Constitution are assumptions that are the taproots of a great civilization. Many of these taproots have been made clear during the past 200 years. They are often given different names, mostly such terms as "equality," "freedom," "justice," "due

231

process," "general welfare," etc. In this paper, three taproots are mentioned: freedom, volunteerism, and individualism.

The taproots of greatness in the Constitution came from many lands and from many countries including Palestine, Greece, Rome, France, and England as well as from other places and times well known to students of history. Taproots of past greatness become the ideals of the present and guidelines for centuries to come.

Our ancestors were aware that the future would hold uncertainties, and to preserve those values named in the Constitution, they spelled out guidelines to protect them, guides such as the "due process" clause, the "general welfare" clause, the Bill of Rights, and a three-fold division of power in government to prevent the centralization of power. Their guidelines are many and these guidelines preserve the great ideals of our Constitution. Our Founding Fathers thus not only wrote a Constitution that created the government of the United States, they expressed ideas and ideals that are the foundations of our American democracy, if not of our western culture.

What are some of the ideals, sometimes referred to as eternal values, named and protected in our Constitution? They are often difficult to name, and more difficult to explain, and yet they are well known to most Americans. In this paper, I name three major human values that I think are the three greatest values in our Constitution. They are:

> 1. *Freedom*, the most successful way to solve life's problems;
> 2. *Volunteerism*, the noblest quality in human life; and
> 3. *Individualism*, the supreme value of creation.

To repeat, these three values are the taproots of greatness in our Constitution, if not in all our western civilization. It is a good time for us to reflect on them. We are fortunate to have the celebration of a bicentennial, not only for our own benefit, but also to remind us of our nation's role of leadership in the world.

We live just now with the challenge of communism. Our best response to it will be to clarify our minds and dedicate our lives to the values preserved for us in the Constitution. They give dignity to human life. They assure us countless possibilities of finding those satisfactions that make our lives glad and beautiful and good. In this world of conflicting values they stand out as the greatest ideas and ideals in the history of mankind. We will need a clear understanding of their meaning in our response to communism.

Freedom

In the hierarchy of human values, freedom is often listed as the greatest. Our Constitution may be regarded as a document about freedom, the inalienable right to think and speak one's thoughts, and within limits, to carry out those ideas about which one thinks and speaks.

As one reflects on history, our species has survived because with freedom we have been able to solve many of our countless problems. We are a problem-solving species. Other species survive mostly by instinct and habit. We also survive by instinct, and by tradition, but much of the success in human life results when there is freedom to reason and choose among various options.

It is a fact of our existence that from the time we are weaned to the time we die we are solving an infinite variety of problems, most of them trivial, but some very important. Over the centuries we have learned that freedom to choose is our best chance for success. This freedom does not guarantee we will find the best solution. Sometimes great freedom can result in great failure. But our belief and hope is that with freedom, we do better, even with our mistakes, than when there is no freedom at all. In any case, human nature generally resents repression and coercion. And so whether the problem we face is personal or social, we have an abiding faith that our best chance for success will be if there is encouragement to thoughtfully reflect upon a problem and freedom within limits to carry out the solution we think is best.

The Constitution is clear about two kinds of freedom: freedom *from*, and freedom *for*. One is freedom from tyranny, the other is freedom for opportunity. One is freedom from dictatorship, where others would compel us to obey, and the other is freedom for opportunity, where choices can be thought about, freely expressed, and, within limits, acted upon.

Our Founding Fathers used the word "liberty" while we more frequently use the word "freedom." They wanted to have liberty, freedom from a foreign dictator. Today we think more of opportunity, freedom for the opportunity to live a brighter future. We always are seeking for a better beyond our present best. In this search, we sometimes define our democracy as a condition of potential perpetual revolution, a constant striving for improvement. Some of our problems are new, and some are age-old problems in the history of mankind.

In responding to the challenge of communism, we can best understand and clarify the meaning of freedom if we divide it into three types. They are: economic freedom, political freedom, and intellectual freedom.

The first, economic freedom, might be defined as the right to own private property and conduct it for a private profit.

The second, political freedom, may be explained as the right to vote privately for a representative who will meet with other representatives and pass such laws as they can agree upon, and such laws as the people are willing to support.

The third kind of freedom might be described as intellectual freedom. This comprises the freedoms to speak, to assemble, to worship, to publish, to learn and to teach, among others.

Reflecting on these three different kinds of freedoms as we celebrate the Bicentennial, we need to be clear about how world governments deal with them. One might divide present major world governments into three kinds: totalitarian, socialistic, and freely democratic. Each deals differently with these freedoms. Communism denies all three freedoms. Socialism denies economic freedom, but allows political and intellectual freedom. A free democracy allows all three freedoms, with one reservation, that economic freedoms be regulated.

In communism, there is no political freedom as we understand a free election. In communism, there are no intellectual freedoms, no freedom to dissent, to be critical or to assemble in opposition. There are no free universities in the Soviet Union.

In socialism, while there is no economic freedom, there are intellectual and political freedoms. The single greatest issue of socialism is whether a power structure like socialism, that combines economic and political power, will run the risk of allowing intellectual freedoms. Will those in power allow criticisms that may endanger their enormous power – brought about when political and economic powers are combined? Or will those with such power curb the freedoms of the mind, the freedoms to speak and publish, the freedom to worship, the freedoms to assemble and criticize?

In our free democracy, all three freedoms are present, if not quite absolute. This is the guarantee of our Constitution. We enjoy complete intellectual freedom, complete political freedom, and complete economic freedom, with the one reservation of limited governmental regulation in our economic affairs. In our free enterprise system, we have learned that some reservations are necessary for the common good. For example, the government must act to preserve free and fair competition. It must protect freedoms that afford to each citizen the chance to try his or her hand in the world of business. But in our political and intellectual life, the Constitution insures complete freedom. We sometimes say that in the world of government regulation there must be no more regulation than may result in the increased freedom for the individual.

Communism makes one attempt to avoid its unbearable oppression over the minds of people. It promises that at some indefinite time in the future there will be a return of intellectual freedoms when the state "withers away." One is to believe that at some time in the future a powerful central committee will voluntarily give up its powers. The question is whether to believe such a state will "wither away," whether men holding such great powers will ever freely step down and voluntarily give up their dominion over the lives of other human beings.

In contrast, our Constitution provides for the peaceful and orderly transition of power. Such a peaceful transition is one of the greatest achievements in all of mankind's political history.

Volunteerism

The second taproot of greatness in our Constitution is the quality of life it affords to each citizen, the chance to be a volunteer. It is sometimes said that the call of communism is: "wanted, conscripts," while the call of our democracy is: "wanted, volunteers." And it is sometimes said that the glory of mankind is a free man or woman who is socially minded, who thinks and acts for the well-being of others. Being free is to have the greatest blessing life can afford, and voluntarily and freely serving others is the greatest happiness one can discover.

Another expression of volunteerism is in going the second mile. Much of life is the necessity of going the first mile, but when we voluntarily choose to go beyond necessity, when we freely and willingly do more than is required, then we live on the highest level of human existence.

Just now you are assembled here as volunteers. What you do to celebrate the bicentennial of our Constitution will be what you freely and voluntarily decide to do. Your reward will be the satisfaction you find in your ideas and plans for the successful celebration of your own organization. To help you and your organization, Congress enacted a law authorizing the three branches of our government to nominate, and the President to appoint, a national commission. And then Congress did more – it appropriated funds to pay for a staff to help you celebrate the bicentennial of our Constitution. A staff of able people will assist you with ideas, but also help you with your own ideas, of how your organization may be successful in this great year of the bicentennial.

The celebration can be done well with your leadership. Your organization can make a difference in the lives of its members by adding to their knowledge about the Constitution, and by helping them achieve a deeper appreciation for such an immortal document.

In the final analysis, the greatest help for your organization will be yourself, your individual leadership. Everything rises or falls depending on leadership. So your greatest contribution will be your own personal commitment, your dedication, your own individual involvement. As private organizations within our great democracy are successful, so also will be our success in honoring our priceless Constitution.

Individualism

The third taproot of greatness in our Constitution we refer to as individualism. It is our belief that the individual is of infinite value, the unit of supreme value in our western civilization.

When this bicentennial year becomes history, what standard may be used to determine the success of our celebration? I think our success will be measured by a new awareness that the supreme value of any civilization is the primacy of the individual. Our response to the challenge of communism will be successful as we realize that the noblest, the highest, the best civilization is one in which the individual citizen, not the state, is the unit of supreme value. The state exists to help and serve the individual. The individual should help the state, but is not a slave to the state.

Granted the value of community achievement, of all social progress, still, society is made up of individuals, one by one, each of infinite value. This recognition of individuals is the great divide between ourselves and communism.

The Constitution is replete with references to the primacy of the individual. Two of them are "due process" and the Bill of Rights. Much of what I have spoken about under the headings of Freedom and Volunteerism refer as well to individualism, of course. I will thus conclude by expressing the hope that we as individuals will strive to exercise those freedoms guaranteed us by the Constitution, that it might also be treasured and celebrated by others another 200 years from now.

V

VALUES

Introduction

L. Jackson Newell

□

Obert Tanner has the mind of a philosopher and the instincts of a man of affairs. Nowhere is this unique blend more evident than in these essays on human values. His impeccable credentials as a capitalist – and his native reasonableness – gave him the credibility to champion the United Nations, world government, disarmament, free inquiry, and cultural diversity as a public figure in a conservative western state from the 1950s through the 1980s. These essays from across those decades deserve our attention as much today as they did when the speeches were given.

A second element that gives Tanner's writing saliency is seeing some of the great ideas of western philosophy expressed through the life and work of a person who knew them intimately and loved them with passion. One would look long to find a better argument for liberal education, or a better case for the relevance of ancient philosophy. Obert Tanner has spent his life searching for ways to understand – and give life to – the notions of truth, goodness, beauty, justice, and liberty. The integrity of

---

Professor Newell is Dean of Liberal Education of the University of Utah.

241

the quest has been his constant concern and three questions have persistently guided his response to value claims: Is it reasonable? Is it probable? Is it good?

One also sees here the work of a catholic mind. Tanner has always taken pride in his state, his country, and his religion, but he has never allowed these loyalties to stand as barriers to embracing other religious traditions, respecting other nations, or loving other peoples. It is quite common to make a show of one's own liberality by putting down one's own origins or culture. Throughout these essays, however, we encounter a person who sees no inconsistency in taking pride in local and regional ties while seeking to know and strengthen larger ones. Tanner's instinct is always to seek the larger loyalties, the higher values. His obvious devotion to Utah's culture and to American institutions enabled him to speak with authority on behalf of global values and universal notions. Obert Tanner's philosophy and ideals are clearly manifest in the speeches contained in this section.

Life Is a Many-Sided Thing

Southern Utah State College Commencement Address
June 2, 1972

☐

I am greatly honored to be your commencement speaker. And I will try to deserve this honor by discussing, with honesty and forthrightness, one of life's greatest problems. The problem is a personal one. It is the search for a measure of good balance and harmony in each one of our lives.

The broad ideal of balance and harmony is considered by many to be the supreme value in our western civilization. Two other values could also rank as supreme in the history of mankind. One is the Oriental—particularly Buddhist—ideal, of Nirvana. The other, also a religious ideal, is the love of God. All three of these values, love of God, Nirvana, and balance, hold a place in man's history as values that have been prized above all other values. They are the three supreme values of the human race.

Harmony and balance, as a supreme value, came into western civilization through the Greeks. The Pythagoreans derived it from the study of music, and they then gave it an ethical meaning. Balance and harmony became the highest good for Socrates and Plato. Plato's *Republic*, second only to the Bible as the most influential document in our western civilization, attempts to show that a good state, a good society, is one of balance and harmony where every citizen performs his appropriate function.

In this address, however, we will not be involved with the great social issues of our country and of the world. Rather, let us turn inward upon ourselves and consider life subjectively, as each one of us will now face it—from our own personal point of view, our own life yet to be. Let us search for some inner harmony that will help match ourselves with the world.

The words, "harmony" and "balance," as we shall use them, and as the Greeks used them, mean the application of reason to life. We mean by harmony, reasonableness applied to life. That is, reason is used to find a harmony among the diverse interests, the various desires that confront our lives. When some of our values oppose each other, when some of our interests appear incompatible, reason may help us find some measure of harmony. Reason, that is, may give balance and good proportion among our various impulses and conflicting desires. To quote George Bernard Shaw, reason can take "a mob of appetites and organize them into an army of purposes and principles." Plato identified reason with harmony.

There is something almost mysterious in this search for inner harmony. It is such a personal matter that no one can speak for another. Each must find his own way.

I do not know what a well-balanced life may be. I am sure that more is involved than neatly balancing life's various interests. For one thing, human values, themselves, are not all on the same level. There is a hierarchy of values. Some values are higher, more important, than other values. Some single value, some higher interest—perhaps of science, or religion, or art, or ambition—alone may give harmony and symmetry to all the lower values.

And while some people appear to achieve a high degree of symmetry and harmony among their various values, it is probably true that all harmonizing of values involves some sacrifice, and more frequently than not, a great harmony may involve a sacrifice of staggering proportions. For example, when two great values confront each other, one value must give way, and then a very great sacrifice may be involved. When two great values are incompatible, the best harmony is no better than some kind of tragic harmony. Among incompatibles, one great value may be lost forever.

I doubt if this point is very meaningful to those on the threshold of life. The price, the extent of this sacrifice involved in big decisions among opposing values is sometimes not known until years after the decision was made. A girl must choose between two fine young men. A person must choose between two attractive vocations.

The point I want to make in this address is this: That every harmony involves some sacrifice; sometimes the sacrifices are small and easily bearable, and sometimes the harmony means a sacrifice that endures for a lifetime.

A poet wrote:

> He who more lives
> Than one would live,
> More deaths than one
> Must die.

I have given this address the title, "Life Is a Many-Sided Thing." I think I may have been influenced by a title of a love song, to the effect that love is a many-splendored thing. Possibly no one has written a song to the effect that life, of itself, is a many-splendored thing. So much of life is not splendor. But life is many-sided. And while many of its sides complement each other and can be easily harmonized, some sides of life oppose each other; and some of this opposition can both make, and also ruin, a lot of happiness. Perhaps a better title for this address might have been, "Life Is a Many-Sided Conflict."

In logical terms, when two values oppose each other, there are three possibilities: one value, possibly the weaker one, gives way to the stronger; or, a second possibility is that the two opposing values may compromise, each side winning something and each side losing something; and, a third possibility is integration. This solution is claimed to be one in which both sides win, and nobody loses. But this is not true. Every integration involves some compromise, some loss.

Let us turn now from logic to life. Logic is formal and unemotional. Not so with life. I believe that finding some harmony in life is the heartbeat of life itself, each day; and if not each day, then at moments of great decision when life is at the crossroads.

All of us want to match ourselves with the world. We want to be well organized. This means we must think our way through life. One is thinking, applying reason to life, when the various alternatives are considered and a course is adopted which promises success. In the problem of achieving harmony, reason is not opposed to our emotional drives, not even our impetuous desires; all are accepted for their potential values. Reason sorts out these impulses, desires, diverse interests, and personal values, and harmonizes them with some overarching value, some great interest, some goal we have set for ourselves.

To achieve some success in finding some harmony and balance, three things are necessary: Self-knowledge, Discrimination, and Renunciation.

Self-knowledge means facing ourselves honestly, appraising as best we can our own abilities, accepting ourselves, not trying to be someone else. Wise ambition means setting high goals for ourselves, but not impossible goals. The dreamed-of self must not be too far from the actual self. A lot of unhappiness is caused by the tension that results when there is a wide difference between the actual and the imagined self.

A character in the play *Green Pastures* relieves some of this tension of unrealistic ambition by saying, "I ain't much, Lord, but

I'se all I'se got." Self-acceptance can bring an inner harmony. "If," as someone has suggested, "you cannot make your life a symphony, you can at least make it a song."

The second requirement for the harmony of a successful life is no easier than the first. It is discrimination, selection. Some values are higher, more important, than others. William James put it this way: "The seeker of his truest, strongest, deepest self, must review the list carefully, and pick out the one on which to stake his salvation."

The third requirement for harmony is renunciation. Herein lies the element of tragedy. Life has not only its inclusions, but also its exclusions. When we say "yes," we also say "no." As the song goes, you can't marry ten pretty girls. You cannot have your cake and eat it too. Whatever is won must be paid for in whatever is lost.

Much is said in favor of becoming a well-integrated personality, and integration is achieved when a person is going somewhere wholeheartedly, without regret or reservation. But there is always a price. Sometimes the total commitment, the strenuous devotion to a single interest, can disturb the harmony of a personality. So Wagner, in a moment of utter despair, wrote of his relation to music: "But I am unhappy in not being able to apply myself to anything but music. . . . While I work I forget my troubles; but the moment I rest, they come flocking about me, and I am very miserable. . . . I am very lonely; I often wish for death. How willingly I would part with the artist's life for a week of real life."

The great student of human values, Professor Parker of the University of Michigan, observes: "I think it is always true that wherever there is strenuous devotion to any of the higher interests, there is some derangement of personality through neglect of the lower."

Whatever the price of specialization, of depth, of great achievement, of total commitment—this is not all of the problem. The devotion to one value often means neglect, if not denial, of another value. Important values frequently oppose each other.

Science may not oppose religion, depending on how one defines both religion and science; but the two disciplines are poles apart both in method and material. And they have fought many wars. And in this warfare, victory for one side meant defeat for the other.

Ambition may not always oppose love, but when ambition means victory in competition, love may be crowded to the wall. Art may not always oppose morality, but complete freedom in the arts can mean considerable indifference to morality. Passion may not oppose convention, but passion and convention do clash, and then a revolution is on. Self-interest may not oppose public interest, but they do clash; and who can tell the right balance between self-interest and public interest?

In this sensitive area, where many public statements and conventional moralists make us feel so guilty about selfishness, about self-love, about self-consideration, we may be justified, especially at this institution of higher learning, to quote a bit of wisdom from the world's greatest genius, William Shakespeare. He said: "Self-love, my liege, is not so vile a sin/As self-neglecting."

You who are graduating should be relieved to know that in your present preoccupation with yourself, your self-preparation, your self-care, your self-concern, your self-regard, you need not feel any twinge of conscience, for the greatest moral law is based upon this: "Love thy neighbor as thyself." No one can improve the world without self-improvement first.

When one contemplates the cost to one's personality of intense specialization and the warfare that goes on between great and precious values—science versus religion, ambition versus love, passion versus convention, self-interest versus public interest—

one is tempted to ask: Is balance and harmony really possible? And if success comes from the imbalance of specialization, and if an integrated personality means going in one direction wholeheartedly, is balance a good thing after all?

Possibly, a better life is not searching for balance and harmony but, rather, achieving imbalance. Are not the highest peaks of happiness found when we are most intense, most exclusive, most free, most independent—are not these moments of abandonment on behalf of some exalting experience the most precious experiences of a lifetime? And is not life more exciting and more interesting, not from harmony, but from the clash and opposition of our interests and values?

Would religion be so interesting without the opposition of science? Would democracy be such a challenge without communism to needle us? Would peace be so precious without war? Is life itself better because of death?

In any case, it appears we will need some new definition of the word "harmony," or qualify the word with the word "tragic"—tragic harmony. Certainly, harmony does not mean some sweet and evenly balanced way of life.

I want to ask several questions. One set of questions relates to a trinity of earthy values that will occupy most of your lifetime. The other set of questions relates to a trinity of ideal values, and these ideal values, for they are all ideal, will disturb you most of your life.

In both trinities, one thing is clear about life—it is not a dull affair. Life is exciting just because our values oppose each other. And even when our values appear to complement each other and we use reason to work out some successful harmony, this is yet not a simple and easy matter.

Consider the values of everyday living. There are three major interests in our everyday living. I have called them our earthy values.

1. Our labor for material goods; simply put, property or wealth.

2. The search for pleasure and happiness, the joys of everyday living; in one word, pleasure.

3. The love of honor, the esteem of others, recognition, influence, prestige, authority; in a word, power—at least some power, some authority, some influence.

Life is spent mostly, but not entirely, in pursuit of these three values. And all agree that a good life would be to harmonize them, enjoy them with some balance and right proportion—that is, without excess, without one of them crowding out the other two.

The question you will ponder many times, however, is this: Which one do you rate the highest, which one will receive your most devoted loyalty? While some balance is good, interest and excitement depend upon having one goal above other goals. Which one gets your majority vote? Would it be wealth, or pleasure, or honor? Which one do you think is the most important?

A further definition of each may help in your choice:

First, consider pleasure. Pleasure may be defined as joy in living, happiness of companionship, love of the beauty of God's out-of-doors (and the beauty of indoors as well), the satisfactions of comfort and of appetite. I have a suspicion that religion, in stressing the spiritual, may have unfairly downgraded these satisfactions of the senses, for they are the joys that give us so much of our happiness.

Would pleasure win first place against wealth and power in your vote?

Second, consider wealth. Wealth may be defined as food, clothing, shelter, and material goods. On the side of wealth it can be said that it is a good thing to live independently, to carry one's own burden, to have the peace of mind that comes with freedom from financial anxiety. To those who call ours a materialistic culture, we would reply, it is not good for one to live by the sweat of another's brow. Moreover, when we are free from poverty, we are free to give ourselves to other and higher values.

Would wealth, then, be the most important of the three? Even slightly more important than pleasure or honor?

Third, consider the love of power. Power may be defined as the human drive for recognition, for influence, for exaltation, for some moments of glory in life. Of this love of honor and power, this much can be said – while man's love of power has written the saddest pages of history, this same value of wanting power and influence, of wanting to be somebody, to have a good reputation, this drive has also been a strong motive for good citizenship, for community service, for a keener sense of social responsibility. To gain a top place, one must serve others well.

When this love of power and influence clashes with pleasure and wealth, would you sacrifice some of pleasure and some of wealth because you supremely enjoy having authority and power over others? If not, will your vote change as you grow older?

I leave you with this trinity of daily values that will involve you the rest of your life.

Turn now to the trinity of ideal values, those that will disturb you the rest of your life. These are Plato's all-inclusive values of goodness, of truth, and of beauty. To be sure, all of us want all three, but the question is whether one of them sits a little higher on the throne than the other two. Again, your choice may be helped with some definitions.

Goodness may be defined as love of God and man. Such goodness is the major concern of religion; but goodness is also the great concern of politics and economics. Perhaps the broadest definition of goodness is this: Goodness is doing whatever will help another person and not doing that which may hurt another person. I suspect that all the law and the prophets might hang on such a definition.

Would you make goodness supreme above the values of truth and beauty? Would service to man—sharing, helping, loving—would you rate this in your personal scale of values above searching for truth or creating the beautiful?

Next, consider truth as a supreme value. There are many definitions, but all might come down to this: Truth, as youth today puts it, is "the way it is." Truth is the actual situation, the real state of affairs, the facts as they are discoverable. Concerning truth, it can be said that nothing can endure for long without at least some measure of truth on its side. Paraphrasing a scriptural passage, one can say they build in vain who build without truth, at least without some truth.

In your personal scale of values, would you place truth slightly above goodness or beauty?

Finally, consider beauty. The beautiful may be defined as a pleasing, aesthetic experience which gives us pleasure, sometimes a deep satisfaction. Beauty is a joyous experience, an experience that can suffuse the whole of life. It can involve the way we dress, talk, and walk; the way we live, our homes, our cities and our wilderness; and the things we create, our surroundings, our work, our play, and our music. While so many joys live only for a day, beauty, as the poet says, is a joy forever.

To which value do you give your supreme loyalty—to goodness, or to truth, or to beauty? Again, you reply, to all three. But again, this is not the question. Everybody loves all three of these supreme values of life. The question is whether, in your personal scale of values, you would give one of them a slightly higher rank in importance. Under which one of the three could you find the harmony you most want for your life?

One thing is certain, a lot of excitement is involved whichever value receives your strongest loyalty.

Loving truth above all else can frequently weaken institutional loyalties concerned with religion, government, and business. Loving truth can mean loneliness. Attempting to harmonize truth with organizations, one can sometimes be hurt. Truth can cause a lot of trouble.

Loving goodness above all else can be frustrating in a competitive world. Love of God and man as the supreme value in everyday life is no easy way to live. Others will oppose you and those loved may not respond, may even return ill will for your goodwill. Attempting to harmonize goodness with a world of so much badness, one can be robbed of peace of mind.

Loving beauty above all can be endlessly painful in a world of so much ugliness. Attempting to harmonize our environment of both beauty and ugliness, one selects a restless way to live.

There is one vast difference between the earthy values of wealth, pleasure, and honor on the one hand, and the non-earthy or idealistic values of goodness, truth, and beauty. Nothing can upset a well-balanced life more surely than excessive preoccupation with earthy values. Excessive pursuit of the values of wealth, or pleasure, or honor can ruin one's life. Not so, however, of goodness, or of truth, or of beauty. The most glorious and well-harmonized lives this planet has ever produced were men and women organized with total devotion to doing good, or finding truth, or creating beauty. Excess, imbalance, total commitment, and a lot of lesser values can be put in their proper places. A person can get well organized with the one supreme value of goodness, or truth, or beauty.

In conclusion, let us turn once more to the concept of tragic harmony. We do so because tragedy is built into life. There is no way to escape adversity, disappointment, failure, sadness – just plain tragedy. Much of life, fortunately, can be a satisfying balance of our lower values; but not the higher values. The higher the value and the stronger our loyalty to it, the greater the chances for both harmony and disharmony.

I have always believed that there is something akin to a sacred obligation for a teacher or a public speaker to tell his students or his audience as best he can, the way the world really is. And instantly let me say to all of you that this is truly a wonderful world. This spaceship we occupy for a few years—this is some spaceship! What a creation, what a Creator!

Even so, it is not an unmixed creation solely for our joy and unending happiness. Sometimes the harmony we find is no better than a tragic harmony.

Our problem is not the tragic harmony itself, but the way we face it, what we do with it. At the beginning we said that for every "yes" to some great value, there must also be a "no." The inclusive also means the exclusive. Every harmony has its price; but with some harmonies the price is so high we lack the personal resources to foot the bill. What we want then is some peace of mind, some serenity, some tranquility in our lives.

At this point, reason cannot help us very much. About all that is possible is some ultimate stand, some unshakable position, some final attitude. The following are four such moods, four ultimate attitudes about life: Resignation, Defiance, Quiet dignity, or Faith.

The first mood, resignation, is deciding that life is a hopeless situation. It is unconditional surrender. There is no way but to give up. Aside from one's own suffering, one is staggered by the sum total of all the misery of the world: prisons, hospitals, mental institutions, bereaved families, war, disease, and poverty. The universe itself, as a poet wrote, is "an eddy of purposeless dust, effort unmeaning and vain."

A second mood in the presence of a tragic harmony is a mood of defiance. This, like resignation, is one of deep pessimism, but a pessimism of strenuous counter-psychological attitude favorable to some activity. We should all remember lines from the poem "Invictus" by William Henley:

> In the fell clutch of circumstance
>   I have not winced nor cried aloud;
> Under the bludgeonings of chance
>   My head is bloody, but unbowed.
>
> . . . .
>
> It matters not how strait the gate,
>   How charged with punishment the scroll,
> I am the master of my fate;
>   I am the captain of my soul.

A third possible mood in the face of tragedy is one of quiet dignity. No borrower of faith or despair, one allows life to be the thing it can be–both good and bad, both beautiful and ugly, both true and false–and walks with serenity to the end with some pessimism and some optimism. One believes that evil can be endured and some good accomplished; that hope, faith, gladness, and goodness may, or may not, someday be vindicated. But whatever, one never loses the highest respect for human dignity, both for one's self and for others. This is the quiet dignity expressed by the poet John Milton in the poem, " . . . Upon His Blindness":

> Yet I argue not
> Against Heaven's hand or will, nor bate one jot
> Of heart or hope; but still bear up and steer
> Right onward.

A fourth approach to tragedy is that of religious faith. This is a mood of reassurance, a belief that in spite of every defeat beyond some tomorrow's sunrise a perfect day will come when hopes and the highest human values will be vindicated by the creation itself. Religious faith is more than just this belief; it is a three-fold activity of careful thought, persistent work, and unselfish prayer.

In the many-sidedness of life, I have included the side of tragedy, hoping that whatever sacrifices are involved in the harmony you make of your lives, you will not finally despair, or be skeptical, bitter, or cynical toward others or your own life. Rather, I entreat you to see the bright side, walk on the sunny side, and remember that if your life cannot be the harmony of a symphony, at least it can be the harmony of a song.

Think Your Way Through Life

Commencement Address, Dixie College
May 30, 1980

☐

It is a great honor to be with you, and a pleasure to congratulate this 1980 graduating class of Dixie College. From the threshold of this college you are about to step into a world of new adventures.

I hope you love adventures, because following your graduation, great adventures lie just ahead of you. But then the whole of life itself may be characterized as a great adventure. Harry Emerson Fosdick portrays this adventurous aspect of human life as follows:

> It is an amazing adventure to be born upon this wandering island in the sky and it is an adventure to leave it when death calls. To go to school, to make friends, to marry, to rear children, to face through life the swift changes of circumstance that no man can certainly predict an hour ahead, these are all adventures. Each new day is an hitherto unvisited country, which we enter, like Abraham leaving Ur for a strange land, "not knowing whither he went" (Hebrews 11:8), and every New Year we begin a tour of exploration into a

257

twelve month where no man's foot has ever walked before. If we all love tales of pioneers, it is because from the time we are weaned to the time we die, life is pioneering.

This Dixie College class is about to enter "an hitherto unvisited country." You are about to begin "a tour of exploration . . . where no man's foot has ever walked before." We all wish you well— your parents, teachers, friends, and community and educational leaders. We want the best for you.

It is my privilege to share with you this important occasion. I am especially pleased to be here because this part of the world is my adopted country. About a half century ago I married a girl from southern Utah, so you will understand the joy we have in our memories as we frequently journey here to places of our romance, the particular place where we became engaged, a place where our car got stuck, etc. And then in later years we brought our children to show them off on Fourth of July celebrations, to have our friends and relatives see and know them, and not least to have them get better acquainted with their grandma and to have her get to know them better and to love them.

I have but a single idea in this commencement address. It is rather an ordinary and commonplace idea, especially so to college graduates. In these remarks I want to make a case for the life of reason, and so I am suggesting to this graduating class that for your future, you think your way through life. I know you are going to do this because thinking goes along with life. In fact, one might say that all, or most all of life, is problem-solving; and, if so, then you will be involved in thought processes most of the time. And because the emphasis in college is on the life of reason, it is appropriate to reflect with you on this subject at your graduation.

My suggestion is that you stress thinking your way through life, that you resolve to emphasize your own personal need for clear thinking. And if you do you will have a good chance, a better chance – not a sure thing – but a better chance of solving your problems well and thereby achieving a better life for yourself.

A thoughtful life has many advantages, and in this commencement address I wish to mention only three. First, as you try to think your way through life, you will have a better chance of finding success, and I assume everybody wants to be successful. Second, as you reason your way through, you have a better chance to live a well-balanced life. Third, if you meditate and reflect upon the various experiences in your life, then at times you may touch the fringes of wisdom.

Granted that wisdom is rare and difficult to find, still there may be a little better chance to become a wise person if you are thoughtful and reflective, if you analyze and think over your past experiences, your mistakes, and how you might have done better, and then make your own corrections and your own resolutions for the future.

This, then, is my case for the life of reason, the case for my suggestion that you think your way through life. First, that thereby you will likely be more successful. Second, that you may achieve a better-balanced life. And third, that you may even go so far as to touch the fringes of wisdom.

Success, balance, and wisdom, on winning these three values, I put my case for the suggestion this evening that you think your way through life.

Let no one suppose that clear and objective thinking is easily done. It may be the most difficult thing you will ever do. Various escapes are used to avoid the pain of facing up to a problem. Rather than courageously looking a problem squarely in the eye, you hedge and dodge and, most tempting of all, let others solve your problem – your peers, your church, or your government. Finally, you cop out rather than be a real man or woman of quality and personal dignity, thinking your own way through life.

The overpowering fact of human life is that almost all of our thinking has a general bias mainly determined by our environment. A baby born in Russia will grow up with more or less fixed beliefs held by the people of Russia concerning religion, politics, economics, social patterns, etc. And so likewise a baby born in China, Iran, France, or the United States; each child in each country will inherit and adopt the prejudices and viewpoints of his native land. And such overpowering environmental influences make objective thinking a near impossibility.

Man is sometimes defined as a rational animal, but he is really more emotional. Some say, and with good arguments, that all thinking, all cognitive activity, is affectively oriented – that is, our thinking judgments are pragmatic and based upon the past experiences of our environment. However technical some of these arguments may be, I think I am clearly understood when I say that there is one great obstacle to objective thinking – it is our emotional life, the emotional aspects of our daily environmental influences. It is the sentimental attachment we have for our peers and the loyalties we feel for those institutions to which we belong. Such loyalties and sentiments become blocks to objective thinking. Even so, such emotions have their rightful place. Not only that, but our emotions are central to the greatest joys in human life. For example we fall in love. We do not reason our way, we fall. When a boy tells a girl he loves her, he does not give his reasons, nor would she care to hear them. He simply says, "I love you." So our emotions, though they impede us as we try to be objective in our thinking, are, nevertheless, greatly important in our journey through life. About all we can do is to try to be as objective as possible. Even in emotional situations we try, as we say, to use our heads, try to do a little thinking for ourselves. So that even when falling in love, a little independent thinking—such as reflections about mutual interests, family background, or common goals for the future—may help to make a good marriage.

Granted that our emotions of loyalty for God and country and peers and loved ones are of great importance, yet even here it is good to have our critical and constructive faculties in good working order and to continue to keep them alive and functioning well. How desperately America needs our best thinking about the international situation today. And how greatly religion is purified from magic and superstition if thought processes are applied that require religious beliefs to be reasonable as well as greatly inspiring.

However, when all has been said in favor of the life of reason, one reservation must be made. It is that even when we forthrightly face a problem and do our best to solve it by our best thinking and reasoning, the final conclusion we reach may be the wrong one. Mistakes and failures are companions of the way in all of human life, and even our best thinking is often no exception.

Even though our emotions and our loyalties (important as they are) often become obstacles to objective thinking, and added to this is the reservation that even our best reasoning may sometimes be in error, I wish now to make the best case I can for the life of reason. I wish to say the strongest things I can to encourage you to think your way through life. So, I will repeat those three propositions on which my case will be made. First, that good thinking will help to assure a successful life. Second, that good thinking will help to assure a well-balanced life. Third, that good thinking may give you a good chance to touch the fringes of wisdom.

Considering the first advantage, that good thinking helps one to be successful, you might reply: "If good thinking is that good, tell me more exactly what good thinking is all about. Be specific, for I would very much like my life to be a success. Just tell me in simple terms the meaning, the ways, the procedures, and the methods of good thinking. What is involved in successful thinking?"

To this I would answer that there are two steps in good thinking that are necessary to solve a problem.

The first step is to decide upon your goal. What is it you want to accomplish? What is your purpose, your dream, your ideal, the end result you hope to realize? The broadest question – What do you want? – you can ask yourself as you begin your day's work or now as you ask yourself what you want to do with your life.

The second step in good thinking is to carefully line up your options, the choices available to you, in accomplishing your goal. I think this second step, sorting out and choosing what you think is your best option, is the heart of the thinking process, and it may be the most difficult part. Certainly it is the step that may spell success or failure.

If I were able to choose what I wish you to remember of this commencement address, it would be the following even though I were given a new name. In later years when one of you meets a classmate and in recalling this evening asks who it was that gave the commencement address, I would be pleased if the other classmate replied, "I can't remember his name, but it was that guy who kept telling us to line up our options." And the other would agree: "Oh yes, it was that 'line-up-your-options' guy."

This remembrance would make me very proud, even for my new name – "line-up-your-options guy." In future years as you face one problem after another, you would be wise to first set up your goal and then line up your options of the best way to achieve your goal.

I said that if choosing what you think is your best opportunity from among your various options is the most difficult part of thinking, the most *important* part, if not the most difficult, is making the decision about what your goal is to be. Just now many of you are trying to decide on a vocation or profession, whether to marry, where to live, etc. These choices of goals are important decisions, and in making them, as you well know, you should do a lot of thinking.

In pioneer days, on a rough frontier road where vehicles had made deep tracks in the mud, this sign was posted: "Be careful which rut you choose. You will be in it for the next twenty miles." So be careful which goals for your life you decide upon, for such goals determine much of what your future life is to be.

The sober fact in choosing life's goals is that once you have made your choice, other possibilities close their doors. So if you choose this, you cannot choose that. If you choose to be an artist you cannot be a scientist; a businessman cannot be a farmer, a commercial aviator cannot be a physician, and so on.

At this time in your life, it may seem a little sad, at least rather sobering, to hear that soon, if not already, your ears will become accustomed to the sound of closing doors. Now at the threshold of your mature life, you are like a person in a room where all the doors are open to many opportunities. But once you make your choice of which door you will go through—for example, which vocation—the chance to select another is not likely to come up again. When you choose some boy or girl to marry, in a figurative sense, you will hear the sound of other doors as they close forever.

The finality of a choice often inclines one to hesitate and postpone one's decision. However, there is a flaw in thinking you can delay for very long. You cannot postpone a decision indefinitely without a grave risk. The risk is that by delay you do not really avoid a decision. Your postponement becomes your decision. If you can't yet decide which vocation to train for, and if you can't make up your mind, this postponement itself may become your decision. The result will be that you become a person who is not trained, which was your decision because you delayed selecting a vocation too long. So, likewise, hesitation about asking a girl to be your wife is likely a decision that she will not be your wife. And one day you may reflect upon the words of John Greenleaf Whittier:

> For of all sad words of tongue or pen,
> The saddest are these: "It might have been!"

The painful truth is that life gets itself made up, one way or another. As William James stated, some of our options are forced; we can't delay, at least not with what James called a live option which he defined as living, forced, and momentous.

In *Julius Ceasar*, Shakespeare described such a forced option this way:

> There is a tide in the affairs of men,
> Which, taken at the flood, leads on to fortune;
> Omitted, all the voyage of their life
> Is bound in shallows and in miseries.
> On such a full sea we are now afloat,
> And we must take the current when it serves
> Or lose our ventures.

But delays may not always be so bad, even if some choices are thereby lost. It may be wise, sometimes, to take the chance of delay until you feel more certain about the wisdom of an important decision. Hasty decisions sometimes make one repent, and, therefore, it may be better to risk a loss than to be too hasty and have cause to regret the decision.

Moreover, once you make your decision there is some comfort in knowing that in some cases, all the doors may not have closed so tightly. Often other opportunities, other doors stand ajar and sometimes you can venture to step inside for an occasional peek and enjoy a brief visit of appreciation. Robert Browning described such possibilities of appreciation in the words:

> I have not chanted verse like Homer, no –
> Nor swept string like Terpander, no – nor carved
> And painted men like Phidias and his friend:
> I am not great as they are, point by point.
> But I have entered into sympathy
> With these four, running these into one soul,
> Who, separate, ignored each other's art.
> Say, is it nothing that I know them all?

So much for these brief remarks about thinking your way to success, about emotional obstacles to clear thinking, and about the situation when thinking does take place. To help insure success in life, you must think and decide upon your goal, think of ways to accomplish such a goal, and face the facts that even with good thinking you may fail. The sober fact is that since life gets itself made up one way or another, you simply have to do some thinking while you can, make your decision, take your chances, and hope for the best. Finally, though this final choice may close out other possibilities, you can look over the fence and enrich your life with appreciation for others and their vocations. You can, as Robert Browning suggests, "enter into sympathy" with many people and their different vocations.

Let us turn now to the proposition that if you think about your way, you may win a well-balanced life. The only way I know that leads to balance, good harmony, and right proportion is by the application of reason. At least this was the basic premise in ancient Greek civilization, and I believe it is just as true today. Thinking leads one to moderation, to a life of balance and harmony.

What does it mean to live a well-balanced life? My answer is that a well-balanced life is one where all the elements of human nature that make for a satisfactory life find expression at the appropriate time. In general terms, a well-balanced life is one that gives opportunity for expression of the many-sidedness of our human natures, albeit the good side, the constructive and positive side. I stress the good side of human nature, for human nature of itself has a potential for both the good and the bad, the tender and the pugnacious, the sharing and the grasping, the serving and the domineering, the altruistic and the selfish. These contrasts are wrapped up together in that complex package we refer to as human nature.

I am limiting myself by saying I plead for a good balance of the good side of our human nature – our rational, emotional, religious, esthetic, practical life. With thought, reflection, and meditation, the good life will surface and turn out to be a life of good balance – a life of harmony that meets all the needs of our complex and wonderful human nature.

Examples of balance and imbalance are easily found in the world of the mind – in ideas and beliefs people hold with deep conviction. We say that some people, for example, are narrow-minded, have tunnel vision, and wear blinders. These individuals have some idea which they hold like a penny so close to their eye that it hides the sun. We frequently reserve such negative judgments and observations for those people who do not agree with us, when all the while it may be our own penny that is hiding the sun.

I can best describe good balance for the mind by reference to the list of courses offered in a college catalog. A college education, if all the courses offered in the catalog were taken by one person, would produce an individual who was well balanced in the world of ideas, and, of course, very interesting to know, surely an interesting conversationalist. But then no one can be that well balanced, and specialization precludes life being as well balanced as we would like. What we are saying is that a good life is not too one-sided, not so specialized that it is blind to new possibilities, new ideas, new methods, and new ideals.

Consider one more example in the search for a well-balanced life. At the beginning of this address I mentioned the value of adventure in one's life – the value of exploration, experimentation, or the search for what a poet has described as "something ever more about to be." But, if such adventure, surprise, and unpredictability were the regular course of events, such a life would surely be quite unsatisfactory. Life needs to be counterbalanced by the value of security, by events that are predictable and people who can be trusted. In short, a life needs to be filled with values that give assurance about the future, a life filled with solid values that favor our peace of mind. Thus, the value of adventure, great as it may be, should be balanced with security. Most people, I think, esteem security as a greater value than the value of adventure. In any case, a good life is balanced with the great value of adventure and the great value of security.

If someone raises the question of whether a well-balanced life is too calculating and selfish – and I think this is a good question – I would reply that if a well-balanced life means a life of fulfillment or an abundant life, then if such fulfillment is claimed to be selfish, mankind's greatest teacher thought differently. He summarized his whole mission to his followers by saying he had come to them that they "might have life and have it more abundantly."

I come now to the last advantage I want to mention, the third benefit for those who try to think their way through life. It is the fascinating and attractive possibility that a thoughtful life may be more likely to touch the fringes of wisdom.

I do not know what wisdom may be, nor do I know a good definition. Wisdom is quite indefinable – like religion, love, beauty, or perfection. Who can describe or define them?

Yet, since definitions are neither true nor false, but hopefully useful and intelligible, let us plunge in and try to say something meaningful about the search for wisdom. If by thinking one's way through life, one has a better chance to find wisdom, the meaning of the word becomes important, however difficult it may be to explain. Indeed, each person must decide for himself or herself what he or she thinks wisdom is. So, I ask each of you: How would you define or describe wisdom? What is wisdom to you? Which are your favorite examples or statements of wisdom?

My favorite description of a wise man, or a wise woman, is a person who sees life steadily, and sees it whole. But, what does it mean to see life steadily and to see it whole? This I do not know. Education may help, but wise men and women are found among those with little formal education. And wisdom appears to surface in unexpected places and from unexpected people. For example, above the locker room door opening onto a football stadium playing field these words are printed in large letters: "Sixty minutes of play: No regrets and no alibis." I think a lot of wisdom is found in those nine words.

There are so many sources to search for wisdom. It may be found in the writings of the prophets, wise men, poets, scientists, statesmen, housewives, businessmen, and schoolteachers. The sources for wisdom are endless.

One of my favorite sources for wisdom is in the writings of the poets. This is not because poets think more clearly than sages and philosophers, but because, like the great prophets, they think with both their hearts and minds, especially on subjects where wisdom is sorely needed. And wisdom is more needed when we confront those ultimates in human life. For example, when we suffer from injustice, grieve over our failures, face life's countless adversities, or are stunned by tragedy or death as all of us are at times, then I think poetry is one source of wisdom that may be helpful.

The poem I love best is Thomas Gray's "Elegy Written in a Country Churchyard." Before quoting from it, I want to tell one or two stories about it. One is that if you visit Stoke Poges in England, where the poem was written, a guide may tell you that

Gray took thirteen or fourteen years to write this poem. Another story concerns the English General James Wolfe who fought the battle for Quebec, Canada, on the plains of Abraham. It may be folklore, but the story is told that one evening before the battle, General Wolfe, reading Gray's "Elegy," put the book down and said, "I would rather have written that poem than win a military victory."

With an awareness that one of life's ultimates is the mystery of death, especially early death, Gray, reflecting on this, wrote in "The Epitaph":

> Here rests his head upon the lap of earth,
> A youth, to fortune and to fame unknown:
> Fair science frown'd not on his humble birth,
> And melancholy mark'd him for her own.
>
> Large was his bounty, and his soul sincere,
> Heaven did a recompense as largely send:
> He gave to mis'ry (all he had) a tear,
> He gain'd from heav'n (t'was all he wished) a friend.
>
> No farther seek his merits to disclose,
> Or draw his frailties from their dread abode
> (There they alike in trembling hope repose),
> The bosom of his Father and his God.

Earlier in the poem, faced with the mystery of a world where so much might have been and so little was realized, so much beauty was to be seen and even more was not seen, Gray wrote:

> Perhaps in this neglected spot is laid
> Some heart once pregnant with celestial fire;
> Hands, that the rod of empire might have swayed,
> Or waked to ecstasy the living lyre:
> . . . .
> Full many a gem of purest ray serene

The dark unfathom'd caves of ocean bear;
Full many a flower is born to blush unseen,
And waste its sweetness on the desert air.

Another ultimate in human life is the need for the wisdom to forgive. In *Idylls of the King*, Tennyson has King Arthur say to Queen Guinevere after she had been captured and convicted of treason against him:

Thou hast not made my life so sweet to me,
That I the King should greatly care to live;
For thou has spoilt the purpose of my life.
. . . .
Yet think not that I come to urge thy crimes,
I did not come to curse thee, Guinevere,

I, whose vast pity almost makes me die
To see thee, laying there thy golden head,
My pride in happier summers, at my feet.
The wrath which forced my thoughts on
      that fierce law
The doom of treason and the flaming death,
(When first I learnt thee hidden here) is past.
. . . .
And all is past, the sin is sinn'd, and I,
Lo! I forgive thee, as Eternal God
Forgives. . . .

We need wisdom to gain peace of mind and find some measure of serenity—as was expressed by John Greenleaf Whittier:

Drop Thy still dews of quietness,
   Till all our striving cease;
Take from our souls the strain and stress,
And let our ordered lives confess
   The beauty of Thy peace.

Breathe through the heats of our desire
   Thy coolness and Thy balm;
Let sense be dumb, let flesh retire;
Speak through the earthquake, wind, and fire,
   O still, small voice of calm!

We need the wisdom of a faith that will not buckle with adversity—as wrote Robert Louis Stevenson:

To go on for ever and fail and go on again,
And be mauled to the earth and arise,
And contend for the shade of a word and a thing
   not seen with the eyes:
With the half of a broken hope for a pillow at night
That somehow the right is the right
And the smooth shall bloom from the rough:
Lord, if that were enough?

Leaving the poets with their great wisdom of heart and mind, we turn to ourselves, to our own thinking. I ask you: Which are your favorite quotations? Which are the ones you think touch the fringes of wisdom? But even more important I ask: Which are your own ideas? Which ideas have you hammered out for yourself because you think they are wise enough to follow? Which ideas or ideals are the products of your own thought? Which ones would you propose as touching the fringes of wisdom?

If you asked me for my own observations and conclusions that I think may be near to wisdom, then with an apology for immodesty and a high risk of being involved with less than wisdom, I offer the following. However, do not think I discovered these ideas easily. They took years in my search for what I think is important, however near or far from wisdom they may be. Here, then, are ten ideas I rate high on my list of wisdom priority.

First, it may be wisdom to see that freedom is life's greatest value, but it is of equal importance to understand that freedom is like a two-sided coin, one side negative and the other side positive.

The negative side of freedom may sometimes be as important to us as the air we breathe, at least when the supply of air has been, or may be, shut off. So, by analogy, sometimes in our lives there are oppressions and exploitations from others that become unbearable. To free ourselves from such tyranny, to get air to breathe, we are sometimes prepared to make almost any sacrifice. This is the important negative side of freedom, namely, the crucial struggles to be free from some personal or institutional tyranny.

The other side of the coin, the positive side of freedom, is more complex. Once freedom from oppression has been won, we face the positive side of freedom and ask, "Freedom for what?"

On the positive side, there are three kinds of great freedoms—economic, political, and intellectual. Wisdom concedes that one way or another, we can struggle through life with reduced economic and political freedoms; but wisdom also tells us that our very civilization would perish if we gave up our intellectual freedoms—that is, the freedom to think, to speak, to publish, to assemble, to teach, to learn, to worship, and, when we desire, to be left alone. The mortal struggle we face with communism concerns all three of our freedoms, but of most importance is intellectual freedom. We can survive with less economic and political freedoms, but our civilization cannot survive if we lose our intellectual freedom, which in essence is the freedom of each individual to think, speak, and act for himself or herself. Such individualism is the very heartbeat of our democracy. This observation is the number one conclusion in my search for wisdom.

Second, it may be wise to agree with the statement of Justice Louis Brandeis that "the right most prized by civilized man is the right to be let alone." However, I would add that it may possibly be even greater wisdom to search within ourselves to discover whether in our thoughts and social actions, with our family and our friends, and in our involvement in business, politics, and religion, we as individuals leave others alone by respecting their personal dignity, their privacy, and the sanctity of their convictions and deeper commitments. We should not invade the private and sacred area of human life that is a matter only between a person and his God.

Third, it may be wisdom to search the creeds of religion and the ethics of philosophers to find their ideas and suggestions for a life of high moral quality. It certainly is useful wisdom to reduce all this search to a simple formula – one simple directive by which one can live each moment, hour, and day of one's life. This absolute constant guide is that it is wrong to hurt a human personality, and it is right to help. To help and not hurt a human personality is based on the wisdom of wise men, of prophets, of mothers, of businessmen, of educators, and applies to all those who wonder how best to live their brief span of life.

Fourth, it may be wisdom to let your conscience be your guide. But if you do, it surely is great wisdom to be as sure as you can be that your conscience is not that of a fool or a fanatic.

Fifth, it may be wisdom to have deep convictions and feel certain you are right to follow through with ideas you think are good enough to live by and share with others. And it may be akin to wisdom to stop and thoughtfully ponder and carefully examine your most cherished idea, and occasionally wonder and ask yourself, as Cromwell did, whether by the grace of God you might be wrong.

Sixth, it may be wisdom to feel that the best part of life is to love and be loved. And it may be wisdom to try to be worthy of being loved and to love others by sharing.

Seventh, surely it is wisdom to work for world peace. And it is a needed wisdom to mix with your thoughts and labors on behalf of world peace that rare and indispensable quality required in our international life, the quality of personal patience.

Eighth, it may be wisdom to search for heroes and heroines to inspire and give direction to our lives—such as Florence Nightingale, Susan B. Anthony, Annie Clark Tanner, Thomas Jefferson, Abraham Lincoln, and David O. McKay. And it surely is wisdom to go beyond hero-worship and care greatly about the ideals they stood for.

Ninth, it surely is wise to live on the sunny side of the street by being cheerful and scattering the sunshine of encouragement to others. And at the same time, it may be wisdom to avoid suffering and guilt and to forge the beatitude to live by: "Blessed is the life that collects no resentments."

Tenth, I hope you will agree that it is great wisdom to think your way through life. And great as the wisdom of stressing a thoughtful life, it may also be wisdom to love people, all people, for the good that is in them and to respect their institutions for the good they accomplish.

My wish for you is the wisdom of that motto over the dressing room door in the football stadium, which I change slightly for this occasion:

"Sixty years of thoughtfulness for each one of you, no regrets and no alibis."

God bless you and thank you for inviting me to be with you on this day of your graduation.

Moral Aspects of the Invasion of Privacy

Great Issues Forum, University of Utah
November 6, 1968

□

Perhaps the foremost question of public morality facing our country today lies within the area of privacy. Other problems, like Vietnam, the cities, crime, and poverty, are difficult to solve, but they are not so much questions of morality as challenges to our will. We know what must be done to solve these problems; the directions we must take are quite clear. The important public problems of poverty and peace, of crime and suffering, raise questions about our will, our determination, or the lack of it. If we have the will to do something, the choice of the means and methods to be used are not really great moral issues.

A great moral issue is raised when a human value is in jeopardy and we do not know how to protect it. The priceless human value of privacy is presently a great moral issue because it is being ignored, denied, eroded, and diminished. It is a great moral issue because we are divided as to its real value, and because we are uncertain as to the means and methods to use in its protection, preservation, and enrichment.

In recent years a revolution has taken place in the technological methods whereby public and private authorities can invade the privacy of an individual. It is true that throughout history public and private authorities in governments, churches, and corporations – in fact, all power structures actively trying to preserve their power – have invaded the privacy of individuals, groups, and other institutions. For example, the merciless invasion of individual privacy by the communist state is perhaps the basis of our deepest antipathy for that political system. But then, churches, too, have ignored the sacred privacy of a person's ultimate beliefs and demeaned his personal dignity by asking questions and probing in an attempt to get him to reveal his inmost thoughts and intimate personal relationships. Corporations and labor unions have secretly monitored the confidential conversations of members and employees.

So, throughout history, institutions have impoverished human personal life, diminished freedom, blighted the spirit, and generally cursed life on earth with fear and humiliation. The barbaric invasions of man's private inward being by institutional surveillance have shattered the walls of privacy, sometimes leaving behind a shambles and the wreckage of one's personal dignity and self-respect.

If all this has been repeated through history, there is now a special devastation exploding the barriers of privacy. It is the revolution in the science of surveillance, the new technology used in invading privacy. Professor Alan F. Westin, of Columbia, in his book *Privacy and Freedom*, describes how modern technology has multiplied the number of invasions, the kinds of invasions, and the thoroughness of these new invasions. He lists these new invasions as "the new means of telephone tapping, electronic eavesdropping, hidden television-eye monitoring, 'truth measurement' by polygraph devices, personality testing for personnel selection, and growing dossiers of personal data about millions of citizens." He then comments: "Some of these accounts of new surveillance technology have gone on to speculate uneasily about future developments in the next decade, from data surveillance by computer systems to drug-aided interrogations and the possibility of brainwave analysis. As examples mount of the uses made of the new technology, worried protests against 'Big Brother' have set alarms ringing along the civic group spectrum from extreme left to radical right. Reflecting this concern, 'invasion of privacy' has become a leading topic in law review articles and social-science journals, as well as the subject of legislative and executive investigations at the state and federal levels and of a growing number of exploratory judicial rulings throughout the country."

In summary, it is submitted that in the remaining years of this twentieth century, no public moral issue will surpass in importance the moral problem of preserving and enlarging the privacy of the individual, of groups, and of institutions. Surely it is true that much of the widespread turmoil in contemporary American public life – protest in universities, dissent in politics, criticism of courts, conflicting personal tastes, and public confusion – is rooted deeply in this problem of privacy. To repeat, the careful balance of privacy, disclosure, and surveillance may well be the single greatest moral issue of this century.

Certainly the size of this great issue diminishes one's ambition to solve it. The most one can hope for is some attempt at clarification. With this more modest goal of clarification, the following will be our outline:

1. To give some meaning to the term "privacy."

2. To point out moral issues involved in some of the various invasions of privacy.

3. To indicate the search for constitutional protection of privacy.

4. To indicate some future directions in defense of privacy.

The Meaning of Privacy

Starting with broad generalizations and then more narrowly defining the concept of privacy, I begin by quoting the former

Dean of the Law School, Daniel J. Dykstra. In his memorable Reynolds Lecture, he said that this area of privacy involves us "with the prying neighbor, the indiscreet associate, the integrity of the home, the sanctity of opinions and thoughts, the right of association, freedom of the press, freedom of speech and religion, and with a vast number of other factors which give dignity and meaning to the life of one man."*

More narrowly, the moral issue of privacy is the difficulty of counterbalancing the need for privacy with the need for disclosure and the occasional need for surveillance. That is, the desire for privacy is never absolute since participation in society is an equally powerful desire. And the value of privacy to an individual or a group may be outweighed by the value of disclosure and social participation.

What then, may be considered as a good definition of privacy? Professor Westin offers this: "Privacy is the claim of individuals, groups, or institutions, to *determine for themselves* when, how, and to what extent information about them is communicated to others." Then he adds this description of privacy: "Viewed in terms of the relation of the individual to social participation, privacy is the voluntary and temporary withdrawal of a person from the general society through physical or psychological means, either in a state of solitude or small group intimacy, or when among larger groups, in a condition of anonymity or reserve."

Before leaving these formal definitions, one might stress the key idea that privacy is something that should only be lost or given up in some voluntary way. The person, the group, or the institution must decide *to what extent* information about them is communicated to others. The essence of the value of privacy, then, is that those who claim it can decide for themselves if any

---

*Daniel Dykstra, "The Right Most Valued by Civilized Man," 1959 Reynolds Lecture, University of Utah.

information, and how much information, may be communicated to others.

So much for definitions. The analysts in philosophy might still press for a clearer meaning of the term "privacy." But privacy is a difficult concept to clarify. It is not difficult to understand the scientific and technological invasions of privacy – at least the methods of these invasions. But to explain our concept of privacy is far more difficult.

Perhaps there are two things we can say about privacy. First, in the manner of the analytical school of philosophy, we can say that privacy is one species of the realm of values. It is something we want and defend, something we find good or important. If we compare it with other values or goods, it seems to fall within that group which are essentially negative goods – that is, those goods which become important when they are not there or are threatened. Liberty is very much like this, and so also is health. It is when we are sick that we really value health, and when we are restricted that we really care about liberty. So, when someone is prying, our privacy becomes important. Other values such as pleasure, beauty, and harmony are more positive, though no easier to define. Pleasure isn't just the absence of pain, nor beauty the absence of ugliness. So also, harmony is something over and above the value of disharmony. Now liberty and health are felt as positive goods, too, but usually just after their absence, or when they are threatened. There is no fine line that divides positive and negative goods, yet privacy may be the clearest example of a negative good. Justice Louis Brandeis's famous description of privacy as "the right to be let alone," while it appears to be empty, is probably most accurate. Privacy is something we want, something we defend. Privacy as such comes from the knowledge or confidence or guarantee that another is not going to do something that will deprive one of his privacy.

The second aspect or characteristic of privacy as goods is that we speak of it as a *right*, and this also makes it conceptually different from other values. Privacy is a *claim right*; that is, it is a right that others do or forbear from doing certain things. A liberty right, on the other hand, is a right to do or forbear from doing something to *one's self*, plus a claim right that others do not interfere. Moreover, privacy is not an absolute right. It is something we voluntarily forfeit in many ways every day for the sake of other goods. Claim rights are rights that can be forfeited. For example, there is an invasion of privacy if a person comes uninvited into one's home, but not if invited in. So, privacy is only one of a number of things we value, a value which has to compete on some occasions with other values such as security and safety.

One last comment about the nature of the value of privacy. It is a simple or pure value. It is sufficient to reply when asked why one does not like invasions of privacy: "I just don't." That is, if one values his privacy, that's an end to it. One simply says, "I don't want the neighbors in my yard, a tap on my phone, my personal diary read, just because I don't." This is a good answer, even if there may be other answers on other occasions. Nor is it necessary for one to value one's right to privacy or one's liberty. You don't have to value a right, in some obvious sense, in order to have a right to it. If one does not value his privacy, he is no less entitled to it as a right.

Our understanding of the concept of privacy might be aided if we say something of its history in human life, and give some examples.

Students of anthropology and sociology contend that privacy as a value derives from man's animal origins, from our evolutionary heritage. While most animals' need for social stimulation is obvious, they also have a need for privacy – temporary individual seclusion or small unit intimacy. H. L. Ratcliffe and R. L. Snyder, in their book *Patterns of Disease, Controlled Populations, and Experimental Design*, report that "studies of crowding in many animals other than rats indicate that disruption of social relationships through overlapping personal distances aggravate all forms of pathology within a group and causes the same disease in animals that overcrowding does in man – high blood pressure, circulatory diseases, and heart disease."

While primitive societies of man always stress social values, and, in some cases, privacy in primitive societies is not greatly observed, the need for individual and group privacy is still virtually universal. Sometimes this is done in an individual's intimate relationships when masks and "distance-setting" are common practices. Concealment of some parts of the body, modesty about natural functions or sexual relations, privacy in household settings, are examples of privacy being sought in virtually all primitive societies.

If privacy is a need in animal life and among contemporary primitive peoples, the crowded cities of modern life greatly intensify such a need. People come to cherish moments of quiet and solitude, the chance to gain some peace of mind. This opportunity for a new perspective, or at least for some reflection and contemplation in achieving personal serenity, is so meaningful in the Orient that one may say that their whole civilization is based upon it.

Moral Issues Involved in Invasions of Privacy

Leaving consideration of the meaning of privacy, we should consider now the moral issues involved when privacy is invaded or when privacy is being eroded and diminished.

The overriding moral problem in all invasions of privacy is the issue of freedom. Privacy-invasion of an individual, a group, or an institution may have almost infinite justifications, such as the need to prevent crime, national security, public morals, or even the need to protect the well-being of the individual whose privacy is invaded as in the case of taking heroin and other drugs. But, in all cases, the invasion of privacy means some loss of freedom. And this loss of freedom usually raises a moral issue.

The moral issue is generally one of balancing the interests of those invaded with those who invade. The problem is to determine whose interests are to have supremacy.

Let us first consider political institutions. In the communist political system, privacy or secrecy is claimed for the regime, but all others under this regime are to live under a searching surveillance. This unfair practice of privacy for government leaders and denial of privacy for all other citizens makes a fair-minded person wonder how such a society can maintain itself against revolution. Recent Czechoslovakian history may illustrate the crass injustice of this unfair balance. It is submitted that, with all the failures in our own democracy, recent political campaigns of exposing all or most of the secret and private actions within our political system are at least not weighted in favor of those in power as they are with fascism or communism.

Consider a value now referred to as "law and order." In dealing with a criminal, the issue is the protection of society, but also the protection of the criminal's right to privacy. How serious is his crime? How great is the harm involved? Sometimes the "little" lawbreaker's privacy is abridged more than the powerful lawbreaker's.

Or consider personnel practices dealing with employment applications. Should a company invade the privacy of an applicant by asking personal questions about attitudes, emotional adjustments, and personal beliefs? There are also invasions of privacy when companies consider students for employment and want to know their grade average or what a teacher may know about something the student has confided. There is no problem if the student consents to his or her grades being disclosed to prospective employers, and a confidence may not be a real issue if our national security is at stake.

There are invasions of privacy in classrooms when microphones are installed by the principal. Here the moral issue may be academic freedom or just the plain dignity of the teacher and the class.

Perhaps the most common unethical invasion of privacy occurs when information given to certain people for a specific purpose is circulated to others to whom it was not intended, such as to credit agencies, survey researchers, welfare agencies, etc.

But of all invasions that raise a profound moral issue, none surpass the ethical questions involved in psychological surveillance – personality and polygraph testing. The heart of the moral issue here is that privacy is invaded without consent; that is, questions are asked which the examinee does not expect, or has not previously consented to answer, questions that were not anticipated when an individual first consented to take the test. Most of these tests raise legitimate questions of privacy. The results of such tests frequently are divulged and misused. This is particularly true when the test results are put in computer banks and used out of context years later. The incompetence of the examiner; the guesswork involved in all personality tests; the freezing of the results for later years; the use of computers to store all the facts, impressions, statements, and opinions of others of every citizen of the United States – all this makes Big Brother look like a poor boy from the country.

The Search for Constitutional Protection of Privacy

I wish to bring the Constitution into the area of privacy because if privacy is a value of the magnitude claimed for it, then, one way or another, the Constitution will be required to be its protector.

When America was founded, our Constitution established a balance among the three values of privacy, disclosure, and surveillance. But this balance was based upon the technological realities then existing. Our Constitution forbade such invasions of privacy as physical entry and eavesdropping. It forbade the then known ways of penetrating the mind through torture and inquisition. We also have several constitutional amendments restricting invasions of the privacy of religion, free speech, free press, peaceful assembly, petition for the redress of grievances, the sanctity of the home, unreasonable searches, and disallowing a person in a criminal case to be a witness against himself. And, with a sweeping declaration on the side of privacy, the Fifth Amendment states that no person is to be deprived of life, liberty, or property without due process of law. Other amendments assure individual protection by giving a right to a speedy trial and an impartial jury, the right to be informed of the nature and the cause of accusation, the right to be confronted by one's accusers, a compulsory process for obtaining witnesses in one's favor, and the right to have assistance of counsel for his defense. These amendments prohibit excessive bail amounts and declare that no man shall be subject to excessive fines or cruel and unusual punishment.

So the framers of our Constitution, drawing heavily from the philosophy of John Locke, made the individual the center of society, freeing him from the kinds of unlimited surveillance used by the kings and lords, churches and guilds, and municipalities of earlier European society.

The before-mentioned references to our Constitution are made because, while there is no direct reference in them to the specific right of privacy, all of the references are now being cited by the courts, in one decision or another, by one judge or another of the Supreme Court, in finding a Constitutional basis for the right to privacy.

There was no protection given by traditional common law to the right of privacy as such. However, the strict and vigorous protection given to a man's property rights, particularly to the sanctity of his home, in effect assured a large measure of privacy in an age when intrusion upon privacy could usually be accomplished only by actual physical violation of one's home. Near the turn of the century, Louis Brandeis and Samuel D. Warren wrote a ground-breaking article entitled "The Right to Privacy" in *Harvard Law Review*, advocating that the courts recognize a separate tort to protect against violation of the right of privacy. It is widely acknowledged that no other article in any legal journal ever had a greater impact on the law or did more to change the law than did this article, in which the authors made the famous statement, "The right most prized by civilized man is the right to be left alone." Although there are still some states in which the right of privacy has not been given overt recognition by the courts and though the manner in which it is enforced among the fifty states varies greatly, today it is a safe generalization that privacy receives protection under the auspices of the law of torts in nearly every jurisdiction in the country.

There are three recent landmark cases in which the Supreme Court has made important decisions that will help chart the future development in the area of privacy. In the case of *Time, Inc.* v. *Hill* (1967), the Court ruled that when privacy is placed against another deep-rooted value of our society – the right to a free press – the right of privacy must be limited. The Hill decision indicates that in some possible clashes between the press and privacy, the latter will prevail. For example, when a newspaper or television intrudes uninvited upon the genuine privacy of a person's home, or where the plaintiff can prove that the defamatory publication of matters private to himself, but for his involuntarily becoming newsworthy, where the defamation was known by the disseminator to be false, the right to privacy will prevail. At most, then, Hill is only a partial limitation of the state-created right of privacy in light of the overriding interest of the First Amendment protecting freedom of the press.

A more difficult problem, from the point of view of constitutional protection, was presented in *Griswold* v. *Connecticut* (1965). In that case, rather than a state-created right of privacy being found in conflict with a federal constitutional value, the Court was asked to extend the protection of the federal Constitution to the area of marital privacy into which the state had sought to intrude. Connecticut had a statute forbidding the sale or use of contraceptives, and in this case a doctor who sought to prescribe contraceptives for married persons was permitted to raise the right of those married persons to be free of state intrusion and regulation in the most intimate and private of places – the marital bed. The theoretical difficulty presented by the case stems from the fact that our Constitution is a written one, and unless one finds in it some verbal formula which can be used to cover the particular case before the Court it is difficult to say that there is a constitutional question at all.

This case clearly delineates the markedly different and conflicting constitutional theories that are employed by the various justices. The Court had a very difficult time deciding this case. To all the judges, the Connecticut law was abhorrent – the problem was in deciding whether it was unconstitutional, and if so, why. Justice William O. Douglas wrote for the Court that in his view all of the Bill of Rights – at least the first eight amendments – are incorporated in the due process clause of the Fourteenth. By examining the various particular provisions of the Bill of Rights, he concluded that implicit in them was a constitutional protection of the right of privacy as such. In his words, privacy falls within the "penumbra" of the Constitution, that area of unspoken but implicit and fundamental rights protected by the Constitution. Justice John Harlan, on the other hand, castigated the Court for attempting to rely either upon the specific words of the Bill of Rights to find a protection for privacy, or upon the strict doctrine of incorporation. But he found the notion of due process itself sufficiently embracive to require this Connecticut law to be struck down. Justice Arthur J. Goldberg, joined by Warren and William J. Brennan (all three of whom had also joined Douglas) felt that in addition to the specific provisions of the Constitution, the notion of rights reserved to the people in the Ninth Amendment was sufficient for finding a constitutional basis for protecting privacy. Justice Byron R. White, without drawing such sharp theoretical distinctions as had Harlan, and more by reliance upon past decisions of the Court, also found the due process clause the proper receptacle in the Constitution for the right of privacy. Justices Hugo L. Black and Potter Stewart, the two members of the Court for whom the explicit words of the Constitution are most binding, felt that abhorrent as the Connecticut law was, there simply was no constitutional base for striking it down as an invasion of privacy. In sum, therefore, though the Court was unable to agree upon a single theory of the Constitution, in this case, however, it clearly ruled that privacy as such is protected by the federal Constitution from state intrusion.

What the limits of the doctrine expounded in *Griswold* v. *Connecticut*, will be, it is impossible to say. Do unmarried persons also have a right to use contraceptives free of state regulations? Does Griswold spell the ultimate demise of state laws forbidding sodomy or other marital sexual practices? And there are other broader questions, all of them as yet unanswered. At base the fundamental problem is to what extent consenting adults in private must be left free of state control and regulation. It is agreed by all (or nearly all) that the state has a special interest in juveniles, that it can legitimately prevent one person from hurting another, that it can properly prevent a person from injuring himself (as by taking heroin), and that it has relatively broad powers in the regulation of public conduct and morality. If there is any particular area, however, in which the moral philosopher can be of great aid in guiding society toward a correct understanding of the proper balance between the public and private, it is in hammering out a solution to the question of just how far the state is permitted to intrude into the purely private, consensual, nonharmful activities of adults. Professor H. L. A. Hart has studied this issue at length in his book, *Law, Liberty, and Morality*. He discusses the problem of whether the state has any legitimate interest in the regulation of morality as such, and he answers with an unequivocal and resounding no.

The third of the three recent landmark cases on privacy deals with the aspect of the question of the right of privacy which in practical terms is the most insistent and pregnant. The general problem is created by the fact that in recent years the burgeoning sophistication in electronics has permitted invasions into privacy never dreamed of a few short years ago. We read almost daily now of bugging and wiretapping, and the technical sophistication of the devices used is quite staggering. Parabolic microphones can pick up a conversation a hundred yards away without the aid of any wires or any instrument on the spot. Transmitters can be made so small that they can be concealed in a martini olive which the eavesdropper places in his glass as he talks to you (while his cohort picks up and transcribes the conversation in another room). The possibility for eavesdropping and wiretapping is almost endless, and we know with certainty that there is a billion-dollar business in this country today engaged in using these devices to steal industrial secrets as well as protect against the stealing of state secrets, and to gather information for blackmail as well as to trap criminals. The question is, what should the law do about it? In the past the Court has been rather timid in this area, again because the Constitution was written at a time when this was not a problem and thus is not directly addressed.

The Fourth Amendment says that "the right of the people to be secure in their persons, houses, papers, and effects, against unreasonable searches and seizures, shall not be violated. . . . " It does not speak of privacy, nor of "conversations" or "acts." In the past, because of the tradition of the common law as well as the explicit wording of the Fourth Amendment, the Court had ruled that the Constitution gave protection to persons against wiretapping or electronic eavesdropping only when there was an actual physical trespassory intrusion into the private property of the person, such as when a microphone was placed in the house or a spike mike driven into the wall. One does not have to enter a house to tap a telephone, however, and no longer must one commit trespass to eavesdrop. Furthermore, many persons speak of private matters in places other than their home, and if trespass were to be required before the Constitution could be invoked, such persons would receive no protection.

Last term, in *Katz* v. *U.S.* (1967), the Court abandoned the trespass test and ruled at last that the Constitution "protects persons not places." It held that when the conversants intended their conversation to be private and had a reasonable basis for expecting privacy, then it is unconstitutional (absent a warrant, the requirements for which the Court indicated at some length in the opinion) to eavesdrop upon that conversation wherever it takes place. This is a landmark decision, and though it leaves many questions unanswered, it marks a significant victory for the advocates of greater protection of privacy. The greatest problems to be solved under this case concern the official use of wiretapping or eavesdropping to protect the national security or to detect or prevent crime. Justice White's concurrence directs itself explicitly to these problems. The Omnibus Crime Prevention and Safe Streets Act, passed this summer by Congress, contains provisions empowering the federal government to engage in wiretapping and eavesdropping under court supervision but without notice to the person being tapped or bugged. It will be soon tested in the Supreme Court for its constitutionality, and once again the Court will have to balance two fundamental rights – the right of each individual to his privacy against society's need to protect itself against crime and treason.

Some Future Directions in Defense of Privacy

The future of privacy is not hopeless. Several promising tendencies are apparent. More people are talking about the value of privacy. This should be encouraged. When privacy and disclosure are balanced, people are alerted to many unwarranted invasions. As science and technology have dissolved the walls and windows, science and technology can replace them with new systems of protection, such as tap-proof waves attached to telephones, scramblers, scribblers, electronic jamming systems, controlling secret codes for unlocking computers, etc. Self-restraint and self-imposed regulations by groups who use personality tests, polygraphs, and physical surveillance – that is, high professional standards discussed and self-imposed – will do much to avoid loss of privacy. When these are inadequate, laws may be necessary to protect the public and private groups from profit-seekers, insensitive researchers, criminal elements, etc.

Above all, since this whole concept of privacy – its value, its invasions – is relatively new, the time has come for widespread discussion. Many violations of privacy, such as churches asking personal questions about one's beliefs, over-zealous government investigators, businesses prying into personality problems – if these and a thousand more invasions of privacy were discussed, privacy would come more and more to be equated with freedom, which is surely the greatest value of our civilization.

I leave the current issue of medical ethics relating to euthanasia. That too is an issue of freedom.

Are Moral Values Absolute?

Great Issues in Philosophy, University of Utah
March 28, 1956

□

The general question we are asking is whether our moral values are determined by some objective standard, or whether our moral values are relative – that is, determined by private opinion or by the customs of a particular group.

Are moral values based upon what *is* right, or upon what is *thought* to be right? Are our moral values relative to time, place, and circumstances? Or, are they objectively true regardless of the time, place, or circumstance?

Is there some intermediate position between moral absolutism and moral relativity? Is there perhaps a standard that is relatively absolute, or a standard that is not absolutely relative, or a standard that is absolutely absolute? The conclusion of this paper is that there is an intermediate position between absolutism and relativity, there is a standard for our moral values that is relatively absolute.

All of us, like it or not, are the products of this Greco-Christian civilization in which we live. One might say that this university represents the Greek tradition in that here is the life of reason, of science. On the other hand, our religion, the Christian tradition, is largely an emotional element in our lives. The result of trying to join these two traditions, reason and religion, creates inevitable tension. Reason favors relativity and religion favors absolutism. So we divide our absolutes and our relativities, and choose one or the other depending on the day of the week. We reserve Sundays for our absolutes and the other days for our relativities.

Institutionally, the church assumes jurisdiction over absolutes, and the university is at home with our relativities. It is frequently uncomfortable to attend both of these great institutions within one week. Students sometimes find it better to give the university and relativities a fling, and later, when swamped by the problems of raising children, revert to the absolutes of their religious training. Religious leaders understand this cycle of conflict and reconciliation and are not too disturbed when the sophomore declares war on the absolutes. University teachers also understand this cycle and are never under the illusion that relativities are permanent.

According to religion, our moral laws issue from the will of God, and there is only one God ruling the universe. He is rational and consistent and, therefore, His commands are the same everywhere for all people in all ages. Such a monotheistic religion entails an absolute morality, unless, that is, one assumes that God is finite, in which case His moral laws may not be absolute.

A university, on the other hand, generally assumes that man is the author of our moral values. Moral customs issue from the will of man. Since there are wide varieties of men, cultures, and moral values, moral relativity is a natural conclusion.

Some students of both religion and science are able to compartmentalize their relativities and absolutes, others live with the tension of conflict, while still others grow weary of the struggle and settle into one camp or the other in peace—peace, that is, if with absolutes, but unceasing disturbance if with the relativities.

It is the general purpose of this paper to work out a compromise between science and religion as they affect our moral values. This can be done by establishing our moral values upon an empirical, factual basis, and then showing that the moral values thus established have always been the supreme moral values taught by religion. In other words, our method will be that of a radical empiricist. The conclusion of this method will be a morality that is in complete harmony with the teaching of religion.

Let us turn first to the method of the radical empiricist or logical positivist. Briefly, this method holds that no word has cognitive meaning unless it refers to something capable (at least theoretically) of being experienced. All concepts are derived from experience, and they must therefore refer to the experience from which they were derived. So, a word or sentence which refers to an entity which could not conceivably be experienced is meaningless. The word "ought" is such a meaningless word. There is no referent or entity corresponding to such a word. And yet this is the key word in the study of morals. Morality means that which men ought to do. We overcome this difficulty by holding that morality is not an end in itself, but refers to an actual situation, a goal or purpose. According to Aristotle, the utilitarians, and many others, the end of moral conduct is happiness. This end or goal of life is likewise held by religion. Jesus prefaced his moral values by saying happy or blessed are you if you do this or that. One sacred scripture says directly: "Man is that he might have joy."

Now, if morality is meant to increase human happiness, then we can avoid a meaningless categorical "ought," and substitute a hypothetical "ought" which is meaningful. Morality now declares: "If you want to be happy, then you ought, for example, to make others happy." The "ought" in this sentence is not without a referent. One could change all hypothetical "ought" sentences to "is" sentences. Thus: "Making others happy is a way to be happy yourself."

This empirical method is important, for we are attempting to establish a principle of morality that is universal – true for all men everywhere. If such a principle is grounded in fact it can be established as a proposition that is true. If it is subject to the same tests that apply to other scientific investigations, then it can be determined to be true or false. If true, it is universal for all men, and moral relativity is false.

Having explained our method, we shall turn now to our analysis of moral values and determine from this analysis whether our empirical method will apply.

We have said with the utilitarians and others that morality is the increase of human happiness. We also hold with the utilitarians that the only sure way to test a moral value is by the results it produces. We think Kant's moral test of a good will is helpful in determining a good man, but a good act is really tested by the consequences. This was the method Christ suggested for our moral values. He said, "by their fruit ye shall know them." It is also thoroughly scientific.

We must divert now from our main argument for a few moments to define what we mean by the word "happiness" and the word "moral," since we have said that morality is the increase of human happiness.

What do we mean by happiness? The term "happiness" is difficult to define. Of itself, it is a mere abstraction. Men do not seek happiness, they seek those activities that make them happy. Perhaps, as Aristotle said, happiness is a by-product of a challenging and successful activity. In any case, it is a matter of fact that we are sometimes happy and sometimes depressed, and that we know when we are in one state or the other. It is factual that we are sometimes elated, full of joy, and cheerful. And it is a fact that some activities produce more happiness than others. It is perhaps not possible to prove why some satisfactions contribute more to happiness.

This much is clear, however: the utilitarians were dead wrong in holding that happiness is an aggregate of pleasures. They were enamored of the quantitative method of science. The larger the quantity of pleasures, the larger the quantity of happiness, like pouring water in a bucket. The facts are against this. Some people with few satisfactions are happier than those with many.

But this is also true: some satisfactions, such as those of the mind (the search for truth or the creation of beauty), contribute more to happiness than do the satisfactions of simple physical pleasures. It is important to see that while basic physical satisfactions – food, sex, drink, wealth, home, occupation, etc. – are conditions important to produce a happy life – it is also true that mental and spiritual satisfactions contribute far more to our happiness. It is important to see this, because our case is that morality, as morality, is defined in terms of these higher satisfactions.

What do we mean by the word "moral"? "Moral values" may be defined in a broad or in a narrow sense. John Dewey gave a broad meaning to the term. He held that morality covers all the rules of conduct, that there is "a better or worse" quality about all our activities. Morality means carrying out every human activity in the best way it can be carried out. Immorality means a worse way, rather than a better way, of carrying out some activity. Dewey wrote: "Morals have to do with all activity into which alternatives enter. For wherever they enter a difference between better and worse arises. . . . Potentially therefore every and any act is within the scope of morals, being a candidate for possible judgment with respect to its better or worse quality."

Such a broad view fails to distinguish between moral values and esthetic values or economic values. I believe there is a better or worse way of painting a picture or carrying out a business transaction that is quite independent of its moral quality. A work of art may be judged esthetically excellent but morally objectionable, or morally edifying but artistically worthless. A business transaction may be carried out well yet be immoral, or it may be moral but carried out poorly.

So, what do we mean by morality? What are moral values? Morality and moral values have to do with the mutual relations of human beings. I agree with Professor W. T. Stace of Princeton who gave a narrower definition of morality than Professor Dewey. He wrote that "morality includes only those universally applicable rules of conduct which seek to control the relations of men with one another." That is, morality does not cover all the rules of conduct. It does not cover dietary regulations or rules of business efficiency. I believe it is possible to isolate from human activities those that are uniquely moral. For one thing, morality arises out of our social environment. Our moral codes are the rules which govern our social environment. It is this common social environment that creates universal needs of men, some of which are moral, some of which are not moral but are dietary or esthetic or something else.

The interpretation of morality that we are assuming in this discussion is taken from the utilitarians. They held that moral actions are not right or wrong in themselves, but that they are moral or immoral depending upon the consequences. A good act produces good consequences, a poor one bad consequences. They further held that good or bad consequences were determined by what they called "human happiness." In this discussion, we have agreed with the utilitarian idea that morality is a means to human happiness, and immorality is a means to unhappiness. Right moral values increase human happiness; wrong moral values increase human unhappiness. While it is difficult to define what we mean by happiness and its increase or decrease, it is also true that most of us know what it means to be happy and when this happiness is increased or decreased.

We come now to two characteristics of any moral act, besides its increase in human happiness. First, it must be unselfish. Second, it must be fair or just.

An act, as Professor Stace pointed out, may increase human happiness but not be moral unless it also has these qualities of altruism and justice. He illustrated it this way: If one is able to distribute ten units of happiness but gives them all to himself, he has increased human happiness, but this is not a moral act. It is a selfish act. Also, if one is able to distribute ten units of happiness to other people (not including himself), and gives all ten to one person, this is not a moral act for it is lacking in justice.

How should one treat one's self to be moral? By considering himself as one, no more and no less. If he asks for special privileges, he moves away from a moral act to a selfish one. However, he may treat himself as well as any other. Jesus put it that we are entitled to love ourselves as much as we love our neighbor. We are to do unto others as we would be done by. The Golden Rule thus satisfies the demand that a moral act be unselfish and also be just or fair.

In substance, we may say that morality is unselfishness, and that immorality is selfishness.

The question now is this: Is this altruism, this unselfishness, this regard for another's welfare, *universal?*

I believe that it is. It is highly developed among some peoples, and poorly developed in others. All moral codes, however well or poorly formulated, state the moral law of altruism in one way or another. After all, morality is nothing but the necessary relations of human beings. It is the rule or set of rules which govern these relations. These rules or practices are based upon mutual consideration. Therefore, the idea of morality or the essence of morality is basically the same everywhere. In some groups it is limited to the family. Others enlarge it to include the neighborhood. Christians enlarge the practice of altruism to include all of humanity.

But this I believe is true: that altruism—unselfishness—is universal, however small or ill-defined it may be. It may be limited to a man for a maid. Then it grows with some to include the children, the tribe, or perhaps the whole human race. But it is present in some degree in all normal human beings, and is therefore universal.

What basis is there for a universal morality? It is this: All men have a common psychological structure. Plato described it as the soul having three parts. He said a man is happy if his soul is healthy. If his reason is in control of the lower two parts (the passions and appetites) he is happy, even if the consequences do not bring external rewards. Plato is affirming one condition for happiness, that a man cannot be happy if he does not control his passions. But the Christians held much more. They have said that a man cannot be happy if he is selfish. Plato did have this accurate insight, namely, that morality grows out of human nature itself. It lies in the structure which is common to all human beings. Plato is saying further that morality means the proper and natural functioning of human personality.

Professor W. T. Stace held, and I agree with him, that there is a common structure of our human nature. Man is a social animal, and is made happy by the happiness of others. Thus, moral values are relatively absolute since they are based on the structure of all normal human nature.

Commitment to Beauty

Utah Meeting of the Newcomen Society, Salt Lake City, Utah
March 26, 1981

□

As I started to write this brief history of the O. C. Tanner Company, I was reminded of a law class at Harvard taught by Samuel Williston, the great authority on contract law. He concluded our discussion of a particular case in a somewhat reflective mood by commenting, "Yes, this was the case of a self-made man who was proud of his maker."

The problem of modesty in relating one's achievements over the years is the difficulty of trying to be accurate, both in our overstatements and in our understatements. It is the belief of the Newcomen Society that a collection of these histories will add meaning to our free enterprise system, and, perhaps more, that they may help to make clear the human value of our culture, if not indeed add something to the understanding of our civilization.

The Search for Beauty

In essence, the history of the O. C. Tanner Company is a search for beauty. One might say the search began in 1927. It was then a search by a high school senior class ring committee, as they were surrounding a table covered with several of my sample class rings. The students wanted to find the most beautiful ring to adopt as their class ring. Then, years later, there was a search by corporate executives. They were selecting a design that might be appropriate as a beautiful corporate emblem, not only to effectively express the meaning of their own corporation, but a design that its employees would be pleased and proud to wear because of its corporate meaning, and also because of its own intrinsic beauty.

Yet the story is not quite so simply stated. Like the various designs of automobiles, Tanner Company has spent years in creating various designs, changing a line here, a curve there, a sharp edge or a folding curve, then a diamond added, or several of them, each variation hopefully adding something to the beauty of a piece of jewelry people like to see and wear.

It may seem a little extreme to compare the changing designs of new model cars with new jewelry designs, but such an effort is not so greatly different. Dozens of Tanner artists work daily from one suggestion to another. On these occasions competitors also submitted their best products, and decisions were made after careful discrimination and judgment. No one knows, of course, whether the final selections were the most beautiful, for beauty itself is one of the most elusive of all human values, its criteria difficult to set and justify.

Yet Plato expressed something profoundly meaningful when he at times placed beauty even above the values of truth and goodness. In any case, beauty does have some objective guidelines, such as the qualities of harmony, variety, proportion, unity and balance. Yet even these descriptions are quite inadequate. Beauty is a quality or property that is indefinable and ineffable; some say that the very idea of beauty is simply a meaningless abstraction; and it is common to argue that judgments of beauty are nothing more than expressions of subjective taste. People do, in fact, like or dislike some pattern or design; they do find some objects more pleasing than others—objects that give more joy and satisfaction not because they are more useful, but because they incite a stronger response to the basic human sensitivity to beauty.

For the Tanner Company, attempting to create the most beautiful designs, this has become a way of life, a basis for our success if not our survival. Dozens of talented Tanner artists examine with utmost care the numerous designs that have been proposed for a specific emblem, and, finally, after days or weeks of creative work and judgment, a selection of a half-dozen or more designs is sent to our prospective customers, corporations whose officials will make the final decisions on emblems which millions of employees will proudly wear.

Parenthetically, if I may be permitted a personal comment, beauty has become my own life's supreme value. At times I shift in my various values, but frequently I give a slight margin of preference to beauty, so that at times my commitment to beauty is equal to or even slightly greater than that to the values of truth and goodness; for, in the final analysis, I think beauty gives more joy to more people, over a longer period of time, than any other human value.

So, admitting to self-interest, I have loved the work of my company, and I feel a satisfaction that in its history there has been some confirmation that beauty is the supreme, or nearly the supreme, value in human life. With this standard, the O. C. Tanner Company has become the world's largest manufacturing firm in its specialty. And though it is true that in a free, competitive market, the three major means of winning a customer are generally by tests of the lowest price, the finest service, and the best quality, there is also a fourth test of authenticity. It is the manufacture of a product that shows not only expert craftsmanship, but also care for every detail in the way it is manufactured.

A Modest Beginning

Let me turn now to a few historical facts about the O. C. Tanner Company. Like so many other companies, the beginning of the firm was modest enough. It was a beginning as near zero as possible. It is not uncommon for many American companies to start at zero – no capital, no customers, not even the necessary skills and equipment to start a company; just a dream of an idea to try out in the business world. So, in relating ever so briefly the history of the Tanner Company, especially the facts of a humble beginning, no claim is made for any special distinction. Here then, are a few background events from which the Tanner Company finally emerged.

In 1921, when I was registering at the age of 17 as a freshman at the University of Utah, I needed a job and found work taking care of about a dozen coal furnaces in large homes near the university. I soon got tired of work where I felt that nothing new might be learned and decided to seek a job from among the affluent people whose furnaces I cared for. The first person I approached was a jeweler. He gave me a job as a salesman in his jewelry store. The hours of work were from 1:00 P.M. to 7:00 P.M. on the five weekdays, and from 8:00 A.M. to 7:00 P.M. on Saturday. Pay for the whole week was a modest $7.00; but I realized that I knew nothing about jewelry and $7.00 could pay my way at the university. A university education was my great ambition. In other words, I did not start in the field of jewelry to make it my life's work, but just as a job to pay expenses while attending the university. Yet it was this beginning as a clerk in a jewelry store that years later resulted in the creation of the Tanner Company. Other significant events in the company's early history followed.

In 1927, six years after my first job as a jewelry clerk, I started my own jewelry company – first, as a sales representative, selling high school class rings and graduation pins. Soon, I ventured to manufacture some of the pins and rings I was selling. I vividly recall the strong pressure that I felt to reach for better quality and delivery, and to attain this I felt compelled to try manufacturing on my own. My first shop was in the basement of my mother's home. There were two basement windows which gave fairly good light. I obtained some 2″ by 12″ boards for the first workbench, bought a polishing motor, some steel saw blades, pliers, some gold plating equipment, etc.—altogether about $500 worth of materials. Our dies were cut in another shop. I began with one employee and our prior experience as manufacturing jewelers was, to say the least, less than modest.

For example, one of our many first experiences in trying to break into the manufacturing jewelry industry was our experiment in building a striking or drop hammer. In a junk yard on the west side of the city we found a railroad car axle made of solid steel. We sawed about two feet off of this axle, which was heavy enough to use as a drop hammer. But because of the weight of such a solid piece of steel, when it was raised by pulleys and dropped to drive the gold into the die, it made such a noise that the neighbors complained of the hammer rattling the dishes in their cupboards. So we moved our shop to the basement of a large theatre building in the downtown area. Then we had a new complaint. The noise from the drop hammers (we now had three of them) disturbed the movie theatre audience upstairs. We tried, with some success, to muffle the noise, but finally gave up; and in the year 1956 we built the first, though small, building at our present location at 1930 South State Street. This original new building was 90′ x 90′—equal to 8,100 square feet. With time, improved technology, devoted employees, and new customers, we moved ahead financially and were able to invest our capital in several additions to the building until now, when this last addition is completed, we will have 200,000 square feet. I might add a cheerful note about drop hammers. Today we have 30 hydraulic and pneumatic hammers, each with pressure from 100 to 500 tons, and each incredibly quiet in its operation. One other comparison, which I must reluctantly mention because it is essential to the story: In 1927, that first year of basement manufacturing, my annual sales volume was about $5,000. Today, in 1981, it is about $100 million.

This growth progression involved two different activities: first, developing a sales department; and second, developing our manufacturing capability. My method of operation in those first years was to travel to big cities, such as Chicago and New York, and with samples from my shop, make the sale, get the order signed, and then literally rush back to Salt Lake to solve the particular problems of how to manufacture the product that would fill the order. Each new order was a little different from the previous one. Thus, the Tanner Company, like many other companies, has been a two-sided enterprise—one of selling and one of manufacturing. I was completely involved with both sides, and frankness compels me to add that no one could have had more to learn, especially on the side of manufacturing. I found selling to be not particularly difficult; but dealing with people completely untrained in jewelry manufacturing, as all of them were, teaching them, being concerned about their goodwill, obtaining capital to purchase equipment—all this was indeed a complex undertaking. Today things are a little different. We now have more than one thousand employees, most of whom are skilled craftsmen.

I may be pardoned if I mention two or three very early memories, memories that are still quite vivid. On one occasion, near the beginning, I was unable to borrow funds which I needed to make a sales trip. With every possible source of a loan exhausted, I took my wife's diamond ring—with her consent, of course—and pawned it in a pawn shop. I could not help feeling very self-conscious in such a transaction, and the loan on the ring was humiliatingly small, at least it seemed so to me. I am pleased to report that later I was able to redeem the ring, and she is wearing it tonight.

Nothing special can be claimed for the modesty of these

first beginnings. But later on, when the company began to grow, other severe problems surfaced, some of them caused by worried competitors. For example, as we became a serious contender for our type of business, a large competitor hired away my sales manager, presumably as a salesman, but in fact it was an attempt to ruin my company. This was to be done by having this former sales manager, who was acquainted with all our people, first hire away the Tanner Company salesmen, and then hire our artists, whom I had sent east years before to be trained at my expense. He was successful in inducing both salesmen and artists to join my competitor. Then this competitor attempted to hire away our die cutters. Because these craftsmen were crucial to my business, I appealed to the Federal Trade Commission to invoke the Fair Trade Practices Act, and won my case. This is now a case of record in the law books.

I relate this event as one of those serious risks that affects one's survival in the business world. Risks are countless in all of human life, and the free enterprise system has a substantial share.

In these first years of history, it is both difficult and perhaps unnecessary to name all of my very first employees; but because "no man is an island," especially in business, I pay tribute to those who first joined me. They must have had a great deal of faith to join their lives with one who really had nothing to go on except faith in the future and a firm determination.

Al Warren was my first associate. He was to do the manufacturing and I was to do the selling. After a few months he said it was too lonely working all by himself, so he quit and went back to his old job. Art Schumann, an engraver, allowed me to move my equipment to the basement of his mother's home for a short time, but within days his mother objected to the noise. I then moved to my own mother's basement. My mother seemed to have infinite patience. I was aware that she hoped I would make enough money to attend the university as soon as possible. Pearse Labrum was my first employee, and though without experience, he was persistent. Pearse is still with me and has become an exceptionally skillful craftsman. He and Newel Barlow each owned a five percent interest in the company but later sold their interest back to the company.

In 1937, I hired my nephew, Norman Tanner, to help me sell high school rings and pins. I liked him as a personable young man. When he left for military service after Pearl Harbor, he had a ten percent interest in the business. Upon his return in the fall of 1945, to encourage him to give the business his best efforts, I gave him an additional ten percent and a contract that would, over 15 years, allow him to increase his share of ownership to thirty-five percent. By 1961, he owned thirty-five percent of the stock of the company; otherwise, substantially all of the ownership of the business has remained in my immediate family. Norman has traveled widely as a salesman, and some who read this Newcomen address may possibly recall his visit to their companies.

As I look back, I may have created a company that is in some respects a little uncommon. For instance, there are a total of twenty-five stockholders in the company, including our children and grandchildren, and none has paid money for the stock he or she owns. My method of getting working capital was to put back into the company every penny of profit. Finally, over many years, and I repeat, many years, the company's assets have grown from the $500 I mentioned in its first year, to now over $50 million. Only in recent years has the company paid dividends.

While I have made almost all the worrisome and unpleasant decisions of company management over the past fifty-four years, this burden has been made easier by my constant practice of discussing business problems with my associates. I have found and made good friends among my company's management personnel. One can easily understand—at least it is easy for me to understand—that I have enjoyed my role as the creator of my company. Nothing has been more rewarding than my personal relations with my associates. I have come to love the people with whom I work. Presently, Don Ostler is the president of the company, and this year I gave him my title as chief executive officer, while I retained the title of board chairman. He is, by every standard, a gentle and brilliant executive. Such qualities are deeply a part of other top executives, Lenny Hilton, Lowell Benson, Bill Paul and others. And also, now retired, Sargent Streeper, a man of sterling qualities.

Our Discovery

I turn now to a discovery of the O. C. Tanner Company. It greatly changed our history and came about in our realization that, while jewelry was a part of the life of high school graduates and fraternal orders, almost no jewelry was used in the life of American industry. With this awareness, we decided to try to sell industrial leaders on the idea of giving an award of a beautiful piece of jewelry to employees of long service. Such emblematic jewelry would be in the form of a tie tac, tie bar, cuff links, bracelets, brooches, necklaces, rings, etc. We also placed the corporate logo on practical gifts, such as watches, clocks, barometers, and leather goods. At first, the idea of a length-of-service emblem wasn't easy to sell. Prior to the Great Depression few such emblems were used. We became pioneers in this field. Some emblems were presented by a few utility companies, but we can accurately claim that the Tanner Company was the main pioneer of manufacturing and distributing industrial recognition service emblems. Soon our competitors were everywhere, and today service award emblems are quite common. Manufacturing service emblems is now about ninety percent of my company's business. Some years ago we gave up the manufacturing of high school and college jewelry and devoted nearly all our attention to manufacturing emblems for industry.

The main value of a service emblem is improvement in employee morale. A service emblem is an award of honor, a tangible recognition, presented to an individual with company executives participating. It is not a *reward*, like fringe benefits such as paid holidays, retirement funding, sick leave, etc. Rather, it is an *award* of distinction, to be worn by employees, and is also something tangible and beautiful to be enjoyed by an employee's family and friends.

I sometimes reflect that O. C. Tanner Company's work, expressed in symbolic terms, is that of putting a drop of oil on the bearings of the free enterprise system. It helps companies run a little more smoothly, with a little less friction, cultivating a more friendly environment where people work.

In essence, the most important thing we sell is not just a piece of jewelry, but friendly and beautiful occasions that are memorable—a bit of happiness where the giver may be even more pleased than the one who receives.

One could say we sell two values, the value of beauty and the value of kindness. We supply the beauty, and our customers supply the kindness. This kindness is a company's willingness to recognize, with dignity, an individual for what he or she has given to that company. After all, giving the productive years of one's life, the daylight hours of each working day, is the ultimate that an individual may give to any company. Saying a sincere and dignified "thank you" with a beautiful gold emblem is really a priceless opportunity for good management.

While our company does not solve any of the usual problems of employer-employee relations, in the presentation of a gold recognition award we are instrumental in bringing about a situation—one might say, a few moments of sunshine—wherein an individual is remembered for his or her years of service. Each year about three million Tanner emblems are awarded to employees of American industry.

The Search for a Company's Durability

Sometimes, in this beautiful valley of the Great Salt Lake, I have compared the craftsmanship of our company with the care for detail that watchmakers achieve who live in the Swiss Alps. So I have dreamed and planned for the perpetuity of the O. C. Tanner Company. I greatly hope it may endure for many, many years.

It has been said by many who visit our plant here in Salt Lake City that we have the most beautiful factory in America. This may well be an exaggeration, but I would like to make our company a friendly place to work. I have come to realize, as many will agree, that there is one sure and successful way to deal with people in our free enterprise system, and that way is the application of the Golden Rule. A company's people know soon enough whether there is success or failure in the daily practice of the Golden Rule.

Our company has a policy of close association with our people. We regularly meet to freely discuss wages, fringe benefits, plans for the improvement of our company to maintain its place as a good national competitor, etc. To insure that all may participate, we hold three meetings each year when all employees are in attendance, and where unsigned suggestions, requests, and criticisms are read, to which management responds. We believe in a situation of opinions and ideas freely expressed.

For nearly all of its years, our company has had a jewelry store. After several different locations, we now have, again to immodestly repeat, what many say is the most beautiful jewelry store in America, located across the street from the Hotel Utah.

Part of a company's planning for perpetuity is helped by the men and women who are selected to be members of its board of directors. With pardonable pride, I wish to list what I regard as a blue-ribbon Board of Directors of the O. C. Tanner Company:

O. Don Ostler	President and Chief Executive Officer
Norman C. Tanner	Stockholder

O. Meredith Wilson	President Emeritus of the University of Oregon and the University of Minnesota, and President Emeritus of the Center for the Study of Behavioral Sciences at Stanford
Victor L. Brown	Presiding Bishop of the Church of Jesus Christ of Latter-day Saints
Roy W. Simmons	President of Zions First National Bank
Carolyn T. Irish	A graduate with distinction from the University of Michigan and Oxford University (she is also my daughter)
Dallin H. Oaks	Former President of Brigham Young University

As mentioned above, I am Chairman of the Board.

A Problem and Its Opportunity

One problem that faces those in the tradition of the Newcomen Society is what should be done with one small margin of its success, the share of profit a company is allowed to deduct from corporate taxes if it gives for charitable or educational purposes. In a strict sense, the profits of a company belong to its stockholders; but in a larger sense, every company is a product of the free enterprise system. And this whole free enterprise system is always under pressure, being tested in the crucible of long-term public opinion, there to be publicly supported and approved, or there to be publicly criticized and disapproved. This long-range goodwill is of importance to stockholders. Industry must help to ensure that free enterprise stays healthy and strong, as it will only if it has broad public support.

I will not speak for other companies. I know that making gifts is a delicate matter, generally confined to the mind and heart of the giver, but I can affirm the ancient wisdom that it is more blessed to give than to receive. In my company the guidelines for giving are decided on the basis of what will bring the greatest joy to the largest number of people; joys that are almost universal to human nature, such as are found in fountains, theatres, libraries, parks, lectureships, and the publication of rare documents.

At the beginning of this paper I mentioned the problem of modesty, and I appeal now for your tolerance as I refer to an educational project that I prize above the others with which I have been associated. It is the Tanner Lectures on Human Values, given each year at six great universities: Cambridge, Harvard, Oxford, Michigan, Stanford, and the University of Utah. Each university selects its own lecturer – a scholar, scientist, or public leader of international reputation and high recognition. These lectures are published in an annual volume and made available to universities, libraries, and the general reader throughout the world. The presidents, or in the case of Oxford and Cambridge, their counterparts, convene to review the program of the past year and plan for possible improvements in the future. Additional universities, up to four, may be added on a one-year basis. While only four years old, the lectureship venture has become widely recognized as one of the world's most prestigious.

Sterling M. McMurrin, former United States Commissioner of Education and now director of the Tanner Lectures, says of them: "In a remarkably brief time the Tanner Lectures on Human Values have achieved international recognition as occasions for major statements on the most fundamental human concerns by philosophers, scientists and statesmen of world stature. The eventual impact of these published lectures is quite beyond estimate. Already they are enriching the thought and knowledge not only of America, but of those other nations where they are delivered, and eventually we may expect they will affect at least the entire English-speaking world." He then adds: "I am proud to say that the Tanner Lectures on Human Values have been funded fully, generously and in perpetuity by an endowment from the resources of the O. C. Tanner Company."

The Greatness of our Civilization

I hold with some deep conviction, the following two propositions:

First, that of the three great freedoms of mankind – political, economic, and intellectual (and by intellectual freedom I mean the freedoms of speech, press, assembly, worship, artistic expression, etc.) – that of these three different kinds of freedom, the third, intellectual, is the most important of all our freedoms.

Second, that economic freedom – our free enterprise system – is mankind's best defense of our intellectual freedom. Put negatively, if economic freedom is lost to the state – that is, if economic and political freedoms are joined into a single power of the state – such a great power structure will inevitably destroy our intellectual freedom. The loss of intellectual freedom, as in Russia, is perhaps the greatest lesson our western civilization has learned in this twentieth century. It is an important lesson to learn, for mankind's intellectual freedom is the widely accepted supreme value of human life. To witness the loss of this freedom has been to witness the ultimate tragedy of communism.

A Recent Event of Great Importance

The business section of *The Sunday New York Times*, August 9, 1981, published a congressional news story of real importance about the business of my company. It will surely help a great many companies, and I add it to this Newcomen Address:

> *Washington* An obscure addition to the new tax bill that does nothing more than increase a business deduction by $300 is being hailed in certain Congressional and busi-

ness circles as a most effective way of meeting the Reagan Administration's vision of increased productivity.

The subject: the trinkets, baubles – and sometimes fine jewelry – offered by corporations to employees in recognition of length of service, salesmanship, safety or success.

Under previous tax law, a company could deduct no more than $100 for, say, the gold watch at retirement. Not enough, felt the O. C. Tanner Company, a Salt Lake manufacturer and wholesaler that claims to be the largest American firm specializing in these "symbolic recognition programs." So Tanner called Senator Jake Garn, Republican of Utah, who decided to do something about it.

He tucked into the tax bill an item that would allow deductions of up to $400 an award, or up to $1,600 an item if the average award in the company program stayed below $400. . . .

"With increases in the price of gold, diamonds, and other gems, it seemed right to try to change the tax law," Charmaine Hart, the Senator's assistant for tax-related issues, said. "Increasing employee pride is a good way to increase productivity."

"It's a low-cost, high-leverage source of motivation," William Paul, in charge of sales at O. C. Tanner contends. "It is born of the frustration of companies tacking on more fringe benefits that no one relates to. An award makes the recipient emotionally involved." . . . He described the awards as "a drop in the bucket" when compared to monetary benefit and incentive programs.

"But our customers tell us this is the most effective thing they do," he said. "It's the experience. Waiting for the award. The presentation as a stimulating experience shared with family and fellow employees.

"And finally, over the years, it serves as a reminder to the employee of a job well done and an appreciative employer."

I conclude, as I began, with a tribute to beauty. Today our customers are many thousands of corporations, each with its own insignia and emblem, awarded to an employee in recognition of a given period of service. And while my company must always face the three competitive tests of price, service, and quality, the Tanner Company counts also on careful craftsmanship to produce "a thing of beauty" so that it may be, as the poet says, "a joy forever."

Business and the Good Society

Brigham Young University School of Business
1963

□

Good business in a good society is that kind of business life that rewards the individual in proportion to the value of his own individual productivity. All else is commentary to this one goal. Individual effort, justly rewarded in wages, fringe benefits, job security, and personal respect is sound business and also helps make a good society. All else is unsound and makes for a bad society.

Individual merit, justly compensated, is a difficult ideal to live up to; yet it forever remains the best standard of good business. It still produces the best society.

The world is full of substitutes for this ideal of *individual merit* compensation. Indeed, many give far more effort to avoid such a standard than to apply it. One main reason for all the substitutes is the difficulty of appraising the value of each individual's worth.

Here are a few of these substitutes, examples of unsound business practices that illustrate bad business and, therefore, a bad society:

1. Labor laws that enable labor unions to get compensation for workers regardless of conscientious individual effort.

2. Corporations which carelessly fail to measure and reward individual productivity.

3. Teacher associations which block efforts to measure more successful teachers and compensate them accordingly.

4. Finally, there are jobs by the million which are carelessly standardized with fixed and unchanging wages or salaries regardless of individual creativity or high achievement. And some jobs are standardized regardless of individual incompetence or just plain laziness. To be more specific, labor unions want only across-the-board wage increases for *all* rather than for *individual* performance. Such a policy of labor unions proves best for collecting greater union dues. So the individual is forgotten at the bargaining table.

Another example of ignoring the individual occurs when corporations market their products by granting territory franchises on total volume of business done rather than by commissions based upon the individual salesman's efforts.

School boards standardize teacher qualifications and salary categories because anything else is difficult. The good teacher and the poor teacher give differently but receive the same. It is easier that way.

We thus tend more and more to practice this unsound business, and the result is bad for any society. If people can receive income for any reason other than hard individual effort, they are only too happy to do so.

But the situation is not hopeless. We do not inevitably gravitate toward standardized wages, thereby becoming a standardized people. Huge corporations, enormous government agencies, even socialism and, rarest of all, communism, ignore individual performance but have cracks in their foundations. Indeed, all of them are eternally splintered and broken by at least two hard realities of life itself. These two realities are everlastingly on the side of our great ideal, namely, that good business rewards each individual according to individual productivity.

The first of these two facts of life is that individuals are the true reality while unions, corporations, and governments are merely abstractions. Any reality—a fact, or an individual—is bound to challenge successfully the artificial realities of corporate entities existing only in the eye of the law. One individual is more real than all the "isms" of politicians and all the statistics of business.

The second basic fact is that man's life on this earth is primarily competitive, and only secondarily cooperative. This basic fact, that all life is competitive, favors individualism. Someone different in personality from every other person is always coming up with a more competitive idea, a more successful way of doing business.

Consider now the first of these great facts—that only the individual is real. We pay lip service to abstractions like nations, corporations, partnerships, trade associations, labor unions, fraternities, societies, churches, and clubs; but only the individual occupies space and exists in time. America is the family of George and Mary and their son, Jimmy. A company is John Smith and Alice Jones. A church is a man in trouble or a widow in need. A union is really not a union but separate people—individuals—one by one.

Sometimes individuals walk alone, sometimes with other individuals in an organization; but he or she as an individual is the only thing that walks. Individuals may band together for great or small business undertakings, but they remain individuals. They are rewarded or cheated, helped or hurt not as corporations or unions, but as single, unique, separate, solitary individuals.

Good business in a good society will think always in terms of individuals. Bad business in a bad society thinks mainly of institutional life—collective results, total achievement, statistical failure, and statistical success. Loyalty to an institution is the easiest and sometimes the cheapest of virtues. Loyalty to an individual, his dignity and worth, and careful reward for his efforts are the measures of a good business in a good society.

The second primary reality of man's life on this planet is that all life is competitive. Nowhere does competition reveal itself more openly than in man's struggle for bread. The fear of poverty, of want, is one of the deepest of man's fears. In business, competition is the most severe and most clearly revealed activity—more so than in man's political, professional, or social activities.

So inexorable is competition for bread, so universal, so unrelenting, so demanding, so stern and sometimes cruel, that man has devised uncounted substitutes for avoiding it. A general term for such an escape is the word "cooperation." Cooperation is the alternative man uses to blunt the harshness of competition. Cooperation is an escape from the hard struggle of competition. But competition still remains the bedrock reality of man's life on this planet. Every conceivable form of cooperation must someday stand the test of competition. Competition, like the mills of the gods, grinds slowly and exceedingly fine. All cooperative ways of living will someday, sooner or later, be tested by a competitor—by competition.

Yet human efforts to avoid competition are as numerous as the sands of the sea. Business corporations, tired and weary of competition, merge with competitors hoping thereby to find prosperity with ultimate peace. Unions, appealing to less successful people in the competitive struggle, promise security and abundance to their membership in general. Governments come to power appealing for cooperation instead of competition, and promising security and generous rewards for all the people of a whole nation.

But companies merging, unions forcing, and governments promising never fully make good. Defying competition is like defying gravity. Day and night, gravity works to bring all things back to earth. And day after day, year after year, the tests of competition are applied against these substitutes, and competition always wins out. From beginning to end, life in all its social and economic forms is primarily competitive – but especially is economic life competitive, deadly competitive.

Perhaps the greatest effort in man's history to escape this competition is the theory and practice of communism. According to communist doctrine there is to be no competition, for the dream of communism is that every man will automatically receive what he needs, and automatically give only as he is able. All one needs to do as a communist is to cooperate – totally.

But this vast monolithic structure of escapism known as communism is now being cracked and splintered. Communism, as such, is failing. Each day its walls show new cracks from the hammer blows of competition, both from within and from without. Within communist countries, communism itself is changing toward more competition. Among free nations, communism is becoming a less attractive competitor. After years of trying, communism is turning out to be inefficient, just because it denies the chance for individual incentive. Communism would shield man from competitive struggle.

If, then, a good business in a good society is one that rewards the individual in proportion to his individual dignity and productivity, then these two hard facts of life – competition and the reality of the individual – despite all the escapes man has devised to avoid them, are on the side of creating good business in a good society.

A recent experience I had may be broad enough to illustrate what I have to say. The State Department in Washington has a practice of referring selected visiting students and professors from the Soviet Union to homes where they will be welcome. My home is fortunate to be one of these. Last Sunday three professors who teach at the University of Moscow were guests in our home, and I was driving them around the city and out to the Kennecott Copper mine. I decided to drive them through one of the streets of Copperton and said: "These are the homes of the workers at the mine."

I thought I could feel something of their shock. The houses were in good repair and beautifully landscaped. One of them said, in what I thought was rather a skeptical tone, "It would be nice if we could go in one of the worker's homes." "You can," I replied. "You pick a place and I will see if the lady of the house will show us her home."

I was fully aware, having traveled widely in communist countries, of their great suspicion and mistrust. They protested that they did not wish to embarrass me by pressing the matter, and I could see they did not really believe these were the homes of the mine workers. So I repeated: "You select the house and I will ask if we can go inside." "When we cross the next street, ask at the third house on the right," one of them specified. With great care we agreed on which house was the third house after crossing the next street.

I stopped the car in front, and at the door I said to the lady, "Madam, I apologize for this strange request, but I have three communists in my car and they would like to see the inside of your home."

Noting her surprise and alarm at the word "communist," I altered my words, saying, "I have three professors from the Soviet Union who have been studying at Columbia for the past year and who are now touring America, stopping only in Los Angeles, San Francisco, Salt Lake City, Denver, and Chicago. Could they inspect your house as an example of one of the mine worker's homes?"

She appeared somewhat relieved, and then looked rather searchingly at me and said, "I believe I know who you are." "I hope so," I replied. "You taught my sister at the Spanish Fork seminary thirty-five years ago." I was never so pleased with my profession of teaching.

She welcomed my three strange guests into her home and they inspected every inch of it, including the refrigerator, washer, television, and piano. Her husband came up from the basement where he was painting the floor and for most of an hour my three guests proceeded to ply him and his wife with questions. How much did he make? How much did food cost? How much was spent for clothing? How many hours a week did he work? Did he like his job?

This was their golden opportunity to investigate firsthand the accuracy of stories they had been told about the exploitation of the workers under the capitalistic system. First of all, here was the hard reality of an individual. Our previous discussions on the abstractions of Marxist theory versus Free Enterprise, our comparisons of buildings, factories, cities, schools, and farms now fell into obscurity compared with the flesh-and-blood reality of a human being whose thoughts they could probe, and whose way of living they could investigate firsthand.

I thought the best witness for our free enterprise system was the man's wife, who showed us examples of her needlework. She brought out clothing purchased for her sons and gave the price of each; she explained carefully her economies of wise purchasing in grocery stores and canning quantities of fruit in the fall. Most of all she was proud of her sons, one of whom she said played the piano well, while her other boy was gifted as a musician on the clarinet. The family had two cars and their home was nearly paid for. This was a better example of the capitalistic system than driving down the streets of one of our big cities.

Driving away, I commented to them that the man was free at any time to accept a job elsewhere if it should compete favorably in wages, fringe benefits, job security, or anything else he considered important. He had the freedom to worship, to think, to dissent, to participate according to his own personal desires. My Soviet friends might argue – and argue we did – but arguments are silenced with facts. No facts are so controlling in human life as the reality of the individual and the reality of free competition in the whole life of man.

A good business lives best by competition, favoring its customers better, if it can, than would any of its competitors.

It is true that cooperation is necessary in human life, not only to achieve great collective results like a huge factory for mass production, but also as the mercy element to soften the harshness of competition. Man is a social being as well as a solitary individual. He lives his fullest self by cooperating with others for the good of all. Yet even in the largest forms of corporate life, no institution can or should try to avoid the bar of judgment – fair treatment of the individual, and fair opportunity to think and speak as an individual and work for improvement based upon personal merit.

Surveying man's economic life today, one sees our drift away from individualism and in the direction of more and more collectivisms – larger institutions and merging corporations. Man is a herd animal. He is also a lazy animal. Labor is hard, rest is sweet. Competition is costly, cooperation is pleasant. So man drifts toward easiness like wood drifts down a river.

But not all human life is like wood drifting down a river. Some of it is more like a giant redwood tree, rooted against the winds, resistant against fire and floods.

A good corporation executive is one who unrelentingly works at the job of rewarding individuals for their special talents, special efforts, and special achievements. A good union leader is not careless of truth, but competes freely with management for positive results. A good teacher endeavors to reach an individual student for his or her personal response. A good government leader aids only when people cannot aid themselves.

All men are different. Their capabilities are different. They need to be so treated. A good business in a good society carefully faces this fact of individual difference and rewards as best it can, each man and each woman according to his or her singular worth and productivity, and also according to the inherent dignity belonging to each human of every race and every nation.